Mathematics

for Retail Buying

Mathematics
for Retail Buying

Revised Fifth Edition

Bette K. Tepper
Fashion Institute of Technology

Fairchild Publications, Inc.
New York

Executive Editor: **Olga Kontzias**

Production Editor: **Joann Muscolo**

Editorial Assistant: **Beth Applebome**

Art Director: **Nataliya Gurshman**

Production Manager: **Priscilla Taguer**

Text & Cover Design: **Nataliya Gurshman**

Cover Illustration: **Nataliya Gurshman**

Full Editorial & Production Services: **Chernow Editorial Services, Inc.**

Agnew's, Inc.

Eighth Printing, 2006
Revised 5th Edition
Copyright © 2002
Fairchild Publications, Inc.

Earlier Editions © 2000, 1996 (Revised 4th Edition), 1994, 1987, 1977, 1973
by Fairchild Publications, Division of Capital Cities Media, Inc. A Capital Cities/ABC Company

Library of Congress Catalog Card Number: 00-102094

ISBN: 1-56367-293-6

GST R 133004424

Printed in the United States of America

Contents

List of Figures

Preface

In the first edition of *Mathematics for Retail Buying,* we stated that operating figures are the language of the retail merchandiser, regardless of the size of the store. In today's highly competitive business environment, it is more important than ever to have comprehension of the mathematical factors involved in profitable merchandising. This fundamental mathematical background gives insight into how merchandising problems are solved mathematically and perception as to why merchandising decisions are based on figures. The most skilled and experienced merchandiser knows that the mastery of mathematical techniques and figure analysis is an essential tool. Additionally, persons in related careers who comprehend the mathematics of profit factors will also benefit by their broader understanding of merchandising situations.

Mathematics for Retail Buying depicts the essential concepts, practices, and procedures as well as the calculations and interpretations of figures related to the many factors that produce profit. The choice of material and the depth of each subject are deliberately confined to that which has practical value for the performance of occupations in or associated with retail merchandising. The book was developed primarily as a learning device to meet the needs of career-oriented students who will be directly, or indirectly, involved in the activities of merchandising and buying at the retail level. In addition to the obvious educational benefits to the students of retailing, *Mathematics for Retail Buying* can serve as a guide in training junior executives, and can be a constant source of reference for an assistant buyer or the merchant who operates a small independent store.

When contemplating the writing or revision of any retailing textbook, the question of practical value inevitably will arise. We feel the contents of *Mathematics for Retail Buying* are not only sensible, but realistic because it has been based on:

■ The personal experience of the author, who was a buyer in a major retail organization.

■ The knowledgable opinions of current retail executives as to the information necessary to prepare prospective retail merchandisers.

■ The insights manufacturers have gained that helped to provide better service and to communicate more effectively with retailers and merchandisers.

■ The tested use of the material by the author and other teachers at the Fashion Institute of Technology, by faculties at other schools, and by retail executives and training departments.

- The favorable comments about the value of the material in relation to career performance by the alumni of the Fashion Merchandising Management curriculum at the Fashion Institute of Technology.

The study and comprehension of the principles and techniques contained in *Mathematics for Retail Buying* will enable the student to:

- Recognize the basic and elementary factors of the buying and selling process that affect profit.

- Understand the relationship of the profit factors and improve profit performance by the manipulation of these factors.

- Become familiar with the use and function of typical merchandising forms encountered in stores.

- Become aware of practices and procedures in stores.

- Become familiar with the applications of computers and computerized forms in retailing.

- Understand and apply the basic mathematical concepts used to solve real-life merchandising problems.

- Comprehend the standard industry terminology employed in retailing and merchandising.

Every effort is still being made to build the contents of the book into a solid foundation for ease of understanding, and not merely to display formulas. Without sacrificing completeness, the material has been structured into a simplified outline form. This step-by-step presentation uses brief explanations stated in basic terms, precise definitions, typical merchandising forms illustrating procedures and techniques, and concepts demonstrated clearly in examples that express the mathematical principles involved. An outstanding feature of the book is that it has the combined advantages of a handbook and the benefits of a workbook. Within each unit, after a major topic, a series of problems is presented that tests the understanding of the fundamental principles discussed in that section. Contained at the end of each unit, there is a large collection of review problems and case studies that utilize practical retailing situations and common difficulties and obstacles encountered in real-life merchandising. These features will further reinforce comprehension of that specific unit, and consequently, the book.

For this Fifth Edition, revised, particular attention has been paid to the comments of the various users, including their own teaching experiences as well as mine. The significant changes in this edition are:

- The Introduction connects the text's contents with an overview of the growth of retailing, impacted by computer technology and the cardinal principles of successful merchandising.

- Units I, III and V have designated spreadsheet problems that apply and help develop their concepts. It is possible to do the required computations for these exercises by computer using spreadsheet software, calculator or hand.

- To become familiar with real-world examples, store forms have been added for the computation of appropriate practice problems.

- To improve clarity of some salient points, sections of the text have been rewritten and/or restructured.

- Important key words have been highlighted throughout the book.

- A Glossary, defining the highlighted terms throughout the book, has been included to facilitate the student's understanding of important key words.

- The improved comprehensive instructor's guide for the entire text, which also includes the computations and answers to the practice problems and case studies for each unit.

- At the end of Units I–VI, additional case study problems have been added to demonstrate the use of that material in a realistic, practical merchandising situation.

- Up-to-date computer store forms present current merchandising procedures and techniques.

- Industry terminology and data is updated and reflected in the text and problems presented.

- The addition of new, up-to-date review problems.

- The sequence within some units has been altered.

In developing and changing the book for this Fifth Edition, revised, I have tried to be sensitive to and concerned about comments from colleagues and students at the Fashion Institute of Technology and from many other colleges relating to the sequence of study units in our book. The old puzzle about "the chicken or the egg" has surfaced time and time again. Why the Profit unit first? Why not the Retail Method unit? Or Dollar Planning? Or Pricing?

We pondered this matter rather endlessly before we attempted the third revision a few years ago. At that time, we happened upon a rather basic principle about the buying/merchandising process: There is no one beginning and no one end. It is a circular process: an unending, interrelated continuum within which all factors influence all other factors. Even though the units are interrelated, each chapter can be used as a separate topic of study, and each can be shifted without losing the continuity of the process. The various facets of the merchandising cycle are an ongoing procedure of monitoring, analysis, and evaluation directed to the purpose of meeting the merchandiser's objective of achieving a pre-determined gross margin which should, in turn, generate an appropriate net profit. This is mentioned here to point out to instructors and students alike (and to merchants who use our book for in-service training purposes) that the study of retail mathematics may begin at any point on the "circle."

In this Fifth Edition, revised, the material is divided into six units. Each unit covers a particular, basic mathematical factor that affects the profits of a retail store. The relationships among these profit factors are stressed throughout the book. The units of study and their subject matter are:

- Unit I, Merchandising for a Profit—introduces the concept of profit, and presents the calculation, interpretation, and analysis of the profit and loss statement.

- Unit II, Retail Pricing and Repricing of Merchandise—discusses and illustrates the basic pricing factors used in buying decisions and presents the calculations used when pricing and/or repricing retail merchandise.

- Unit III, The Relationship of Markup to Profit—explains the importance of markup to profitable merchandising, and illustrates the calculations of the various types of markup, i.e., cumulative, initial, and maintained, that, when understood and implemented, achieve the desired results.

- Unit IV, The Retail Method of Inventory—presents and explains this proven, reliable procedure as a mechanism and system of determining the total value of the stock-on-hand and shortages.

- Unit V, Dollar Planning and Control—includes the analysis of possible sales, the planning and control of stocks and purchases, and the techniques used to accomplish these objectives.

- Unit VI, Invoice Mathematics—Terms of Sale—is concerned with discounts, dating procedures, and shipping terms that a retail buyer must know to buy effectively and profitably at wholesale.

The idea for this book originated with the many faculty members who helped develop some of this material to meet the needs for teaching merchandising mathematics at the Fashion Institute of Technology. The author is indebted to those faculty members for their contributions and to the many students and alumni for their constructive criticism and suggestions that were used in preparing this book. The enthusiastic response provided the incentive to complete this revision.

We would like to thank the following people for their constructive, helpful, and thoughtful reviews and critiques of the revision in all of its various forms and states: Tim Christiansen, Purdue University, West Lafayette, IN; Victoria A. Deyoe, FIDM, Woodland Hills, CA; Ann Fairhurst, University of Tennessee, Knoxville; Georgia Kalivas, Fashion Institute of Technology, New York, NY; Gail Moran, Harper College, Pallatine, IL; and Lesley D. Stoel, University of Kentucky, Lexington, KY.

Special thanks go to my coauthor of earlier editions, Professor Newton E. Godnick. He was actively involved in sharing and participating in all phases of the original and subsequent editions. His contributions are still evident in this book.

Personal thanks go to my colleague, Helen Sampson, Associate Professor at FIT, who unstintingly critiques each edition with helpful, astute comments and suggestions in a quest to provide the best possible teaching vehicle.

I want to acknowledge and give special thanks to the following people for their valuable assistance in the revision of this edition: R. J. Asher, Jr, Director Executive Recruitment and College Relations, Central Human Resources, Macy's East, for his helpful suggestions and confirmation concerning the training necessary for a successful retail career in today's environment; Bernadette M. Commisa, Manager Merchant Training, Macy's, for evaluating the material in the text that relates to current industry procedures and practices, and Jack Tepper, former Vice President/Divisional Merchandise Manager of Ohrbach's, and International Consultant to Mondial International, to whom I am indebted for providing the criticism, advice, guidance, inspiration, and steadiness in presenting practical, merchandising situations in the text, problems, and case studies; Karen Dubno, editor, for her initial diverse suggestions, and Barbara Chernow, editor, for her support, diligence, and professionalism.

Bette K. Tepper

Mathematics
for Retail Buying

Introduction

At the beginning of a new millennium, it is not possible to predict or visualize the various organizational and/or ownership alternatives retailers will pursue or changes that will result from future hi-tech innovations as each retailer struggles for a uniqueness in the marketplace. However, we can foresee in the future, as in the past and the present, significant and rewarding career opportunities in the traditional retail institutions—e.g. department and specialty stores—the wide variety of more recently developed retail formats—e.g. manufacturers' outlets—and the latest types of electronic retailing. Chances for success are more favorable than ever due to the rapid increase in the type, size, and number of retailers in plentiful geographic locations.

Merchandising strategies are conceived by the retailer and executed by the buyer. The buyer knows that the basic mathematical elements involved in profitable buying must be coordinated and correlated with the principles and concepts that are applied to the function of buying at cost, selling at retail, and producing a profit from these activities. The most cardinal principle is that it does not matter what product you buy, or which diverse retailer offers the product, or what the industry is, be it in the fashion, hardware, or supermarket areas, the same set of concepts and mathematical calculations are connected to the three elementary factors of retail, cost and profit. Their application to any product in any particular store and/or industry is identical. The emphasis on these elements may differ because the retailers' policies may not be alike. It is understandable, for example, that the calculation of a markup percent for a specialty store like Bergdorf Goodman and a discounter like Target Stores is computed identically, yet the markup percent considered acceptable by each is different. We can better appreciate the interlinking of the retailer or any other alternate merchandise distribution choice, with the buyer as we consider their common goals and their effect on each other's function.

By definition, **retailing** is the term used to describe the many activities involved in selling small quantities of goods and/or services, at a profit, to the ultimate consumer. **Merchandising** combines having the right merchandise, in the right place, in the right quantities, at the right price, at the right time. Performed by the buyer, this task—to go into a market buying what a customer wants and having it ready when it is wanted—seems simple. In practice, retail management today has become quite complex and difficult because the growth of retailers fosters keen competition and has seriously reduced the possible profit margin. Therefore, it is more important than ever that the buyer who fulfills the merchandising function has a basic knowledge of the mathematical factors involved in profitable merchandising. Without this background it is difficult to comprehend the operation of either a small store, a department in a large store, or a non-store based retailer such as mail catalog, or an Internet operation. This fundamental mathematical background gives insight into *how* merchandising problems are solved mathematically and *why* merchandising decisions are based on figures. The financial personnel in many major organizations like Sears and Home Depot use preset programs and spreadsheets for analysis and profit planning. Nevertheless, the buyer's ability to understand and manipulate the profit factors is essential because everyday problems and situations that arise from figuring profits can be a basis in earning future maximum profits. In a computerized organization, the buyer can go "on line" and instantly retrieve a particular desired merchandising figure. However, if the computer "is down" and the data necessary to take immediate action is not available, the buyer who can compute and supply the necessary information has a decided advantage.

The Growth of Retailing

In America, retailing first began with the Indian trading posts of the frontier days. After 1850, such pioneers as R. H. Macy and Marshall Field established the department stores. By 1900, there were department stores in all major cities and this was the retail format recognized as the mass distributor of goods. The mail order houses were given a substantial boost by the adoption of rural free delivery by the post office, while the chain store, established in the middle of the nineteenth century, rose to maturity in the twentieth century.

The consolidation and growth in American retailing was the period between the two world wars. After 1945, there were revolutionary changes with the appearance of planned shopping centers, which often led to direct competition between retailers. The latter part of the twentieth century saw variation in retailing format with the inception of discounters, closeout stores, manufacturer's outlets, and warehouse clubs, to name just a few. In addition, direct selling, and television-shopping channels became the convenient techniques by which to buy merchandise in a nonstore environment. There was an another unprecedented phenomenon in 1994 when the competitive strategy changed with the acquisition of R. H. Macy's by Federated Department Stores, as store size changes with a trend toward larger or smaller stores than their past counterparts. Today, retailing is fast-paced and requires the ability to adapt and be flexible as the basic concepts and principles are applied.

Computer Technology in Retailing

In the late twentieth century, high tech made its mark everywhere including retailing. Success in the contemporary retail environment relies heavily on records that are the basis for analysis, planning, making decisions and acting quickly. The first generation of electronic computers started in 1951, when the growth of multistore operations mandated a need for prompt, accurate, and complete facts to make merchandising decisions.

Since the 1960s, data processing systems have provided retailers with an uninterrupted flow of information. In more recent years, the increased use of Electronic Data Processing (EDP) systems by department stores and retail businesses, as well as by mass merchandising chains, has had a major impact on the management of merchandise inventories and other areas of recordkeeping. Today, because retailers locate their stores in distant geographic markets, the computer as a tool not only furnishes data that identifies problems but also facilitates and accelerates the decision-making process. Computers assist retailers not only with merchandising functions, but also with information that enables them to integrate and improve merchandising, buying, customer service, store operations, and the financial management of the business.

All retailers agree about the value of computer usage in their individual stores. This powerful force that processes information accurately and promptly is particularly appreciated in the volatile retailing industry because it has resulted in much improved control and management of merchandise and finances. The network of computers that allows a continual flow of information to be electronically exchanged between retailers and manufacturers results in this control at a lower cost. Ideally, a computerized merchandising system should provide data about the physical stock that is in tandem with dollar control. Management has an almost unlimited choice concerning what programs should be instituted, maintained or eliminated. The benefits of the computer to a particular organization can easily be determined through analysis of sales, productivity, and profit.

The quick evolution of technology has become critical to a retailer's success. The major mass retailers of the 90s, WalMart and Home Depot, as well as the sophisticated specialty stores like Saks Fifth Avenue have a major competitive advantage as they reap the benefits from their capital investments in technology. Their programs touch every aspect of their operation. They include executive information systems that analyze and report the detailed performance of what merchandise is selling, use historical performance to plan data to determine quantities, and improve the efficiency of the buying process by providing better distribution of merchandise by the store based on customer profiles. Internal and external communications are changed by the use of E-mail. Vendor partnerships through development of replenishment systems, that is, Quick Response ensure that the merchandise wanted by the customer is in the store when they want it. Standardized bar codes printed on the tickets enables retailers to move merchandise quickly from distribution centers to selling floors at lower costs. These are just some of the processes currently used to achieve the important goal of having what the customers want, where they want it, and in precisely the right quantity.

History records past events. We know the merits and influences of the computer on the development of retailing, as it is known today. The future will reveal how this or other major innovations will facilitate the degree or the speed of electronic progress as it is known today. It is equally difficult to predict the impact of the Internet as a retailing venue.

Mathematics for Retail Buying delineates the essential concepts, practices, and procedures, as well as the calculations and interpretations of figures related to the many factors that produce profit. The choice of material and the depth of each subject are deliberately confined to that which has practical value for the performance of occupations in or associated with retail merchandising.

The study of retail mathematics may begin at any point of the buying/selling "circle." The six units in this text are interrelated with the various phases of merchandising; therefore, each unit can be used as a separate topic of study, and each can be shifted without losing the continuity of the process. Here is an overview of the units and their role in the buying/selling circle.

Merchandising for a Profit: Unit I

Logically, the study of the mathematics involved in retail buying should begin with the analysis of a profit and loss statement, the subject of Unit I. This statement reports a summary of the achievements of a particular department, store, or company as it reveals whether or not the activities involved in operating this unit for a specified time period has been profitable. Profits are mainly the results of how much merchandise is sold (known as sales volume), the cost of the merchandise that is sold, and the expenses incurred in buying and selling this merchandise. The buyer is the force that buys, prices, reprices, and negotiates the merchandise found in a retail store and/or featured on the Internet. These functions are the responsibilities of the buyer who must have the ability to understand the linkage of the profit elements. The fundamental relationships among the profit factors are repeated throughout the book. In the calculation of a profit and loss statement, there is emphasis on an exact and rigid order of the factors included. Although adding and subtracting the appropriate figures can determine a correct profit result, the standard arrangement provides an analytical picture that allows a determination of the store's strengths and weaknesses and facilitates comparisons with other counterparts. The buyer must critically examine these figures and then make a determination of causes from these results.

Retail Pricing and Repricing of Merchandise: Unit II

This unit presents the relationship and calculations of the basic pricing factors, the various pricing situations used in making buying decisions, the techniques involved in repricing goods, and the effect of each on gross margin (the difference between the sales and the cost of those sales) and profit. The approach to pricing is presented from the standpoint of who sets the selling price on goods purchased for resale. In economics, the central idea is use, which is closely associated with the idea of choice and value. Without going into the realm of psychology on this concept, it is easy to understand that before anything is consumed, somebody must choose to use it. The choices made determine the relative value. Prices reflect these uses and choices. Some of the influences on the pricing strategies within the merchandising framework are store type and policy, for example, department stores versus "off-price" stores and the choice of fashion versus staple goods in addition to customer demand as it relates to the supply-demand theory and competition.

The buyer guided by a prescribed price-line structure plans purchases and merchandise offerings that fit into this framework. The buyer sets the retail price on each item purchased. The mathematical skill of the buyer helps to produce an assortment balanced in variety, breadth, and depth by retail price lines, while satisfactory costs are obtained that will eventually yield a profit on the goods purchased.

Retail stores buy and sell. All the buying and selling activity is in terms of price. There is great interest in the relation between the buying price and the selling price because the difference between these two largely determines profit.

The Relationship of Markup to Profit: Unit III

The overall effectiveness of buying and pricing is measured by the buyer's ability to achieve a markup established by management and designed to produce the desired profit. As merchandise is purchased, it is neither common nor desirable to require that each item be retailed with the same markup percent. The results would be disastrous! Yet, it is the buyer's responsibility to meet the overall target figure for profit. Never can the buyer forget that goods must be priced to sell. Therefore, during a season, there are many considerations that affect the pricing of merchandise at the time of purchase, and many of these, in addition to others, cause goods actually to sell at a lower price. The ability to recognize that this results in different markups allows the buyer to make the necessary adjustments. The buyer constantly has an opportunity to average high and low markups to reach the required pre-determined average.

The Retail Method of Inventory: Unit IV

An essential feature of retail merchandising is to determine the total value of stock on hand. The value of inventory is significant for planning specifically how much to buy and for the determination of the proper valuation of inventory for profit figuring purposes. Unit IV discusses the Retail Method of Inventory because it is the accepted, proven system that provides this information. We familiarize ourselves with the general procedures used in implementing this system, and the calculation and records required to maintain it. A probable amount of stock on hand can be known at any time without counting the merchandise, and a shortage figure can easily be derived through a comparison between the actual physical inventory and the computed records. The mathematical calculations involved in this method are not performed by the buyer, but the accuracy depends on the buyer's prompt and accurate classifying of records that pertain to price changes. This system helps the buyer to constantly track the amount of stock on hand while protecting the gross margin, the difference between sales and the cost of those sales to be attained.

Dollar Planning and Control: Unit V

The most talked-about topic in retailing is the budget of stocks and sales more commonly known as a six-month dollar plan. This is the subject of Unit V. The six-month plan is an attempt to set in advance realistic projected goals for stocks in ratio to sales, the amount and timing of markdowns, an average markup for the season, and the correct amount and proper timing of purchases. This "calendar" plans, forecasts, and controls the purchase and sale of merchandise. It is designed to protect the store's inventory investment and produce a profit as it controls the above factors. The projection of planned sales is the hub of the buying/selling wheel or circle, and all of the other elements are predicated on this figure. Although the estimation is based on actual past performance plus external and internal sales-related conditions, it is not an exact process. It is a judgmental decision and, therefore, it is not always possible to predict all possible contingencies.

The buyer, who is responsible for interpreting and achieving the goals set, constantly monitors the sales in order to adjust the elements of the plan that rely on the amount of sales generated. The six-month dollar plan, in action, helps the buyer to keep score of whether the correct balance between sales and stocks is maintained. The procedure of planning the various elements and the calculations that produce the desired outcome give insight into why and how this technique produces a profitable operation.

Invoice Mathematics—Terms of Sale: Unit VI

After the buyer has decided "what to buy," great care must be taken in finalizing arrangements with the seller. One usually thinks of negotiations as associated with price, but there are other matters that must be agreed upon by the buyer and seller that can result in eventually producing profit. It is only the buyer who negotiates prices, delivery dates, discounts, shipping terms and terms that pertain to payment of the merchandise purchased. These matters are called "terms of sale." These are the subjects of Unit VI. While fulfilling the duty of obtaining the lowest prices, the buyer must realize the impact of credit, shipping terms and the eligibility of possible available discounts on the cost of the merchandise purchased. The buyer must know what discounts are available and how they are calculated to determine the true cost. The buyer must also push for discounts and extended credit terms that pertain to payment and provide specific shipping instructions that relate to transportation costs and transit insurance. Many of these elements can be negotiated. Each of them can help increase significantly the gross figure that leads to improved profits.

The problems, cases, and spreadsheet situations to be solved in *Mathematics for Retail Buying* focus mainly on situations prevalent in the women's, children's and men's apparel, and home furnishing industries because fashion is such an important factor in our economic system and affects the major industries of retailing, manufacturing, and marketing. Practical and realistic examples follow the theories, principles, concepts, and calculations that through application test the reader's understanding of the fundamentals of each major topic discussed in that section.

For the future, the function in retailing of maintaining assortments appropriate for selected customers, in quantities that provide efficient use of investment, at prices that create a constant flow of merchandise, while assuring a profit focused on the buying/selling process will continue. The principles by which this will be achieved will remain constant, as they accommodate to the mode and tempo of life in the twenty-first century. As additional traditional retailers join Macy's, WalMart, and Internet-only retailers with web sites, on-line selling will grow rapidly. New rules and standards that pertain to return policies and company-wide coordination will have to evolve. However, the basic profit elements, as we know them, will continue to guide and measure success.

Bette K. Tepper

Unit I

MERCHANDISING FOR A PROFIT

Objectives
- Recognition of the importance of profit calculations in merchandising decisions.
- Identification of components of a profit and loss statement.
- Completion of a profit and loss statement, including the calculation of:
  Net sales.
  Cost of goods sold.
  Gross margin.
  Operating expenses.
  Profit.
- Identification of types of business expenses and their impact on profit.
- Utilization of profit calculations to:
  Make comparisons between departments and/or stores.
  Detect trends.
  Make changes in merchandising strategy to achieve an increase in profits.

Key Terms

alteration and workroom costs	indirect expenses
billed cost	inward freight
cash discounts	net loss
closing inventory	net profit
contribution	net sales
controllable expenses	opening inventory
cost	operating expenses
cost of goods sold	operating income
customer returns and allowances	profit and loss statement
direct expenses	retail
final profit and loss statement	sales volume
gross margin	skeletal profit and loss statement
gross sales	total merchandise handled

Why is the study of the calculation of profit necessary? An individual involved in retailing inevitably will have many opportunities to become involved with the concept of profit. An employee of a private organization should be aware of corporate profits. For example, many companies offer a profit-sharing plan, which is now a frequent form of incentive in many industries. An individual may be a possible investor of personal funds in publicly owned corporations. To an employee of a publicly owned corporation, profit is a significant goal in the sale of shares. Since the beginning of the twentieth century, the U.S. government has requested that all entrepreneurs declare the profits or losses of all business ventures. The profits are taxed. Competent accounting methods require a statement of net profit before and after taxes.

Because one of the major responsibilities of a merchandiser in retailing is to attain a profit for the department,[1] store, or retail business being supervised, it is logical to begin by learning the elements of profit. The merchandising executive uses the calculation of profits to:

■ Exchange data and compare stores to determine relative strengths and weaknesses.

■ Indicate the direction of the business and whether it is prosperous, struggling for survival, or bankrupt.

■ Provide a statement for analysis so that knowledgeable changes in management or policy can be made.

■ Improve the profit margin by using this analysis.

This unit examines the basic profit elements, their relationships to each other in profit and loss statements, and methods to manipulate these elements to improve profits. After these topics have been studied, the meanings understood, the calculations learned, and the existing interrelationships discerned, it is possible to determine analytically whether an organization is operating at a profit or a loss.

I. Defining the Basic Profit Factors

The function of the retail store is to sell merchandise to consumers at a profit. These sales are the store's source of operating income. Before merchandise can be sold, however, it must be bought. Even in a computerized organization in which financial personnel may preset programs and spreadsheets, the buyer is ultimately responsible for creating a merchandise assortment. This selection occurs after planning and predicting what, when, where, and how much to buy

---

[1]Department (Merchandise Department): A grouping of related merchandise for which separate expense and merchandising records are kept for the purpose of determining the profit of this grouping. It is not merely a physical segregation.

and what to pay for these purchases. **Cost** is the amount the retailer pays for these purchases. **Retail** is the price at which stores offer merchandise for sale to the consumer.

In retailing, one of the most important financial records is the income statement, commonly known as a **profit and loss statement.** This statement, prepared periodically by the department, store, or organization summarizes the basic merchandising factors that affect profit results. It is used to measure profitability as it evaluates the results of current performance and allows for comparison of present and possible future trends. Because the buyer buys and prices the merchandise offered for sale in a retail store, the buyer must have the ability to know, manipulate, and understand the interaction among the three basic profit factors, which are: the **operating income,** also known as sales or **sales volume,** which indicates in dollars how much merchandise has been sold; the **cost of goods sold,** which shows the amount paid for the goods sold; and the **operating expenses,** which refers to those expenses, other than the cost of the goods, incurred in the buying/selling process.

Gross sales are the entire dollar amount received for goods sold during a given period. This total sales figure is calculated by multiplying the retail price of the individual items of merchandise by the number of pieces actually sold to consumers. The accurate calculation of gross sales, however, must also take into account adjustments because of returns and price reductions. Stores typically give customers the privilege of returning merchandise. When merchandise is returned to stock and the customer receives a cash refund or a charge credit, these returns of sales are called **customer returns.** In addition, if a customer receives a price reduction after the sale is completed, it is known as a **customer allowance.** These two adjustments are referred to collectively as **customer returns and allowances.** When a customer return or allowance takes place, the previously recorded sale must be canceled and subtracted from the gross sales amount. When customer returns and allowances are subtracted from gross sales, the resulting total is the net sales figure. Thus, **net sales** is the sales total after customer returns and allowances have been deducted from gross sales. Net sales represent the amount of goods that actually stay sold. When retailers calculate profit, the net sales figure is the more significant because a firm can only realize a profit on goods that remain sold at the retail price. For this reason, the term sales volume is always a net sales figure.

Merchandisers must determine and balance the retail price for the items they purchase for sale to customers with, among other factors, how much they can afford to pay a vendor for merchandise. Cost of goods sold is simply the cost of the merchandise that has been sold during a given time period. This concept is simple, but the actual calculation is complex because other necessary adjustments must be made to the cost or purchase price that appears on the bill or invoice (vendor's bill). These adjustments are transportation costs, known as **inward freight,** which is the amount a vendor may charge for transporting merchandise to the designated premises of the retailer; **alteration and workroom costs,** which is a charge to a selling department when it is necessary to treat merchandise so that it will be in condition for sale (i.e., assembling, polishing, making cuffs, etc.); and **cash discounts,** which vendors may grant for payment of an invoice within a specified period of time.

In addition, the retailer must maintain a place of business from which the goods are sold, and to maintain this place, it must incur operating expenses. Operating expenses usually fall into two major categories and are charged to a merchandise department to determine the net profit for that department. Expenses that are specific to a given department and that would cease if that department were discontinued are called **direct expenses.** These include salaries of the buyer, assistant buyer, and salespeople; departmental advertising; selling supplies; and customer delivery expenses. Store expenses that exist whether a department is added to or discontinued are **indirect expenses.** These include store expenses that are prorated to all selling departments on the basis of their sales volume, such as store maintenance, insurance, and salaries of top management.

A. Elements of Each Basic Profit Factor

Each of the basic profit factors needs to be dissected because each consists of elements that contribute to profit. The calculations involved highlight the meaning and importance of each element.

Operating Income (Sales)

Gross Sales

Gross sales are the total initial dollars received for merchandise sold during a given period.

CONCEPT:

Gross sales = Total of all the prices charged to consumers on individual items × Number of units actually sold.

PROBLEM:

On Monday, an accessories department sold 30 dolls priced at $15 each, 25 dolls priced at $25 each, and 5 dolls priced at $30 each. What were the gross sales for that day?

SOLUTION:

30 dolls @ $15 each =	$ 450
25 dolls @ $25 each =	625
5 dolls @ $30 each =	150
Gross sales =	**$1,225**

Customer Returns and Allowances

Customer returns and allowances are profit factors because the customer receives either a complete refund of the purchase price or a partial rebate. Thus, the retailer must make a corresponding deduction from the gross sales figure because these transactions result in some cancellation of sales. This dollar figure is usually expressed as a percentage of gross sales.

CONCEPT:

Dollar customer returns and allowances = Total of all refunds or credits to the customer on individual items of merchandise × Number of units actually returned.

PROBLEM:

On Saturday, the junior petite department refunded $98 for one velour jacket, $75 each for two wool skirts, and $55 each for two velvet tops. Other returns for the week amounted to $400, and the weekly total of allowances given was $57. What was the dollar amount of customer returns and allowances?

SOLUTION:

$98 × 1 velour jacket	=	$ 98
$75 × 2 wool skirts	=	150
$55 × 2 velvet tops	=	110
Customer returns for Saturday	=	$358
+		
Total weekly customer returns	=	400
+		
Total weekly customer allowances	=	57
Customer returns and allowances (for week)	=	$815

CONCEPT:

Customer returns and allowance percentage = The dollar sum of customer returns and allowances expressed as a percentage of gross sales.

$$\text{Customer returns and allowances \%} = \frac{\text{\$ Customer returns and allowances}}{\text{Gross sales}}$$

PROBLEM:

Last week, the junior petite sportswear department had gross sales of $20,375. Customer returns and allowances for the week totaled $815. What was the combined percentage of allowances and merchandise returns for the week?

SOLUTION:

$$\text{Customer returns and allowances \%} = \frac{\text{\$815 Customer returns and allowances}}{\text{\$20,375 Gross sales}}$$

Customer returns and allowances % = 4%

Conversely, dollar customer returns and allowances can be computed when the gross sales and customer returns and allowances percentage are known.

CONCEPT:

Dollar customer returns and allowances = Gross sales × Customer returns and allowances percentage.

PROBLEM:

Last week, the junior petite sportswear department reported gross sales of $20,375, with customer returns and allowances of 4%. What was the dollar amount of customer returns and allowances?

SOLUTION:

Dollar customer returns and allowances = $20,375 gross sales

× 4% customer returns
and allowances

Dollar customer returns and allowances = $815

Net Sales

Net sales are the sales total for a given period after customer returns and allowances have been deducted from gross sales.

CONCEPT:

Net sales = Gross sales − Customer returns and allowances.

PROBLEM:

A housewares department sold $65,000 worth of merchandise. Customer returns were $6,500. What were the net sales of this department?

SOLUTION:

Gross sales	= $65,000
− Customer returns and allowances	= −6,500
Net sales	= $58,500

In retailing, the operating income is known as net sales. The net sales figure, also called sales volume, is used to designate the size of a particular store or a merchandise department. For example, last year, Department #37 had a sales volume of $1,000,000. This dollar figure is generally the sales volume for the year.

Retailers use net sales to measure a department's performance or productivity. It is common practice to calculate the percentage of sales that an individual department has contributed to the store's net sales. This type of analysis allows a retailer to compare a particular department of one store with other departments or stores within the company, as well as to compare this selected department's sales with industry figures. These figures are published annually by the National

Retail Federation in the *FOR/MOR, the Combined Financial Merchandising and Operating Results of Retail Stores.*

CONCEPT:

The individual department's net sales are expressed as a percentage of the store's total net sales.

$$\text{Department's net sales \% of total store sales} = \frac{\text{Department's net dollar sales}}{\text{Store's total net dollar sales}}$$

PROBLEM:

The costume jewelry department had net sales of $900,000. For the same period, total store sales were $45,000,000. What is the costume jewelry department's net sales percentage of the total store's net sales?

SOLUTION:

$$\frac{\text{Department's net sales}}{\text{Total store net sales}} = \frac{\$\ \ 900,000}{\$45,000,000}$$

Department's net sales % of total store sales = 2%

Because net sales are determined by the adjustment of customer returns and allowances to gross sales, it is also possible through this relationship to calculate, when desired, a gross sales amount—provided an amount of the dollar net sales and the percentage of customer returns and allowances are known.

CONCEPT:

$$\text{Gross sales} = \frac{\text{Net sales}}{100\% \text{ (Gross sales)} - \text{Customer returns and allowances \%}}$$

PROBLEM:

The net sales of Department #93 were $460,000. The customer returns and allowances were 8%. What were the gross sales of the department?

SOLUTION:

$$\frac{\text{Net sales}}{100\% - \text{Customer returns and allowances \%}} = \frac{\$460,000}{100\% - 8\%}$$

$$\text{Gross sales} = \frac{\$460,000}{92\%}$$

Gross sales = $500,000

For assignments for the previous section, see practice problems 1–10.

Cost of Merchandise Sold

The control of the cost of goods sold is crucial to profitability. The buyer, who decides what merchandise to buy, also makes decisions regarding the cost, transportation, and credit terms as they relate to these purchases. In actual practice, to determine the accurate cost of goods sold, there must be a complete calculation to represent the total cost of goods purchased, which begins with an invoice or billed cost to which the following factors are adjusted:

Billed cost is the purchase price that appears on the invoice (i.e., vendor's bill)

PLUS

Inward freight or transportation costs. This is the amount that a vendor may charge for delivery of merchandise. Inward freight plus billed cost is called the billed delivered cost.

PLUS

Alteration and workroom costs. It is accepted practice to treat this figure as an additional cost because it applies only to merchandise that has been sold and not to all purchases.

MINUS

Cash discounts.[2] These are discounts that vendors may grant for payment of an invoice within a specified time. For example, a vendor may offer a 2% cash discount (deducted from the billed cost) if payment is made within a designated time period. The discounts are offered in the form of a percentage and are deducted from only the billed cost, but the dollar discount earned is used in the calculation of the total cost of sales. For example, a 2% cash discount given on a billed cost of $1,000 translates into a $20 deduction:

$$\begin{array}{r} \$1,000 \text{ billed cost} \\ \times\ 2\% \text{ cash discount} \\ \hline \$ = \$20 \text{ dollar cash discount} \end{array}$$

CONCEPT:

Total cost of merchandise = Billed cost + Inward transportation charges + Workroom costs − Cash discount.

PROBLEM:

An activewear department, for a six-month period, had billed costs of merchandise amounting to $80,000; transportation charges of $2,000; earned cash discounts of 7 1/2%, and workroom costs of $500. Calculate the total cost of merchandise.

---

[2]In Unit VI, Invoice Mathematics—Terms of Sale: The other discounts, in addition to cash discounts, that can reduce the cost of the goods are discussed.

SOLUTION:

	Billed costs	=	$80,000
+	Inward freight	=	+ 2,000
	Billed delivered cost	=	$82,000
+	Workroom costs	=	+ 500
	Gross merchandise costs	=	$82,500
−	Cash discount (7 1/2% × $80,000)	=	− 6,000
	Total cost of merchandise		$76,500

For assignments for the previous section, see practice problems 11–17.

Operating Expenses

Because the expenses of operating a business determine whether or not a net profit is achieved, the control and management of operating expenses are of major concern. For the purpose of analysis, the expenses incurred by the retailer (e.g., maintenance of store space, salaries, etc.) are classified to measure the performance of the designated function or activity. There are various approaches to classifying these items and, although there are many different kinds of expenses, each can be easily identified as just that. However, there is a variation in the format used to record them. Traditionally, operating expenses fall into two major categories and are charged to a merchandise department to determine its net profit. These major categories are direct and indirect expenses.

Direct Expenses

Direct expenses exist only within a given department and cease if that department is discontinued. These might include salespeople's and buyers' salaries, buyers' traveling expenses, advertising, selling supplies, delivery to customers, and selling space. For the purpose of expense analysis in retailing, the amount of floor space occupied that generates a given department's sales volume is allotted by the square foot and is charged directly to that department even though there is no cash outlay. Each expense and/or the total direct expenses are expressed as a percentage of net sales. For example, if the net sales of a department are $100,000 and $3,500 is spent on advertising, the percentage of advertising expenses would be $3,500 ÷ $100,000, or 3.5%.

Indirect Expenses

Indirect expenses are store expenses that will continue to exist even if the particular department is discontinued. These might include store maintenance, insurance, security, depreciation of equipment, and salaries of senior executives. Many indirect expenses are distributed among individual departments on the basis of its sales volume (e.g., if a department contributes 1.5% to the store's total sales, the indirect expenses charged to this department are 1.5%).

CONCEPT:

Operating expenses = Direct expenses + Indirect expenses

PROBLEM:

A children's department has net sales of $300,000, and indirect expenses are 10% of net sales. Direct expenses are:

- Selling salaries   = $24,000
- Advertising expenses =   6,000
- Buying salaries   =   12,000
- Other direct expenses =   18,000

Find the total operating expenses of the department in dollars and as a percentage.

SOLUTION

Indirect expenses (10% × $300,000) = $30,000
Direct expenses:

Selling salaries	=	24,000
Advertising	=	6,000
Buying salaries	=	12,000
Other	=	18,000

Total dollar operating expenses   = $90,000

$$\text{Operating expense } \% = \frac{\$90,000 \text{ operating expenses}}{\$300,000 \text{ net sales}} = 30\%$$

Controllable and Noncontrollable Expenses

There are additional expenses that further complicate expense assignments. Many, but not all, direct expenses are **controllable expenses.** For example, the rent for branch store Y is directly related to this store, but is not under the control of the present store manager because this expense was previously negotiated. Utilities are another example of a direct expense to a store, but an indirect expense to a particular department. The rates are not controllable, but the utilization is.

Because retailers do not always agree on the handling of expenses, some firms use the contribution technique to evaluate the performance of a buyer or store manager. **Contribution,** also known as controllable margin, includes those expenses that are direct, controllable, or a combination of direct and controllable (e.g., selling salaries). Contribution is the amount the department contributes to indirect expenses and profit as seen in Figure 1.

In learning situations, it is more important to identify expense items and to understand the control, management, and relevancy to profit of those expenses

Figure 1. Contribution Operating Statement

		Dollars	Percentages	
Net Sales		$500,000	100.0%	
(minus) **Cost of Merch. Sold**		−266,000	−53.2%	
		$234,000	46.8%	
(minus) **Direct Expenses**				
Payroll	$73,000			
Advertising	13,000			
Supplies	7,000			
Travel	5,000			
Other	12,000			
		−110,000	−22.0%	$110,000
				$500,000
Contribution		124,000	24.8%	$124,000
				$500,000
(minus) **Indirect Expenses**		106,500	21.3%	$106,500
				$500,000
Operating Profit		$17,500	3.5%	

than to make the accounting decision as to which expense is direct, indirect, controllable, or noncontrollable. To eliminate the confusion of how to classify and charge a particular expense item, in this text, expenses are listed individually or are referred to simply as operating expenses.

For an assignment for the previous section, see practice problem 18.

B. The Relationships Among the Basic Profit Factors

The following examples show the relationships among the three fundamental factors on which the amount of profit depends. For comparison, these factors are expressed in percentages as well as in dollars. The net sales figure is the basis for determining profit computation, and so is considered 100%. The other factors involved are shown and stated as a percentage of net sales.

EXAMPLE:

Net sales (operating income)	=	$10,000	100%	
− Cost of merchandise sold	=	− 5,500	− 55%	= ($5,500 ÷ $10,000)
− Operating expenses	=	− 4,300	− 43%	= ($4,300 ÷ $10,000)
Profit	=	$ 200	2%	= ($200 ÷ $10,000)

Notes

PRACTICE PROBLEMS[3]

Operating Income

1. Customer returns and allowances for department #620 came to $4,500. Gross sales in the department were $90,000. What percentage of merchandise sold was returned?

2. The gross sales for store B were $876,500. The customer returns and allowances were 10%.

      (a) What was the dollar amount of returns and allowances?

      (b) What were net sales?

3. The net sales of department X were $46,780. The customer returns were $2,342. What were gross sales?

---

[3]When the final answer to a practice problem is a percentage, it should be expressed to one digit to the right of the decimal (e.g., 6.8%). If the solution is expressed in dollars, the final answer should be expressed as, for example, $29.98.

4. The gross sales of store C were $2,500,000. The customer returns and allowances were $11,360. What were net sales?

5. The net sales of department Y were $36,000. The customer returns and allowances were 10%. What were gross sales?

6. After Mother's Day this year, the loungewear department had customer returns of 10.5%. The department's net sales amounted to $635,380. As the buyer reviewed last year's figures for the same period, the customer returns were 12.5%, with gross sales of $726,149.

       (a) Compute the department's performance for this year and last year, in regard to gross sales, customer returns, and net sales.

       (b) Compare this year's results to last year's performance. Discuss the performance from a profit viewpoint.

7. For this year, department store G's sales volume was $550,000,000. The junior dress department had net sales of $8,250,000, and the misses dress department had net sales of $24,750,000. What were the net sales percentages of each department to the total store?

8. Branch store H had total sales of $30,000,000. The hosiery departments sales were 1.9% of store H's total sales. The handbag department's sales were 2.1% of the total branch sales. What were the dollar net sales for each department?

9. Discussion Problem: Explain why a merchant should be alarmed if customer returns are excessive. How does a merchant determine what is an excessive percentage of returns? What can be done by the department itself to correct a problem rate of returns?

10. The customer returns for the Fall season were 10% on gross sales of $900,000. For the Spring season, gross sales were $850,000, and customer returns were $70,000. What was the percentage of customer returns for the entire year?

Cost of Merchandise Sold

11. A luggage buyer purchased 72 attaché cases that cost $40 each. The cash discount earned was 2%, and the store paid transportation charges of $95. Find the total cost of the merchandise on this order.

12. The petite sportswear buyer placed the following order:

- 36 pants costing $10.75 each
- 48 pants costing $15.50 each
- 24 pants costing $17.50 each.

Shipping charges (paid by the store) were 6% of the billed cost. Find:

  (a) The dollar amount of shipping charges.
  (b) The delivered cost of the total order.

13. A gift shop has workroom costs of $575. The billed cost of merchandise sold amounted to $59,000, with cash discounts earned of $1,180, and freight charges of $650. Find the total cost of the merchandise.

14. A specialty dress shop made purchases amounting to $3,700 at cost, with 8% cash discounts earned, workroom costs of $100, and no transportation charges. Determine the total cost of the merchandise.

15. A sporting goods buyer placed the following order:

- 18 nylon backpacks costing $22 each
- 12 two-person tents costing $54 each
- 6 camp stoves costing $55 each.

Shipping costs, paid by the store, were $60 and a cash discount of 1% was taken. Find:

(a) Billed cost on the total order.
(b) Total delivered cost of the merchandise.

16. Discussion Problem: Explain why control of inward transportation costs and workroom (alterations) costs is vital. Can a merchandiser help to control these factors. If so, how?

17. Why is cash discount calculated on billed cost?

Operating Expenses

18. Analyze the expense section of the following statement:

JOHNSTON CANDY COMPANY

Operating Expenses	Last Year	This Year	Plan
Advertising	$ 28,500	$ 24,300	$ 27,700
Sales salaries	74,000	75,100	75,300
Misc. selling costs	8,300	8,300	8,500
TOTAL	$110,800	$ 107,700	$111,500
Net sales	$900,000	$1,140,000	$980,000

(a) What is the percentage of advertising expenses for each year?

(b) What is the percentage of sales salary expenses for each year?

(c) What is the percentage of miscellaneous selling costs for each year?

(d) What is the yearly percentage of total operating expenses shown?

(e) What is the trend of operating expenses?

(f) What is the trend of net sales?

Notes

II. PROFIT AND LOSS STATEMENTS

Businesses must keep accurate records of sales income, merchandise costs, and operating expenses to calculate profit. Periodically, the income and expenses are summarized on a form known in retailing as a profit and loss statement. {In other types of organizations, this statement is frequently called an income statement.} A **profit and loss statement** shows the difference between income and expenses. Generally, the accounting department keeps a continuous record of sales income and expenses. At set intervals, this statement is analyzed to determine whether these transactions have resulted in a profit or loss. {The interval might be a year, three months, or one month.} If income exceeds expenses, the result is profit. If expenses exceed income, the result is a loss. It is a summary of the business transactions during a given period of time expressed in terms of making or losing money. A profit and loss statement should not be confused with a balance sheet, which shows the assets, liabilities, and net worth of a business.

Because this is a retailing text, the profit and loss statement will not be analyzed as a bookkeeping procedure, but in terms of how a merchant can use the data it contains to improve a merchandising operation. It is a fundamental merchandising concept that one of a buyer's chief responsibilities is to ensure that a store or department earns a profit on the merchandise sold specifically during the accounting period under consideration.

The difference between net sales and the total cost of goods sold is the **gross margin.** This figure must be large enough to cover operating expenses and allow for a reasonable profit. It is calculated for a given period of time by subtracting the total cost of goods sold from net sales for the period under consideration. Gross margin is also frequently known as gross profit because it is an indicator of the final results.

CONCEPT:
  Gross margin = Net sales − Total cost of goods sold.

PROBLEM:
  A department had net sales of $300,000 with the total cost of goods sold at $180,000. Determine the dollar gross margin.

SOLUTION:

Net sales	= $300,000
− (Total) cost of goods sold	= −180,000
Gross margin	= $120,000

The difference between gross margin and operating expenses is **net profit,** which is calculated by subtracting operating expenses from gross margin. To compare profits among retailers, it is necessary to know how the expenses are treated because, in accounting, there are acceptable variations in how expenses are recorded. In this text, expenses will continue to be listed individually or referred to merely as operating expenses. In performing the calculations necessary to answer the problems that apply the profit concepts and principles, the focus is on adjusting the proper element to the appropriate basic profit factor. For example, cash discount is an adjustment to the cost of goods sold factor.

CONCEPT:

Net profit = Gross margin − operating expenses.

PROBLEM:

A department has a gross margin of $120,000, with operating expenses of $105,000. Find the net profit or loss.

SOLUTION:

Gross margin	=	$120,000
− Operating expenses	=	−105,000
Net profit	=	$ 15,000

A department with a gross margin of $120,000 has operating expenses of $135,000. Find the net profit or loss.

SOLUTION:

Gross margin	=	$120,000
− Operating expenses	=	−135,000
Net loss	=	$ 15,000

The five major components of a profit and loss statement are:

- Net sales.
- Cost of goods sold.
- Gross margin.
- Operating expenses.
- Profit or loss figure.

Profit and loss statements can show the performance of a department, division, branch, or the entire organization. The basic format of a profit and loss statement is as follows:

Net sales
− Cost of goods sold

= Gross margin
− Operating expenses

= Net profit or loss

A. Skeletal Profit and Loss Statements

A **skeletal profit and loss statement** does not spell out all transactions in detail, but it is a quick method to determine, at any particular time, any given department's profit or loss. It contains the five major components of a profit and loss statement and is expressed in both dollars and as a percentage.

EXAMPLE:

Net sales	=	$300,000	100%
− Cost of goods sold	=	−180,000	60%
= Gross margin	=	$120,000	40%
− Operating expenses	=	−105,000	35%
= **Net profit**	=	15,000	5%

The value of a profit and loss statement is that it can be used to compare previous statements or compare a company's figures with industry-wide figures to help improve profit or adjust any of the other factors mentioned in the example. Therefore, it is vital to think in terms of percentages as well as dollar amounts. For example, a buyer's statement that a net profit of $2,869 was earned during a given business period has no real meaning unless the dollar amount for each of the other contributing factors is also stated. The profit figure could be phenomenally high or dismally low by industry standards, depending on the dollar net sales volume of the department. Unless the figures for all other factors are available, it is impossible to determine which departmental operations excelled or faltered. The only meaningful way to compare departmental performances is to compare the respective results expressed as a percentage of the net sales volume. From this information, the deduction can be made that profit will vary upward or downward as one or more of the three major factors (i.e., net sales, cost of goods sold, or operating expenses) vary.

CONCEPT:

$$\text{Cost of goods sold \%} = \frac{\text{Cost of goods sold (in dollars)}}{\text{Net sales}}$$

$$\text{Gross margin \%} = \frac{\text{Gross margin (in dollars)}}{\text{Net sales}}$$

$$\text{Operating expenses \%} = \frac{\text{Direct and indirect expenses (in dollars)}}{\text{Net sales}}$$

$$\text{Net profit \%} = \frac{\text{Net profit (in dollars)}}{\text{Net sales}}$$

PROBLEM:

The junior sportswear department in Store A had net sales of $160,000; the cost of goods sold was $88,000 and operating expenses were $64,000. The junior sportswear department in store B, for the same business period, had net sales of $260,000; the cost of goods sold was $135,200 and operating expenses were $109,200. Which store earned a higher net profit percentage?

SOLUTION:

	STORE A		STORE B	
Net sales	$160,000	100%	$260,000	100%
− Cost of goods sold	− 88,000	− 55%	−135,200	− 52%
Gross margin	$ 72,000	45%	$124,800	48%
− Operating expenses	− 64,000	− 40%	−109,200	− 42%
Net Profit	$ 8,000	5%	$ 15,600	6%

As a basis for comparison, the percentage figures give the clearest picture. Upon examination of this skeletal profit and loss statement, the reader can see that the junior sportswear department in Store A spent 55 cents of every dollar of sales on the cost of merchandise sold, while Store B spent 52 cents. Respectively, Store A spent 40 cents and Store B spent 42 cents of every dollar of sales on operating expenses. Gross margin, net profit, and individual transactions can be more accurately compared when these figures are recorded in a complete profit and loss statement. Also, all other figures in the skeletal profit and loss statement are then expressed as a part or a percentage of net sales. Conversely, when the respective results for cost of goods sold, gross margin, operating expenses, or net profit are expressed as a percentage of net sales, the dollar amounts of each factor can be determined.

CONCEPT:

$ Cost of goods sold = Cost of goods sold % × net sales.
$ Gross margin = Gross margin % × net sales.
$ Operating expenses = Operating expenses % × net sales.
$ Net profit = Net profit % × net sales.

PROBLEM:

The junior sportswear department in Store A had net sales of $160,000. The cost of goods sold was 55%; gross margin was 45%; operating expenses were 40%; and net profit was 5%. What were the dollar amounts of each?

SOLUTION:

Net sales	=	$160,000	
− Cost of goods sold	=	− 88,000	($160,000 × 55%)
Gross margin	=	$ 72,000	($160,000 × 45%)
− Operating expenses	=	− 64,000	($160,000 × 40%)
Net profit	=	$ 8,000	($160,000 × 5%)

For assignments for the previous section, see practice problems 19–34.

B. Final Profit and Loss Statements

A **final profit and loss statement** shows the basic profits factors developed in detail, so that every transaction is clearly seen. The skeleton format discussed earlier shows the basic factors—that is, sales and cost of goods and expenses, provides a quick method of monitoring profit or loss, but it is also necessary to have more detailed information on these basic factors to detect weaknesses that need strengthening or to illuminate strengths that bear repetition.

Thus, a final profit and loss statement includes additional information pertaining to stock levels. Bearing in mind that profit occurs only when the merchandise sold remains sold, the retailer must be able, from an accounting viewpoint, to determine the value of inventory or merchandise sold. Generally, retailers use an accounting method known as the Retail Method of Inventory,[4] in which the retail stock figure at the end of the accounting period provides the basis for determining the cost value of stock. An **opening inventory** figure refers to the retail value of the merchandise in stock at the beginning of the accounting period. It is established by a physical count of the merchandise in stock at current retail prices; this figure is then converted to a cost amount. The **closing inventory** figure is the amount of merchandise in stock at the end of the period under consideration. The opening inventory, at cost, is added to the cost of new net purchases and the transportation charges {inward freight} to determine an amount known as **total merchandise handled.** Total merchandise handled is the sum of merchandise, at cost, available for sale. To determine the cost of only the merchandise that was sold, the final profit calculation requires a total merchandise handled amount. It can be determined at cost or at retail. The gross cost of goods sold can be calculated when the closing inventory, at cost, is subtracted from the total merchandise handled amount.

---

[4]In Unit IV, Retail Method of Inventory, this prevalent retail accounting method is discussed in detail.

EXAMPLE:

Opening inventory, at cost		$100,000
+ Billed costs		+500,000
+ Inward freight		+ 1,000
Total merchandise handled, at cost	=	$601,000
− Closing inventory, at cost		−159,000
Gross cost of goods sold	=	$451,000

With this information, it is now possible to determine the net cost of goods sold by the other adjustments, {e.g., cash discounts}. For a better understanding of the detailed final profit and loss statement, shown on page 29, refer to the definitions that accompany Figure 2.

For assignments for the previous section, see practice problems 35–40.

Figure 2 illustrates a final profit and loss statement, which is an amplification of the skeletal profit and loss statement. The basic profit factors (that is, sales, cost of goods sold and expenses) are developed in detail so that each transaction is clearly seen. To analyze the results, each factor must be presented in a standard accounting arrangement. The final profit and loss statement is the only way to make a valid comparison among departments or stores because the detailed information supplied by this statement is necessary to compute the cost of goods actually sold.

- **INCOME FROM SALES** is divided into such categories as:
  Gross Sales ($450,000): the retail value of total initial sales.
  Customer Returns and Allowances ($25,000): the total value of cancellation of sales by customer credit, refund, or partial rebate.
  Net Sales Figure ($425,000): the figure derived by subtracting customer returns and allowances from the gross sales of a period. It is the dollar value of sales that "stay sold."

- **COST OF MERCHANDISE SOLD** is divided into such categories as:
  Opening Inventory, at Retail ($100,000): the amount of merchandise at the beginning of a period, counted and recorded at the current selling price.
  Opening Inventory, at Cost ($52,000): the figure derived from the retail figure by applying a markup percentage to the total merchandise handled.
  New Net Purchases ($258,000): the billed cost of merchandise purchased. The gross purchases minus returns and allowances to vendors.
  Inward Transportation ($2,000): the cost of transporting goods to the premises.
  Total Cost of Goods ($260,000): the combination of the cost of merchandise purchased and inward transportation.

Figure 2. Profit and Loss Statement

Profit Factors		Cost		Retail		%
Income from sales						
	Gross Sales				$450,000	
	– Customer Returns & Allowances				– 25,000	
	Net Sales				$425,000	100%
Cost of Merchandise Sold						
	Opening Inventory		$ 52,000	$100,000*		
	New Net Purchases	$258,000				
	+ Inward Transportation	+ 2,000				
		$260,000				
	+ Total Cost of Goods		$260,000			
	Total Merchandise Handled At Cost		$312,000			
	– Closing Inventory At Cost		– 65,000			
	Gross Cost of Goods Sold		$247,000			
	– Cash Discount		– 13,000			
	Net Cost of Goods Sold		$234,000			
	+ Alteration & Workroom Costs		+ 1,000			
	Total Cost of Goods Sold		$235,000		–235,000	55.3%
GROSS MARGIN					$190,000	44.7%
Operating Expenses						
	Total Direct Expenses		$101,250			
	Total Indirect Expenses		67,500			
	Total Operating Expenses				$168,750	39.7%
	Net Profit				$ 21,250	5.0%

*$100,000 represents the opening retail inventory figure (determined by physical count), from which $52,000, the opening cost inventory figure, is derived by applying a markup percentage.

Total Merchandise Handled at Cost ($312,000): the sum of the opening inventory plus the total cost of the purchases.

Closing Inventory, at Cost ($65,000): the figure derived from the retail inventory figure that represents the merchandise in stock at the end of an operating period.

Gross Cost of Merchandise Sold ($247,000): the total merchandise handled less the cost of the closing inventory.

Cash Discounts ($13,000): adjustments made to the cost of goods sold from paying bills in a specified time.

Net Cost of Goods Sold ($234,000): the gross cost of merchandise sold minus cash discounts.

Alteration and Workroom Costs ($1,000): the cost of preparing goods for resale. It is another adjustment to the cost of goods sold.

Total Cost of Goods Sold ($235,000 or 55.3%): the figure that results when the gross cost of merchandise sold is adjusted by subtracting cash discounts and adding alteration and workroom.

Gross Margin ($190,000 or 44.7%): the difference between net sales and total merchandise cost. This is often called gross profit.

■ **OPERATING EXPENSES** are divided into such categories as:

Direct Expenses ($101,250): expenses that come into being with a department and cease if it is discontinued.

Indirect Expenses ($67,500): expenses that continue even if a department is discontinued.

Total Operating Expenses ($168,750): direct and indirect expenses combined.

■ **NET (OPERATING) PROFIT** ($21,250 or 5%): the result of the relationship among sales, cost of goods, and expenses. When the gross margin is larger than the operating expenses, a net profit is achieved.

PRACTICE PROBLEMS

Profit and Loss Statements

19. Determine the net profit or loss in dollars and as a percentage for a small leather goods department if:

Net sales	=	$278,000
Cost of goods sold	=	191,600
Operating expenses	=	78,300

20. Calculate the net profit or loss in dollars and as a percentage if:

Net sales	=	$30,000
Cost of goods sold	=	52%
Operating expenses	=	48%

21. A drugstore has net sales of $490,000, with the cost of merchandise sold at $240,000. If the buyer must achieve a 5% net profit, calculate the allowable expenses in dollars and as a percentage.

22. The housewares buyer was allotted a newspaper and television advertising budget of 2.5% of net sales, with 60% designated for newspaper advertising. The net sales for this department were planned at $725,000. What is the dollar amount available for television advertising.

23. The swimwear department of the ABC Department Store had the following records:

Net sales   = $132,000
Cost of goods sold   =   118,000
Operating expenses   =   11,500

What is the net profit or loss?

24. The Rappapart Ribbon Company had the following records:

Gross sales   = $110,000
Customer returns and allowances   =   10,000
Cost of goods sold   =   80,000
Operating expenses   =   35,000

What is the net profit or loss?

Skeletal Profit and Loss Statements

25. Note the following figures:

Net profit	2.5%
Gross margin	$7,000
Operating expenses	6,600

Find:

    (a) The cost of goods in dollars.

    (b) The percentage of operating expenses.

26. The net profit in an appliance of department for the Spring/Summer period was $20,000, which represented 2% of net sales. Operating expenses totaled $480,000. Find:

    (a) The dollar amount of gross margin.

    (b) The net sales figure.

27. The linen department had net sales of $80,000. There was a 2% loss, and the gross margin was 46%. Determine the operating expenses of the department and express the result in dollars and as a percentage.

28. Calculate the percentage of operating expenses for a home furnishings department that has the following figures:

Gross sales	$476,000
Customer returns	4,000
Advertising costs	10,000
Salaries	101,000
Miscellaneous expenses	6,160
Utilities	9,000
Insurance	11,000
Rent	70,000

29. Set up a skeletal statement that shows the following figures as dollars and as a percentage:

Net profit	$5,500
Net profit	2.5%
Operating expenses	47.5%

30. Suppose that the estimated net sales for the coming year are $100,000; estimated cost of merchandise purchases is $52,000; and the total estimated operating expenses are $43,000. The buyer's goal is a net profit of 5%. Determine the percentage of gross margin on sales needed to achieve this desired profit.

31. Using the following figures, set up a skeletal profit and loss statement that shows each factor in dollars and as a percentage.

Net sales	$85,000
Net profit	1,700
Cost of goods sold	45,000

32. What is the profit or loss in dollars if gross sales are $218,000, customer returns and allowances are $3,000, cost of goods sold are 55%, and the operating expenses are 41%?

33. Find the gross margin percent when:

Gross sales	$435,000
Customer returns and allowances	49,000
Billed cost of goods	195,000
Freight charges	1,800
Cash discounts	4%

34. Discussion Problem: In measuring gross margin performance, which is more significant: the dollar amount or the percentage figure? Why?

Final Profit and Loss Statements

35. Review this store's performance by analyzing the following figures:

Opening inventory, at cost	$120,000
New purchases (billed cost)	140,000
Transportation charges	1,000
Closing inventory, at cost	122,000

(a) Determine the total merchandise handled at cost.

(b) What is the gross cost of merchandise sold?

36. A retailer, contemplating the purchase of a small children's shop, found the previous owner had an inventory at cost of $30,000. For that period, this retailer was given the following figures:

Sales	$60,000
Closing inventory, at cost	33,000
New purchases, at cost	40,000
Transportation charges	500

What was the gross cost of merchandise sold?

37. During the year, a stationery store achieved the following results:

Sales	$585,000
Purchases, at cost	548,000
Transportation charges	5,000

Inventories at cost:

Beginning of year	555,000
End of year	500,000

Determine the gross cost of merchandise sold.

38. Find the net profit or loss as a percentage and the gross margin as a dollar amount:

Gross sales	$200,000
Customer returns and allowances	15,000
Opening inventory, at cost	38,000
Billed cost of goods	99,000
Inward transportation	5,000
Cash discount	6,000
Closing inventory, at cost	36,000
Payroll	48,000
Occupancy	28,000
Wrapping and packing	1,200
Utilities	2,000
Delivery	2,800

39. Construct a profit and loss statement using the following departmental figures and show the dollar amounts for net sales, total cost of goods sold, gross margin, expenses, and profit:

Gross sales	$82,000
Customer returns and allowances	4,000
Inward freight	2,000
Workroom costs	1,000
Opening inventory, at cost	17,000
Closing inventory, at cost	14,000
Purchases, at cost	36,000
Cash discounts	8%
Advertising	5,000
Rent	12,000
Salaries	17,000
Miscellaneous expenses	2,500

40. Construct a final profit and loss statement from the figures listed below and calculate the major factors as percentages and dollar amounts.

Opening inventory	$ 74,200
Gross sales	248,000
Advertising	15,000
Misc. expenses	18,000
Purchases, at cost	120,000
Closing inventory	78,000
Customer returns	25,800
Salaries	26,000
Transportation charges	8,000
Rent	39,000
Cash discounts	3%

III. HOW TO INCREASE PROFITS

Realistically, it is impossible to list everything a retailer needs to know to merchandise at a profit because the factors that govern profits are variable and net profits do not represent any fixed sum. As a frame of reference, Figure 3 lists various types of retail stores and their profit performances. These results illustrate that the amount of profit generated can be different depending on the type of organization and is rarely, if ever, constant. For each store type, the actual figures will change annually, but the information required for analysis will remain constant.

After reviewing a profit and loss statement, however, to determine how each of these factors affects profit, certain measures can be taken to improve profits. However, because these three factors (that is, sales, cost of goods sold, and operating expenses) are always interrelated, the adjustments made must keep all three factors balanced in relationship to one another. Fundamentally, profits can be improved through the following three approaches:

1. Increase sales with only a proportionate increase in the cost of the merchandise and little or no increase in expenses.
2. Decrease the cost of merchandise sold without a decrease in sales (e.g., sell a larger proportion of higher markup merchandise or decrease the net cost of goods sold by lowering shipping charges and/or obtaining greater cash discounts).
3. Reduce expenses.

Figure 3. Profit Performance by Store Type

Store Type	Profits		Profits to Sales		
	Last Year	This Year	% Change	Last Year	This Year
Department stores	$1,470,655	$1,580,722	+ 7.5	3.3%	3.5%
Mass merchandisers	1,896,700	2,033,300	+ 7.1	2.8	2.8
Specialty stores	555,579	568,774	+ 2.4	4.4	5.0
Discount stores	335,336	432,774	+29.1	3.4	3.3
Off-price stores	24,143	32,073	+32.9	5.4	5.2
Miscellaneous	478,326	461,537	− 3.5	2.3	2.6
Total	$4,762,739	$5,109,000	+ 7.3	3.0%	3.2%

EXAMPLE:

The following example shows the application and effect of each approach. For the accounting period under consideration, a merchant estimated sales at $100,000, merchandise purchases at $70,000, and total operating expenses at $25,000. If the merchant wants to increase the previous 5% net profit, which approach should he take?

Actual Estimated Performance

		Dollars		Percentages
Sales		$100,000		100%
− Cost of goods sold		− 70,000		− 70
Gross margin	=	30,000	=	30
− Operating expenses		− 25,000		− 25
Net profit	=	$ 5,000	=	5%

APPROACH #1:

Increase sales with only a proportionate increase in cost of goods sold and little or no increase in expenses.

		Dollars		Percentages	
Sales		$110,000		100 %	(Increased sales)
− Cost of goods sold		− 75,900		− 69	(Decreased % of cost of goods sold)
Gross margin	=	34,100	=	31	(Increased $ and % of gross margin)
− Operating expenses		− 28,050		− 25.5	(Increased $ and % of opererating expenses)
Net profit	=	$ 6,050	=	5.5%	(Increased net profit)

APPROACH #2:

Decrease the cost of goods sold without decreasing sales, which is equivalent to a larger gross margin.

		Dollars		Percentages	
Sales		$100,000		100 %	(Constant)
− Cost of goods sold		− 69,500		− 69.5	(Decreased cost of goods sold)
Gross margin	=	30,500	=	30.5	(Larger gross margin)
− Operating expenses		− 25,000		− 25	(Same expenses)
Net profit	=	$ 5,500	=	5.5%	(Increased net profit)

APPROACH #3

Lower or reduce expenses.

		Dollars		Percentages		
Sales		$100,000		100 %	(Constant)
− Cost of goods sold		− 70,000		− 70	(Constant)
Gross margin	=	30,000	=	30	(Constant)
− Operating expenses		− 24,500		− 24.5	(Reduced expenses)
Net profit	=	$ 5,500	=	5.5%	(Increased net profit)

Practice Problems for Review

41. The following figures are for your department:

Net sales	$490,000
Billed cost of goods	265,000
Freight charges	11,160
Rent	56,640
Salaries	111,600
Miscellaneous expenses	25,260
Cash discounts	37,000
Insurance	27,800
Advertising	16,740
Opening inventory (cost)	117,000
Closing inventory (cost)	120,000

(a) Calculate the total cost of goods sold.

(b) Determine the operating expenses in dollars.

(c) Determine the profit or loss in dollars and as a percentage.

42. If profit is $8,000 and profit percentage is 4%, what is the net sales figure?

43. If expenses are $85,340 and gross margin is $90,960, express operating profit or loss in dollars.

44. Find the net profit or loss in dollars and as a percentage if:

Opening inventory (cost)	$ 70,000
Operating expenses	180,000
Closing inventory	72,000
Net sales	400,000
Inward freight	5,000
Purchases, at cost	210,000

45. Gross sales are $25,619; customer returns and allowances are $2,791.32; purchases at billed cost are $12,585; inward freight is $932.45; and cash discounts earned average 2%. What is the gross margin in dollars?

46. If a department experiences a loss of 3% during a six-month period and its gross margin is 43%, what must its expense percentage be?

47. Gross margin in the shoe department was $185,000. Operating expenses were $178,000, and the net profit was 2% of net sales. What were the net sales?

48. Determine the net sales when:

Operating expenses	$57,750
Gross margin	56,650
Net loss	1%

49. Express the gross margin as a percentage if:

Gross sales	$283,000
Customer returns	7,000
Billed cost of goods	137,000
Inward freight	5,000
Workroom charges	3,000
Cash discounts	6%

50. Set up a final profit and loss statement using the following figures.

Inward freight	$ 3,000
Workroom and alteration charges	600
Opening inventory (at cost)	14,400
Closing inventory (at cost)	14,600
Customer returns	8,000
Gross sales	82,000
Purchases (at cost)	35,000
Promotional expense	3,500
Rent and utilities	10,000
Payroll	15,500
Miscellaneous expenses	2,000
Cash discounts	3%

Express results in dollar amounts and as a percentage for:

(a) Net profit or loss.
(b) Cost of goods sold.
(c) Gross margin.
(d) Operating expenses.

Then, analyze the above figures. Discuss the relationship of expenses to net profit and the size of the gross margin. Suggest strategies to improve profit.

51. Determine the dollar profit or loss in a department in which sales were $1,950,000, cost of merchandise sold was 50%, and operating expenses were $925,000.

52. Prepare a skeletal profit and loss statement showing both dollars and percents for a department showing the following figures:

Net sales $280,000
Cost of merchandise sold 150,000
Loss 3%

53. Determine net sales for a handbag department with the following figures:

Gross margin $11,500
Operating expenses 11,000
Net profit 2%

54. Prepare a profit and loss statement for a boutique with the following figures and determine if the store operated at a profit:

Gross sales $104,000
Customer returns 5,000
Billed costs 49,000
Inward freight 10,000
Advertising 7,500
Rent 12,000
Alterations 1,000
Salaries 16,000
Miscellaneous expenses 5,000

55. Find the gross margin percentage when:

Gross sales	$566,000
Customer returns	10%
Billed cost of goods	258,000
Inward freight	9,000
Workroom charges	2,200
Cash discounts	6%

56. Set up a profit and loss statement, showing dollar amounts only, using the following figures:

Gross sales	$127,000
Closing inventory, at cost	29,000
Opening inventory, at cost	33,000
Miscellaneous expenses	5,000
Customer returns	6,000
Purchases, at cost	60,000
Rent and utilities	23,000
Payroll	30,000
Transportation charges	1,700
Cash discounts	8%
Advertising	6,000

57. Construct a skeletal profit and loss statement from the figures below, expressing all factors in both dollars and as a percentage.

Billed cost of goods	$ 90,000
Alteration and workshop charges	2,400
Cash discounts	1,800
Freight charges	3,000
Direct expenses	36,000
Customer returns	9,000
Indirect expenses	31,200
Gross sales	177,000

58. Determine the percent of profit or loss if:

Gross sales	$180,000
Direct expenses	52,000
Opening inventory (at cost)	39,000
Indirect expenses	27,000
Purchases (at cost)	95,000
Customer returns	8,000
Inward freight	1,000
Closing inventory (at cost)	44,000
Cash discounts	4%

59. Discussion Problem: Your merchandise manager has pointed out that the profit percentage in your department for the most recent period was extremely poor. In conjunction with your assistant buyers, make a list of as many ways as possible that you, as the buyer, can attempt to improve the situation directly.

60. Discussion problem: Set up a mathematical demonstration example to show how increased profit percentage might be achieved in a department operation despite reduced volume. Explain.

The housewares department in a specialty store had net sales of $1,500,000. The direct expenses during the period under consideration were:

Buying salaries	$125,000
Selling salaries	275,000
Advertising	90,000
Receiving & marking	15,000
Wrapping & packing	10,000

The gross margin achieved during this time was 34.0%. After reviewing this performance, management decided that expenses must be reduced. The manager was given the choice of either reducing the advertising budget to a maximum of $50,000 or eliminating a salesperson which would reduce selling salaries by $50,000.

Which plan of action would you choose? Why? Explore the two options mathematically, and then state your choice. Justify your decision. Discuss the impact your strategy will have on net profit.

ANALYSIS OF PROFIT AND LOSS STATEMENTS

Ms. Kane, the China and Glass buyer of Crystal Clear, Inc., was asked to present a yearly profit and loss in skeletal form to the divisional merchandise manager. In addition, she wanted to prepare a summary of comments that included a comparison of her performance this year with that of her major competitor, China Seas, Ltd. Ms. Kane obtained the following information from Crystal Clear's statistical department:

Gross sales	$135,000
Alteration and workroom costs	1,000
Opening inventory, at cost	49,500
Closing inventory, at cost	61,000
New purchases, at cost	77,500
Inward freight	1,500
Cash discounts	4%
General overhead	11,000
Advertising	9,000
Salaries	20,000
Rent	8,600
Customer returns and allowances	15,000

Ms. Kane obtained, from outside research, profit and loss data on her competitor, China Seas, which had the following results for the same year:

Profit	6% or $7350
Operating Expenses	40%

Ms. Kane then prepared a skeletal profit and loss statement for her department and for that of her competitor China Seas. Upon completion of this task, she compared the two statements. Based on this study, where and how did Ms. Kane determine that she could take action that would give immediate results and have an impact on the department's profitability? Support the suggested action mathematically.

For the past two years, Ms. Rose has been the owner of My Secret Love, a trendy boutique specializing in moderate-priced handbags. Her previous training and experience as an assistant buyer in a major department store were instrumental in the development of a successful and profitable business. Lately, however, she has realized that current economic conditions are less favorable for her. Sales have been sluggish, and she could see that maintaining the current level of her expenses was becoming increasingly difficult. As a result, she decided to target another customer group for the next season by adding a high-priced designer line to her assortment. To properly merchandise this new classification, she wants to hire another part-time salesperson skilled in selling this type of goods and to use additional sales promotion techniques to launch the new line. Most important, however, she wants to maintain her current profit percentage even though sales are soft and her expenses will increase.

In the first year, My Secret Love's net sales were $450,000, expenses were at 40.5%, and the profit margin was 4.5%. Ms. Rose was pleased with her venture. The second year, sales grew to $481,500 and her profit increased to 5.0%, with expenses totaling $192,600. She felt she was moving in the right direction. Now, her goal is to increase sales by 7%, with expenses estimated to reach 41%.

(a) How, if at all, will her change in sales and expenses affect her profit?
(b) As you review Ms. Rose's performance and future goals, what suggestions can you offer to help her meet them?

Spreadsheet Analysis

Use the facts and figures from Case Study 3, Merchandising for a Profit. The opening of a new mini-mall near Ms. Rose's trading area is predicted. Therefore, as she does her projections for the next two years, she recognizes that the increased competition could decrease the rate of sales growth for her fourth year from 7% to 6%, yet she wishes to maintain a 5% net profit and offsetting expenses at 41%. Prepare a spreadsheet from the following data.

	Year 1		Year 2		Year 3		Year 4	
	$	%	$	%	$	%	$	%
Growth rate				7%		7%		6%
Net sales	$450,000.00	100%	$481,500.00		$515,205.00		$546,117.30	
Cost of goods	247,500.00							
Gross margin	202,500.00							
Operating expenses	182,250.00							
Net profit	20,250.00							5%

Using Year 1 as a base, complete the chart for the subsequent years by calculating the following in dollars and as percentages:

(a) Cost of goods sold.
(b) Gross margin.
(c) Operating expenses.
(d) Net profit.

What can Ms. Rose do to retain the gross margin percentage that provides the net profit percent? Compare the yearly results. What, if any, adjustments in the third and fourth years should be made to reach the 5% net profit goal?

Unit II

RETAIL PRICING AND
REPRICING OF MERCHANDISE

Objectives

- Identification of activities that retailers can use to maximize profits.
- Understanding of price lining and identification of the types of prize zones.
- Recognition and identification of the three basic pricing elements and how they relate to each other.
- Calculation of markup as dollar amounts and percentages for individual items and groups of items.
- Establishment of retail prices.
- Ascertainment of the types of price adjustments and confirmation of their importance as merchandising decisions.
- Calculation of markdowns as dollar amounts and percentages.
- Delineation of the procedures for making price changes.
- Recognition of the impact of pricing and repricing decisions on profit.

Key Terms

additional markup	net markdown
cost complement	point-of-sale markdown
employee discount	prestige price zone
gross markdown	price line
markdown	price lining
markdown cancellation	price range
markdown percentage	price zone
markup	promotional price zone
markup cancellation	retail reductions
markup percentage	volume price zone

Every business aims to yield the largest possible total profit. One way a retail merchandiser attempts to secure maximum profits is through the skillful pricing of goods offered for sale. Price is a strong motivation in consumer buying habits. It is a competitive weapon and, very frequently, it is the only way to attract customer patronage when merchandise assortments are comparable, if not identical. Because many factors influence pricing, it can be considered an art as well as a science.

In large industrial organizations, the actual pricing decisions are generally the responsibility of management. In large retail stores, the actual pricing of merchandise is determined by individual departmental buyers or a comparable person designated by the particular organizational structure. Top management, however, does formulate the basic price policies of the store, such as the implementation of a policy of underselling the competition by 10% on all items. Although the retailer establishes the price of individual items as they are offered for sale, ultimately, the total of all purchases must realize maximum profits. In the final analysis, the volume of sales as an aggregate figure must be great enough to cover not only the costs of merchandise sold, but also to provide a profit. Pricing, therefore, is an integral part of merchandising that requires training and skill.

I. RETAIL PRICING

Pricing refers to **price lining,** which is the practice of predetermining the retail prices at which an assortment of merchandise will be carried. A retail buyer selects and offers a merchandise assortment to the consumer at a specific price point, or **price line,** such as $15, $20, and so on.

A. The Structuring of Price Lines

A buyer creates a stock assortment by considering what price lines to carry and the depth of assortment offered at the various price points. The number of price lines, and those particular price lines in the assortments, can help reflect the desired character that management wishes to project. The emphasis of a stock by price lines depends on the composition of the consumer segment that management wishes to attract. Usually, there is a price structure around which buying for a specific retail establishment is concentrated. For example, the sportswear department stocks tops to retail for $25; this price line may cover a variety of types, fabrics, and sizes. The buyer, with the proper source of information, knows that this particular store's customers will pay $25 for a top.

The sportswear department, however, may stock a variety of tops that retail from $8 to $40. This is called the **price range,** which refers to the spread from the lowest to the highest price line carried. Most customers generally prefer to

Figure 4. Price Line Structure Promotional Chart

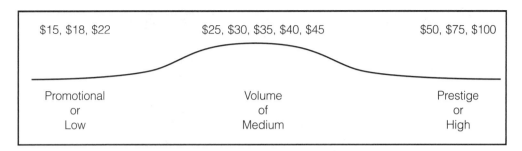

$15, $18, $22	$25, $30, $35, $40, $45	$50, $75, $100
Promotional or Low	Volume of Medium	Prestige or High

concentrate their purchases at either one price line or several that are relatively close to each other. **Price zone** refers to a series of price lines that are likely to appeal to one group of the store's customers. When more than two price lines are stocked, a price zone situation exists. The price zones can be referred to as **volume price zone, promotional price zone,** and **prestige price zone.** Figure 4 illustrates three possible price zones for a price range from $15 to $100.

Generally, the promotional price zone refers to the lower price lines carried; the volume price zone is the middle price lines where the largest percentage of sales occur; and the prestige price zone refers to the highest price lines carried in a department, which "tone up" the assortment. This distribution curve typically occurs within a price range, regardless of the price lines.

B. Setting Individual Retail Prices and/or Price Lines

The pricing of individual items and the establishment of price lines require experience and skill. When pricing merchandise as it is bought, a buyer must always consider its salability in terms of its retail price, remembering that the aggregate of all prices must be high enough to cover merchandise costs, operating expenses, a fair profit return, possible reductions, shortages, and discounts to employees. Variations in pricing occur because there are some noncontrollable factors that influence pricing decisions, such as the volatility of ready-to-wear. Because they influence the setting of the retail price, the basic factors to consider in pricing are:

- Wholesale costs.
- Competition.
- Price maintenance policies of manufacturers, such as "suggested" retail prices.
- Handling and selling costs.
- Store policies, such as "off-price" policy.
- Nature of the goods, such as markdown risk in fashion goods.
- Correlation among departments.
- Supply and demand factors.

Figure 5. Price Line Report by Classification

(1) Code No.	(2) Code Description	(3) Store	(4a) Net Sales Units — This Week Ending 02/07	(4b) One Week Ago Ending 01/31	(4c) 2 Weeks Ago Ending 01/24	(4d) Last 4 Weeks Ending 01/10	(4e) Season to Date 02/07	(5) On Hand Units	(6) On Order Units	(7a) MTD Receiving	(7b) MTD Trans-fer	(7c) Markdown $	(7c) Markdown %	(7d) Net Sales $	(7d) Net Sales %	(7e) Inventory $	(7e) Stock Sales Ratio	(7f) Open Order	(7g) Inventory + On Order	Code No.
96	JEANS																			96
	$15.01 – $20.00	01					48	51	120											
		05					34	15	84											
		08					31	13	48											
		10					13	1	48											
		14					26	24	48											
		15					25	25	60											
	TOTAL UNITS						177	129	408											
96	TOTAL DOLLARS						3142	2310	6528											
96	JEANS																			96
	$20.01 – $29.00	01	4	1		5	5	5–												
		05	3			3	3	3–												
		08	2	1		3	3	3–												
		10	4	1		5	5	5–												
		14	2	1		3	3	3–												
		15	1	3		4	4	4–												
	TOTAL UNITS		16	7		23	23	23–												
96	TOTAL DOLLARS		464	203		667	667	667–												
96	JEANS																			96
	PRICE LINE–ALL	01	6	3	1	11	391	199	120					1	30	28	20	19	47	
		05	3		3	8	325	66	84					1	19	8	9	13	21	
		08	2	5	1	8	259	111	48					1	12	14	24	8	21	
		10	4	2	3	12	188	14	48					1	25	1	1	8	9	
		14		2	6	9	238	100	48						7	14	41	8	21	
		15	2	4	1	11	285	76	60						7	11	32	10	20	
	TOTAL UNITS		17	16	15	59	1686	566	408											
96	TOTAL DOLLARS		468	320	188	1099	23005	7656	6528					5	100	75	16	65	140	
96	CLASS TOTALS																			90
	PRICE LINE–ALL	01	108	154	302	884	7673	2394	1192					11	28	264	24	140	404	
		05	67	131	93	362	3475	1636	958	16				8	20	172	22	109	281	
		08	30	121	67	258	3054	1136	906					3	7	112	41	107	219	
		10	65	118	65	317	2680	1072	708	12				7	18	107	15	79	186	
		14	49	56	72	225	2609	1162	796					5	12	114	24	91	205	
		15	69	92	86	327	3610	1319	792	14				6	16	135	22	87	222	
	TOTAL UNITS		388	672	685	2373	23101	8719	5352											
90	TOTAL DOLLARS		3965	6019	5385	20605	239725	84680	77191	42				40	100	905	23	612	1516	
99	INVALID CODES																			99
	PRICE LINE–ALL	01		1	1	1	3	52	530	29						62–		80	18	
		05	1–	1–	2	3–	33–	84	378					13		5–	62	58	53	
		08				1–	31–	35	378									58	59	
		10		3		4	20–	53	378					24			2	58	58	
		14	1–	1–	1–	3–	84	70–	378					63		10–	25	58	48	
		15		1–		2	19–	29	378							7–		58	51	
	TOTAL UNITS		2–	1	2		16–	183	2420											
99	TOTAL DOLLARS		62–	10–	37–	330–	4875–	3751	37204	29		638–	1–	100		84–	133	372	288	

1 = Code Number: Designates code within a classification, example: Code 96.

2 = Code Description: Description of codes separated by price lines, example: Jeans are separated as $15.01–$20.00. Totals include:

  a = By Code: Example: under STD (season-to-date) for all price lines in the code both by units and dollars, 1,686 total units, $23,005 total dollars.

  b = By Classification: Example: under STD (season-to-date), all codes and all price lines, both in units and dollars, 23,101 total units, $239,725 total dollars.

  c = By Department: All classifications, codes, and price lines both in units and dollars. (Not shown.)

3 = Store: Designates by store, each store, example: 01.

4 = Net Sales Units: Permits analysis of unit sales. This category is divided into the following sections:

  a = This Week Ending: Net units sold for the week ending indicated, example: 02/07.

  b = One Week Ago Ending: Net units sold for the week previous to the date of this report, example 1/31.

  c = Two Weeks Ago Ending: Shows the net sales for the week, two weeks previous to the date of this report, example 01/24.

  d = Last Four Weeks Ago Ending: An accumulated statistic of net units sold over the total last four weeks, example 01/10.

  e = Season to Date: A cumulative statistic of units and/or dollars from the beginning of the season's accounting period to present date, example: 02/07.

5 = On-Hand Units: Net units on hand as of the date of the report, example: code 96, Store 01—51 units.

6 = On Order Units: Numbers that are shown are obtained from an order file of the purchase order, example: Store 01—Jeans $15.01–$20—120 units.

C. Advantages of Price Lining

The practice of offering merchandise for sale at a limited number of predetermined price points creates several merchandising problems, but the practice is prevalent because the advantages are numerous and significant. The advantages of price lining are that it:

- Simplifies customer choice, which facilitates selling.
- Enables the store to offer wide assortments at best-selling price lines.
- Simplifies buying by limiting the range of wholesale costs.
- Reduces the size of stock, resulting in more favorable stock turnover and decreased markdowns.
- Simplifies stock control.
- Decreases marking costs.
- Provides a basis for stock/sales control of customer preferences by price.

D. Price Line Reports

Reports by price line make possible an analysis of an entire department's sales trend. The control of planning and purchasing a stock that reflects customer demand is improved by a knowledge of net sales. The information of stock on hand, outstanding orders, receipts, transfers, and markdowns as well as the stock/sales ratio for each group aids present and future buying decisions.

Figure 5 shows a typical report of price line by classifications and presents a complete selling history by dollars and units of merchandise by classifications or groupings. Only two price lines are included because of space. The practice problem following this report show the value and application of this report analysis.

For an assignment for the previous section, see practice problem 1.

Figure 5. (*Continued*)

7 = Dollars to the Nearest Hundred: Financial figures that reflect the actual value of the indicated transactions. This category is divided into the following sections:

a = MTD Receiving: Net receipt to inventory, month to date.

b = MTD Transfers: Cumulative transfers between stores during the current month.

c = MTD Markdown: Cumulative markdowns processed for the current month in both dollars and percentages.

d = MTD Net Sales: Cumulative dollar sales for the current month, by price line for each store, plus the percentage of the total company's business equaling 100% for each total.

e = Inventory: The stock to sales ratio is calculated by stock-sales ratio = Current dollar inventory/Net sales previous week. This can be looked upon as "week's supply," example: 20 stock-sales ratio means if a particular price line continues to sell at the rate of last week's sales, and nothing new is received, it will sell out in 20 weeks.

f = Open Order: Dollar value of the outstanding orders.

g = Inventory and On Order: Total liability calculated by adding the on hand to the on order figures.

E. Basic Pricing Factors and How They Relate to Each Other

Merchandising, or the act of buying and selling, is performed by the retailer, who selects and buys merchandise that is offered for resale to the consumer. To make a profit, the retail merchandiser must set the proper price on the merchandise. Although the profitable pricing of selected individual items cannot always be done by applying a mathematical formula, the three basic elements involved in the pricing of all goods are the cost of the merchandise, the retail price, and the difference between them, which is referred to as markup (MU). **Markup** is the amount that is added to the cost price of merchandise to arrive at a retail price. This amount must be large enough to cover the cost of the merchandise, the expenses incurred to sell it, and the desired profit. The aim of proper pricing can be expressed by the following:

Cost of goods
+ Markup
= **Retail price**

{ Expenses
Markdowns, shortages, employee discounts[1]
Profit

If one knows any two of the basic pricing factors, the third can be calculated both in dollar amounts and/or in percentage relationships. The following formulas show the relationship, in dollars, of the three basic pricing elements.

Calculating Retail When Cost and Dollar Markup Are Known

CONCEPT:
Retail = Cost + Dollar markup.

PROBLEM:
A retailer buys a top for $10 and has a markup of $8. What is the retail price?

SOLUTION:

Cost	=	$10
+ Markup	=	+ 8
Retail price	=	$18

---

[1]Markdowns, shortages, and employee discounts must be considered in determining the original retail price that is set when the merchandise is received into stock because these factors reduce the value of total purchases.

Calculating Dollar Markup
When Retail and Cost Are Known

CONCEPT:

Dollar markup = Retail − Cost.

PROBLEM:

A retailer buys a top for $10 and decides to price it for $18. What is the dollar markup on this item?

SOLUTION:

Retail	=	$18
− Cost	=	−10
Dollar markup	=	$ 8

Calculating Cost When Retail
and Dollar Markup Are Known

CONCEPT:

Cost = Retail − Dollar markup.

PROBLEM:

What is the cost of an item that retails for $18 and has a dollar markup of $8?

SOLUTION:

Retail	=	$18
− Dollar Markup	=	− 8
Cost	=	$10

Although retailers pay for and sell merchandise in dollars, knowing the relationship of the three basic pricing elements (i.e., retail, cost, markup) in percentages and dollars is useful to the merchandiser. Frequently, the retailer thinks in terms of dollars only, as for example, "My customers prefer tops that retail for $18 to $25," or a resource quotes the cost of an item to a retailer at $10 each. At other times, the retailer is concerned about achieving a 44.4% markup on an item that retails for $18 and costs $10. If this markup percent is perceived as low, it may determine whether a particular item will be purchased. At still another time, the buyer thinks simultaneously in terms of dollars and percentages. For example, in determining the dollar cost of an article to be purchased, a buyer must balance the retail price the customer is willing to pay with the particular markup percentage required by management.

Calculating Cost and Markup Percentages
When Dollar Cost and Retail Are Known

To fully understand the relationship among the three basic elements in percentages, it should be understood that the retail of the basic equation is always 100%, and the dollar cost and markup can be converted from dollars to percentages by expressing each as a part of the retail.

CONCEPT:

$$\frac{\$\ Cost}{\$\ Retail} = Cost\ \%$$

$$\frac{\$\ Markup}{\$\ Retail} = Markup\ \%$$

PROBLEM:

What is the cost percentage and the markup percentage of a top that costs $10 and retails for $18?

SOLUTION:

$$Cost\ \% = \frac{\$10\ Cost}{\$18\ Retail}$$

$$Cost\ \% = 55.6\%$$

$$Markup\ \% = \frac{\$\ 8\ Markup\ (\$18\ Retail - \$10\ Cost)}{\$18\ Retail}$$

Markup % = 44.4%

Therefore:

	Dollars		Percentages	
Retail	$18	=	100.0%	
− Cost	−10	=	−55.6%	($10 ÷ $18)
Markup =	$ 8	=	44.4%	($8 ÷ $18)

The markup percentage is commonly called the **cost complement.**

PRACTICE PROBLEMS

Price Line Reports

1. Answer the following questions based on the data in Figure 5.

    (a) What is the price line with Code 96 that generates the major unit and dollar sales?

    (b) Which store has the best performance for Class Totals, Code 96? How many units were sold STD?

    (c) Which two stores contributed 49% of the MTD sale in Code 96 Jeans?

    (d) In the Jeans $15.01–$20.00 price lines, which store requires a "rush" delivery of its order so it can stay "in business" with this price line in this classification? How many units does this store have on hand?

    (e) Consider the Inventory and On Order figures for 96 Class Totals—Price Line–All. Which two stores require adjustments to an order because of the relation between their stock-sales and their MTD net sales percentage? What adjustments should be made?

    (f) For each store, calculate the percent increase or decrease in sales from the previous week to the current week. Which store has shown the largest increase?

    (g) What reasons might explain a decline in sales from one week to the next?

    (h) Since January 24, which stores show a continuous decline in sales of this merchandise classification?

    (i) Why must changes be made in merchandising strategies at these stores?

    (j) What changes in merchandising strategies would you suggest?

Retail Pricing

2. A merchant buys a sweatshirt for $15 and has a dollar markup of $14.95. What is the retail price?

3. The toddler's department buyer purchases some wool robes that cost $30 each and prices them at $65 each. What is the dollar markup on this item?

4. What is the cost of a set of golf clubs that retails for $250 and has a markup of $157?

5. What is the markup percentage on a coat that costs $49.75 and retails for $125?

6. What is the cost percentage for a sweater that retails for $38 and has a 55% markup?

Notes

II. MARKUP

Markup, as defined in this text, applies to an individual item, a group of items, or the entire merchandise stock of a department or a store, and it can be expressed in either dollars or percentages. For comparison and analysis, it is the markup percentage (rather than the dollar amount) that is significant. To understand the effect of markup on buying decisions, it helps to know the basic markup equations and their relationship to other pricing factors.

A. Basic Markup Equations

Markup percentages can be computed as a percentage of the retail or cost price. Because the retail method of inventory is prevalent in large stores, it is more common to calculate the markup percentage on the retail price. The cost method of calculating markup, considered relatively old-fashioned, is still used by some retailers.

Calculating Markup Percentage on Retail Using the Retail Method of Inventory

CONCEPT:

$$\text{Markup \%} = \frac{\text{Dollar markup}}{\text{Retail}}$$

PROBLEM:

What is the markup percentage on an item when the markup is $8 and the retail is $18?

SOLUTION:

$$\text{MU \%} = \frac{\$ 8 \text{ Dollar markup}}{\$18 \text{ Retail}}$$

$$= 44.4\%$$

Calculating Markup Percentage on Cost

CONCEPT:

$$\text{Markup \%} = \frac{\text{Dollar markup}}{\text{Cost}}$$

PROBLEM:

What is the markup percentage on cost, when the markup is $8 and the cost is $10?

$$\text{MU \%} = \frac{\$ 8 \text{ Markup}}{\$10 \text{ Cost}}$$

SOLUTION:

$$\text{Markup \%} = 80\%$$

(Note: Markup percentage calculated on cost is higher than markup percentage on retail.)

Generally, the retail calculation of markup is more acceptable because retailers also figure expenses and profits as a percentage of retail sales. Thus, they tend to consider price lines, stocks, and customer demands in retail values when making plans, and the calculation of markup on retail price is consistent with this approach. In this book, discussions and problems on markup will use the retail basis for all further calculations.

B. Markup Calculations Used in Buying Decisions

The retailer faces numerous purchase planning and merchandise pricing problems when buying goods for resale. To achieve maximum profits, the same estimated initial (original) markup percentage is not applied to all purchases. The astute merchandiser sets an ultimate goal, but realizes that unexpected situations may cause deviations as goods are sold to individual purchasers. Therefore, manipulation of the markup and sales volume ultimately will provide the largest possible dollar profit. Calculations of the various buying and pricing situations that may occur in merchandising are expressed in formulas that must be understood by all retail merchandisers.

Calculating Markup Percentage When Individual Cost and Individual Retail Are Known

CONCEPT:

$$\text{Markup \% (on retail)} = \frac{\$ \text{ Markup}}{\text{Retail}}$$

PROBLEM:

What is the markup percent on an item that costs $6.50 and is priced at $12.75?

SOLUTION:

Given:

Retail	=	$12.75
− Cost	=	$ 6.50
Markup	=	$ 6.25

$$\text{Markup \%} = \frac{\$ 6.25 \text{ Markup}}{\$12.75 \text{ Retail}}$$

Markup % =   49%

When the individual cost and the individual retail do not change, but the number of purchased pieces varies, the markup percentage is the same whether it is calculated for one piece or for the entire quantity purchased. The following calculations illustrate this principle:

PROBLEM:

What is the markup percentage on a purchase of 12 pieces that cost $6.50 each and are retailed at $12.75 each?

SOLUTION:

Total retail	=	$153 (12 pieces × $12.75)
− Total cost	=	− 78 (12 pieces × $6.50)
Dollar markup on entire purchase	=	$ 75
Markup %	=	$ 75 Markup
		$153 Retail

Markup % on entire purchase = 49%

While:

SOLUTION:

Individual retail	=	$12.75
Individual cost	=	−$6.50
Markup	=	$ 6.25
Markup %	=	$ 6.25 Markup
	=	$12.75 Retail

Markup on individual item = 49%

As a buyer evaluates a particular item, the markup percentage on the individual piece will generally be used to determine its salability. Once an order is placed, however, the markup percentage will be calculated on the basis of the entire quantity to be purchased.

Calculating Markup Percentage on a Group of Items with Varying Costs or Retail Prices

In the final analysis, purchases are evaluated on an overall basis. The following variations on markup formulas illustrate this concept in that the markup percentage is calculated on the total amounts ordered, rather than on an individual basis, so that the total purchase can be evaluated.

CONCEPT:

$$\text{Markup \% on entire purchase} = \frac{\text{Total \$ markup}}{\text{Total retail}}$$

Calculating the Markup Percentage When Writing Orders Placed for a Variety of Items and Prices

Currently, some stores are using computer-generated purchase order systems and automated replenishment systems. Although the mechanics of order writing can vary, determining the markup percentage on the entire purchase always requires a calculation of the total cost and total retail to determine the overall percentage on the purchase.

PROBLEM:

A buyer ordered 10 coats at a cost of $59.75 each to retail for $100 each and 6 coats costing $79.75 each to retail for $150 each. What is the markup percentage on this entire purchase?

SOLUTION:

Total retail = $1,900.00

↓

10 pieces × $100 = $ 1,000.00
6 pieces × 150 = + 900.00
_____
$ 1,900.00

− Total cost = −1,076.00

↓

10 pieces × $59.75 = 597.50
6 pieces × 79.75 = + 478.50
_____
$ 1,076.00

Dollar markup on entire purchase = $ 824.00

Markup % = $ 824.00 Total dollar markup
_____
$1,900.00 Total retail

Markup % on entire purchase = 43.4%

Varying Retail Prices of Either a Classification or a Group That Has the Same Cost

PROBLEM:

A buyer bought 150 handbags that cost $22.50 each. The buyer then retailed 50 pieces for $40 each, 75 pieces for $48 each, and the balance for $55 each. What is the markup percentage on this purchase?

SOLUTION:

Total retail = $6,975

↓

50 pieces × $40 = $2,000
75 pieces × $48 = $3,600
25 pieces × $55 = $1,375
_____
$6,975

− Total cost = − $3,375

150 pieces × $22.50 = $3,375
_____

Dollar markup on entire purchase = $3,600

Markup % = $3,600 Total $ markup
_____
$6,975 Total retail

Markup % on entire purchase = 51.6%

Offering Merchandise with Varying Costs at the Same Retail Price

PROBLEM:

A jewelry buyer has an unadvertised promotion on rings at a special price of $25 each. The group consists of 75 pieces that cost:

> 15 pieces @ $10.00 each
> 40 pieces @ $12.50 each
> 20 pieces @ $16.00 each

What is the markup percent on this group?

SOLUTION:

Total retail　　　　　　　　　　= $1,875

　　　　　　↓

75 pieces × $25　　= $1,875
− Total cost　　　　= − 970
　　　　　　　　　　 ‾‾‾‾‾‾

　　　　↑

15 pieces × $10.00　= $　150
40 pieces × $12.50　=　　500
20 pieces × $16.00　= +　320
　　　　　　　　　　　　　　　− $970
　　　　　　　　　　　　　　　 ‾‾‾‾‾
Dollar markup on entire group　=　$905

Markup % = $　905 Total dollar markup
　　　　　　 ‾‾‾‾‾
　　　　　　 $1,875 Total retail

Markup % on entire purchase = 48.3%

Calculating Retail When Cost and Desired Markup Percentage Are Known

Although cost prices can be quoted by individual prices or by-the-dozen prices, in pricing an item for retail the merchandiser "thinks" in terms of unit retail and therefore uses the cost per piece as a basis for calculating the retail per piece.

CONCEPT:

$$\text{Retail} = \frac{\text{Cost}}{100\% - \text{Markup \%}}$$

PROBLEM:

A manufacturer quotes a cost of $42 per dozen for a visor; the markup that the buyer wants is 51.7%. At what retail price should the item be marked to obtain the desired markup?

SOLUTION:

Given: Cost = $42 per doz.

= $42 ÷ 12

= $3.50 per piece

Retail = $$\frac{\$3.50 \text{ (Cost per piece)}}{100\% - 51.7\%}$$

= $$\frac{\$3.50}{48.3\%}$$

Retail = $7.25

Calculating Cost When Retail and Markup Percentage Are Known

In maintaining established price lines, a retailer who knows the required markup must be able to determine the maximum affordable price to pay for an item so that it can be sold profitably.

CONCEPT:

Cost = Retail × (100% − Markup %)

PROBLEM:

A children's underwear buyer plans to retail pajamas for $10.95 with a 48% markup. What is the maximum price the buyer can pay for the pajamas to be sold at this price line?

SOLUTION:

Given: Retail = $10.95

Cost = $10.95 (Retail) × (100% − 48%)

= $10.95 × 52% (Cost complement %)

Cost = $ 5.69

For assignments for the previous section, see practice problems 7–28.

PRACTICE PROBLEMS

Markup

7. Fill in the blank spaces for each of the exercises below. (Note: Several of the examples may be done without written calculations.)

	Retail	Cost	$MU	MU%
a.	$ 5.00	$ 2.70		
b.	$ 14.95	$ 7.50		
c.	$200.00		$ 90.00	
d.	$ 1.75	$ 9.60/doz.		
e.	$ 29.95	$ 14.50		
f.	$ 10.00	$ 60.00/doz.		
g.		$ 15.00 each		48%
h.		$ 42.50 each		46.6%
i.		$106.00/doz.		45%
j.		$ 15.00/doz.		47.5%
k.	$100.00			49%
l.	$ 80.00			50%
m.		$ 16.00	$ 14.00	
n.		$ 55.00	$ 45.00	
o.	$ 75.00			52%
p.	$ 3.98			37.8%
q.		$ 21.60/doz.		46.5%
r.	$ 9.95	$ 72.00/doz.		
s.	$465.00	$235.00		
t.	$590.00	$310.00	$280.00	

8. A buyer purchases dresses at $42.50 each.

    (a) At what must these dresses be marked to achieve a 52% markup?

    (b) At what actual customary price line are the dresses most likely to be marked?

    (c) What would be the percentage of markup if the dresses were priced at $79.50?

9. A buyer purchased:

- 500 nylon windbreakers costing $12 each, to sell at $22 each.
- 700 sweatpants costing $9 each, to sell at $17.50 each.
- 300 acrylic sweaters costing $16 each, to sell at $30 each.

What is the markup percentage for this order?

10. Apply the following "typical" departmental markups to find the cost of an item that retails for $49.95 in each department:

    (a) Girls (4–6X) Department: 59%.

    (b) Electrical appliances: 27.8%.

    (c) Junior sportswear: 55.8%.

    (d) Gifts and clocks: 56.2%.

What would cause the wide range of markup percentages among the various products?

11. A buyer of men's furnishings paid $96 per dozen for wool blend knit neckties. If the desired markup was 58%, what was the exact retail per tie? What price line would the buyer probably use in ticketing the ties for the selling floor?

12. A buyer is interested in a group of tweed jackets costing $35 each. If the required markup is 53.6%, what would be the minimum retail price for each jacket? If the buyer had previously bought these jackets at $39.75 and retailed them for $79.50, what was this previous markup percentage?

13. For a holiday catalog, a buyer makes a special purchase of infant knit shirts that cost:

- 40 dozen at $60/dozen.
- 20 dozen at $72/dozen.
- 18 dozen at $66/dozen.

If the shirts all retail at the same unit price of $11, what markup percentage will be yielded?

14. The accessory buyer buys straw visors at $45 per dozen and sells them at $7.50 each. What markup percentage has been achieved?

15. A toy buyer planned a special sale of dolls to retail at $25 each. If the overall markup on the purchase was 46%, what was the cost per doll?

16. Men's walking shorts that cost $132/dozen require a markup of 50%. What should be the retail price of each pair?

17. A suit that costs $67.50 has a markup of 62.5%. What should be the retail price of each suit?

18. A buyer purchased 50 assorted leather attaché cases that cost $79.50 each, and subsequently merchandised them as follows:

- 25 pieces to retail for $175 each.
- 10 pieces to retail for $150 each.
- 15 pieces to retail for $125 each.

Find the markup percentage on this purchase.

19. An outerwear buyer arranges a special purchase from a manufacturer who offers a group of 150 raincoats (with varying costs) at one low price of $25 each. The buyer decides to price this purchase as follows:

- 50 pieces to retail at $35.95 each.
- 50 pieces to retail at $45.00 each.
- 50 pieces to retail at $55.00 each.

What markup percentage is realized on this purchase?

20. A special promotion, consisting of 10 dozen novelty sweaters, is purchased at the cost of $240 per dozen. Determine the retail selling price of each sweater if the buyer wants a 52% markup.

21. After its arrival in the store, the buyer (in Problem 20) reviewed the shipment of raincoats and decided to include this purchase in a store flyer featuring a group of sweaters retailing for $42 each. What markup percentage was achieved on this particular purchase?

22. If the shoe buyer wants to buy some leather sandals to retail for $49.50 each and needs to obtain a markup of 53.4%, what is the most that these sandals can cost?

23. Calculate the markup percentage on the following order placed by the hand-bag department:

- 3 1/2 dozen, costing $180 per dozen to retail for $32.50 each.
- 15 pieces, costing $37.50 each to retail for $79 each.

24. The jewelry buyer wants to spend $15,000 at retail. The department maintains a 56.7% markup. The buyer needs a minimum of 600 pairs of earrings to cover each branch with an adequate assortment.

(a) What should be the retail price per pair?
(b) What should be the cost per pair?

25. The sportswear buyer wants to spend $84,000 at retail. Orders for $18,500, at cost, have already been placed. If the planned markup percent to be achieved is 52.5%, how much, in dollars, does the buyer have left to spend at cost?

26. On Figure 6 (purchase order), write and complete this order.

(a) Style #300: 25 leather attaché cases, costing $79.50 each, retailing for $169.99.

(b) Style #401: 10 leather folders, costing $55 each, retailing for $125 each.

(c) Style #411: 15 leather briefcases, costing $69.50 each, retailing for $150 each.

Figure 6. Purchase Order Form

DATE SHIPPED	TO BE SHIPPED FROM	DELIVERY DUE	F.O.B.	Charges on shipments bought FOB New York or our premises must be prepaid	FREIGHT ALLOWED	TERMS
						Dating Is From Date of Receipt of Goods

CLASS.	HOUSE # STYLE # LOT #	DESCRIPTION	1	2	3	4	5	6	7	8	9	QUAN.	UNIT COST	TOTAL COST	UNIT RETAIL	TOTAL RETAIL
												TOTAL				

THIS ORDER IS PLACED SUBJECT TO CONDITIONS ON BOTH SIDES   M.U.%

Signed _____
DEPT. MANAGER

Countersigned _____
MDSE. MANAGER

Date _____ 19 _____

27. On Figure 7, write and complete this order. As the men's raincoat buyer, a manufacturer offers you a group of 225 pieces at one low price of $50 each. You decide to price this group as follows:

    (a) Style #132: 25 pieces, retailing for $75 each.
    (b) Style #145: 50 pieces, retailing for $90 each.
    (c) Style #160: 50 pieces, retailing for $125 each.
    (d) Style #165: 100 pieces, retailing for $138 each.

Figure 7. Purchase Order Form

DATE SHIPPED	TO BE SHIPPED FROM	DELIVERY DUE	F.O.B.	Charges on shipments bought FOB New York or our premises must be prepaid		FREIGHT ALLOWED	TERMS Dating Is From Date of Receipt of Goods

CLASS.	HOUSE # STYLE # LOT #	DESCRIPTION	1	2	3	4	5	6	7	8	9	QUAN.	UNIT COST	TOTAL COST	UNIT RETAIL	TOTAL RETAIL
														TOTAL		

THIS ORDER IS PLACED SUBJECT TO CONDITIONS ON BOTH SIDES

M.U.%

Signed _____ Countersigned _____
     DEPT. MANAGER   MDSE. MANAGER

Date _____ 19 _____

28. On Figure 8, write and complete this order. You purchase the following from a glove resource:

    (a) Style #321: 20 dozen children's wool gloves costing $66 per dozen.

    (b) Style #492: 30 dozen men's wool gloves costing $72 per dozen.

    (c) Style #563: 10 dozen women's wool novelty gloves costing $78 per dozen.

You decide to price them all at the same retail of $12 per pair.

Figure 8. Purchase Order Form

DATE SHIPPED	TO BE SHIPPED FROM	DELIVERY DUE	F.O.B.	Charges on shipments bought FOB New York or our premises must be prepaid	FREIGHT ALLOWED	TERMS Dating Is From Date of Receipt of Goods

CLASS.	HOUSE # STYLE # LOT #	DESCRIPTION	1	2	3	4	5	6	7	8	9	QUAN.	UNIT COST	TOTAL COST	UNIT RETAIL	TOTAL RETAIL
													TOTAL			

THIS ORDER IS PLACED SUBJECT TO CONDITIONS ON BOTH SIDES   M.U.%

Signed _____
DEPT. MANAGER

Countersigned _____
MDSE. MANAGER

Date _____ 19 _____

III. REPRICING OF MERCHANDISE

The dynamic nature of merchandising makes the repricing of goods in retailing universal. Price adjustments are made to either increase or decrease the original retail price placed on merchandise. These changes in prices must be properly recorded to:

- Achieve an accurate book inventory figure used in the retail method of inventory.
- Plan initial (original) markup goals when pricing goods.
- Control and manage the amount received in an attempt to merchandise at a profit.

The repricing of goods for sale is constant, the causes are numerous, and the skill required is considerable. It is rare that a retailer makes an upward adjustment to the retail price, and often a buyer is forced to make a downward retail price change on a significant portion of sales. In a profit and loss statement the downward differences frequently have a group heading of **retail reductions** that include:

- Markdowns.
- Employee discounts.
- Shortages.[2]

Although all retail reductions have an impact on markup, they are, for the most part, considered a necessity. Their study is of major importance, for only with complete understanding of their use can the retailer turn them into a dynamic and advantageous merchandising tool.

A. Markdowns

The most common and important type of price adjustment is technically called **markdown** (MD). It is the lowering or reducing of the original or previous retail price on one item or a group of items. For example, a sweater that was retailed for $25 when it was received in the store was reduced to $18 because it became soiled. This price adjustment is called a markdown because the retail value of the merchandise was lowered. The difference between the new selling price ($18) and the former price ($25) is $7. The amount by which the retail value has been lowered is called the markdown and is the meaningful figure to the merchandiser. The merchandiser expresses markdowns as a percentage of net sales of all goods during a period, month, or year. Frequently, the merchandiser needs to calculate the **markdown percentage** that is necessary to sell a group of items. When this occurs, the markdown is still expressed as a percentage of the net sales figure.

---

[2]Shortages will be discussed and calculated in Unit IV: Retail Method of Inventory.

The Purpose of Markdowns

Markdowns are "a cure, not a curse." This merchandising tool can be used to good advantage if the retailer realizes the objectives of markdowns. The major aims of reductions are:

- To stimulate the sale of merchandise to which customers are not responding satisfactorily.
- To attract customers to stores by offering "bargains."
- To meet competitive prices.
- To provide open-to-buy money to purchase new merchandise.
- To create special "promotions," or sales (e.g., Birthday sales).

Causes of Markdowns

By analyzing all the possible causes of markdowns, a merchandiser can make an effort to minimize them. The most common causes (not in order of importance) are listed below:

- Buying errors, which include:
  Overbuying in quantities.
  Buying of wrong sizes.[3]
  Buying of poor styles, quality, materials, and colors.
  Poor timing in ordering goods.
  Receiving and accepting merchandise that has been shipped late.
- Pricing errors, which include:
  Poor timing of markdowns.
  Setting the initial price too high.
  Not being competitive in price for same goods.
  Deferring markdowns too long.
  Calculated risks of carrying "prestige" merchandise.
- Selling errors, which include:
  Poor stockkeeping.
  Careless handling that results in soiled and damaged goods.
  Failure to display merchandise properly or advantageously.
  Uninformed salespeople.
- Special sales from stock, which include:
  Off-price promotions.
  Multiple sales (e.g., 3 for $1.00).
- Broken assortments, remnants, and so on.
- Necessary price adjustments.
- Remainders from special sales.

---

[3]Because of unbalanced buying or the accepting of merchandise that is sized contrary to order.

Timing of Markdowns

Accurate timing of markdowns can help reduce the amount of the markdown needed to sell the merchandise. It is suggested that merchandise be analyzed and reduced when:

- Merchandise becomes "slow selling."
- The customer demand is sufficient to sell the merchandise with a minimum price reduction.
- The consumer's interest in the merchandise in stock may diminish because of the appearance of a new fashion or product, or of a lower price.

The Amount of the Markdown

Judgment is required to determine the price at which items can be cleared quickly. The pricing of goods is a major factor in the control of markdowns. It is difficult to generalize on the amount of the markdown to be taken because the "right" price depends on:

- The reasons for the reduction.
- The nature of the merchandise.
- The time of the selling season (the proper moment during the selling season).
- The quantity on hand.
- The original (initial) markup.

Because the purpose of a markdown is to sell the merchandise quickly, the size of the markdown must be large enough to produce the desired results. Some rules to be considered in repricing are:

- The first markdown should be sharp enough to move a considerable amount of the goods.
- The markdown should be sufficiently large to attract customers who rejected the merchandise at its original price.
- The price may be reduced sufficiently to appeal to the next price zone customer.
- Markdowns should not be so large as to invite customer suspicion.
- Small markdowns are ineffective.
- Small, successive markdowns may increase the total loss.

Markdown Calculations

Calculating the Dollar Markdown

To find the dollar amount of markdown taken when there is a group of items, it is customary to first determine the difference per piece between the present and new retail prices, and then to determine the total cost of the markdown.

CONCEPT:
Dollar markdown = Original retail price − New retail price

PROBLEM:

A buyer reduces 93 calculators from $15 to $10. What is the total markdown in dollars?

SOLUTION:

Original or present retail	$15.00
− New retail	−10.00
Dollar markdown	= $ 5.00 per piece

Total Dollar Markdown = 93 pieces × $5.00 = $465

However, the retailer frequently advertises markdowns as a percentage off the current retail price; for example, "25% off the selling price."

CONCEPT:

Dollar markdown = Percentage off × Present retail price

PROBLEM:

A store advertises 25% off on a group of 50 chairs currently retailed at $100 each. What is the total dollar markdown?

SOLUTION:

Percentage off	= 25% × $100 Retail
Dollar markdown	= $25
	= 50 pieces × $25
Total Dollar Markdown	= $1,250

Calculating the Total Dollar Markdown When a Second Markdown Is Taken

Even with the markdown, not all merchandise will sell. Therefore, after a reasonable period of time, an additional reduction must be made to move the remaining goods of that style and/or group.

CONCEPT:

Total dollar markdown = First total dollar markdown + Second total dollar markdown

PROBLEM:

The men's clothing buyer had a group of 50 jackets priced at $225 each that were selling very slowly. To stimulate sales of these jackets, the buyer reduced the price of jackets in that group to $175. At this price, 40 pieces were sold in a short time. At a later date, the remaining pieces became shopworn and needed a further reduction to clear them from stock. The buyer reduced them to $100 each and at that price they all sold out. What was the total dollar markdown taken?

SOLUTION:

First Markdown on Group

Original retail price	$ 225
− First markdown price	− 175
Amount of markdown per piece =	$ 50
× Number of jackets	× 50
First dollar markdown =	$2,500 $2,500

PLUS

Second Markdown on Group

First markdown price	$ 175
− Second markdown price	− 100
Amount of markdown per piece =	$ 75
× Number of jackets	× 10
Second dollar markdown =	$ 750 + 750

Total Dollar Markdown on This Group = $3,250

Calculating the Planned Dollar Markdown When the Markdown Percentage and Net Sales Are Known

Once an estimated net sales figure for an accounting period has been projected and the markdown percentage allowed is known, the total amount of markdown in dollars can be determined. Because markdowns are taken in dollars off the retail price, a buyer's thinking and decisions in merchandising markdowns alternates, according to circumstances, from percentages to dollars and vice versa.

CONCEPT:

Planned dollar markdowns = Net sales × markdown %

PROBLEM:

The sales in the men's footwear department were planned for $560,000 and the markdown percent was estimated at 5%. Find the dollar amount of markdowns that would be permitted.

SOLUTION:

Total planned dollar markdowns	= $560,000 Net sales
	× 5% estimated markdown %

Total Planned Dollar Markdown = $ 28,000

Calculating the Markdown Percentage

Markdowns taken are expressed as a percentage of the net sales for an accounting period. It is important to control and plan markdowns within a store. Markdown percentages can be calculated for an entire department, as shown in the following calculations:

CONCEPT:

$$\text{Markdown \%} = \frac{\$ \text{ Markdown}}{\$ \text{ Net sales}}$$

PROBLEM:

In March, Department #33 had net sales of $5,000. The markdowns taken for March totaled $500. What was the markdown percentage for March?

SOLUTION:

$$\text{Markdown \%} = \frac{\$ \ 500 \text{ Markdown}}{\$5,000 \text{ Net Sales}} = 10\%$$

Also, markdown percentages can be used to evaluate a group of items and/or a vendor. The following shows this type of calculation:

CONCEPT:

$$\text{Markdown \%} = \frac{\$ \text{ MD}}{\text{Total dollar sales of group's final selling prices}}$$

PROBLEM:

A buyer had a special selling price group of 100 faux snakeskin belts marked at $16 each. At the end of the season, the 15 pieces that were unsold were reduced to $10 each and sold out immediately. What is the markdown % on this purchase?

SOLUTION:

Step 1: Determine markdown per piece.
$16 to $10 = $6 each

Step 2: Determine markdown amount.
15 pieces reduced = 15 pieces × $6 = $90 Markdown

Step 3: Determine final selling price sales of group.
85 pcs × $16 = $1,360
15 pcs × $10 = + 150
Sales of group = $1,510

$$\text{Markdown \%} = \frac{\$ \ 90 \text{ Markdown}}{\$1,510 \text{ Sales of group}}$$

Markdown % = 5.96% or 6%

For assignments for the previous section, see practice problems 29–44.

Calculating Markdown Cancellations

It is easier to describe a markdown cancellation than to define it. When the markdown price is raised to a higher retail price, it is considered a cancellation of a markdown. Cancellations may occur after special sales from stock, if the remaining merchandise is repriced upward. The restoration of a markdown price to the former retail is a **markdown cancellation.**

Currently, markdown cancellations are much less common because most large stores electronically program temporary markdowns into the cash register. This means of recording the markdown as the reduced offering when an item is being sold is called a **point-of-sale (POS) markdown.** It eliminates the need to mark the goods with the reduced price, and, subsequently, to remark the goods to the original price. Figure 9 shows a sales slip recording the purchase of a pair of comfort shoes selling for $52, less 30%. The $15.60 is an example of a POS markdown.

Figure 10 is a credit slip indicating the return of "sale" merchandise and shows how the $15.60 markdown taken at the time of purchase was canceled. The amount of markdown taken on this simple transaction is zero because the $15.60 markdown recorded by the cash register on the purchase was neutralized by the return of the goods.

For those firms that are not yet using the POS system of recording and canceling markdowns, the following material, though not popular, is included to show the basic principles for the manual procedure. (Note: There are no review problems that illustrate this material.)

CONCEPT:

Markdown cancellation = Higher retail − Markdown price

PROBLEM:

After a one-day sale, a buyer marked up the remaining 12 pieces to the original price of $50, which had been reduced to $43 for the special event. What was the amount of the markdown cancellation?

SOLUTION:

Markdown cancellation   = $50 Higher retail
                                  − 43 Markdown price

                              = $ 7 Difference per piece
                              =   12 Pieces × $7 Difference

Markdown Cancellation = $84

Figure 9. POS Markdown Receipt

Figure 10. POS Credit Slip

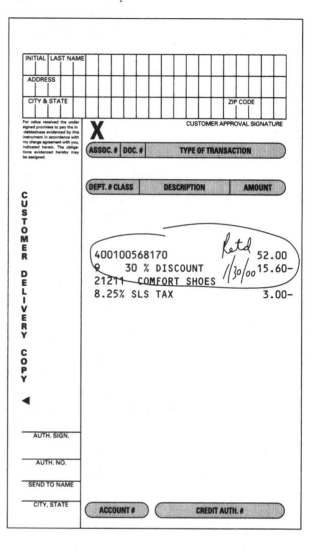

INITIAL	LAST NAME																
ADDRESS																	
CITY & STATE												ZIP CODE					

For value received the under signed promises to pay the in -debtedness evidenced by this instrument in accordance with my charge agreement with you, indicated herein. The obligations evidenced hereby may be assigned.

X _____
CUSTOMER APPROVAL SIGNATURE

ASSOC. # | **DOC. #** | **TYPE OF TRANSACTION**

CASH

DEPT. # CLASS | **DESCRIPTION** | **AMOUNT**

```
21211   COMFORT SHOES
400100568170              52.00
9     30 % DISCOUNT       15.60-
         8.25% SLS TAX      3.00
```

CUSTOMER DELIVERY COPY ◄

AUTH. SIGN. _____

AUTH. NO. _____

SEND TO NAME

CITY, STATE

```
184060 02172    1/30/00    39.40
```

ACCOUNT # | **CREDIT AUTH. #**

```
184060 02172    1/30/00    39.40
```

TRANSACTION NO. | **DATE** | **AMOUNT**

CUSTOMER RECEIPT

TRANSACTION NO. | **DATE**

RETURN POSTAGE GUARANTEED

ADDRESS LABEL / SEND TO	NAME														CONTENTS MERCHANDISE
	STREET										APT. NO.			
	CITY & STATE									ZIP CODE			
	DEPT. #	DELIVERY INSTRUCTIONS		PHONE NO.		

(5/87)   PARCEL MAY BE OPENED FOR POSTAL INSPECTION IF NECESSARY

Calculating Net Markdown

When a reduction in price is made originally, it is called the **gross markdown.** The difference between gross markdown and markdown cancellation is called the **net markdown** figure or the amount of the permanent markdown.

CONCEPT:

Net markdown = Gross markdown − Markdown cancellation

PROBLEM:

A buyer reduces 75 pieces from $50 to $43 for a one-day sale. After the sale, the remaining 28 pieces were marked up to the original price and were sold out at that price.

(a) What was the gross markdown in dollars?
(b) What was the markdown cancellation?
(c) Find the net markdown in dollars.

SOLUTION:

(a) Determine gross markdown.

Gross markdown	= $50 − $43 = $7 per piece
	= 75 pcs. × $7 Markdown
Gross markdown	= $525

(b) Determine markdown cancellation.

Markdown cancellation	= $43 to $50 = $7 per piece
	= 28 pcs. × $7 Markdown cancellation
Markdown cancellation	= $196

(c) Determine net markdown.

Gross markdown	= $525
− Markdown cancellation	= −196
Net markdown	= $329

B. Employee Discounts

It is common practice for a retail store to give its employees a reduction off a retail price. This type of retail reduction is called an **employee discount.** As noted previously, this is another type of price adjustment that must be recorded because it lowers the value of merchandise. This reduction is generally stated as a percentage off the retail price (e.g., a 20% discount). It must be recorded by the statistical department of the accounting division for accuracy of the book inventory figure under the retail method of inventory. The cumulative amount of employees' discounts is usually shown on the profit and loss statement under the general heading of **"retail reductions."**

PROBLEM:

Store X grants its employees a 20% discount on all merchandise purchased. If a salesperson buys an item that retails for $16.95, what is the employee discount in dollars? What is the amount paid for the item?

SOLUTION:

Retail price of item	=	$16.95
Discount allowed	=	20%
	=	$16.95 × 20%
Employee discount	=	$ 3.39
Employee's Price	=	$16.95 − $3.39 = $13.56
or	=	$16.95 − 20% = $13.56

C. Additional Markup

An **additional markup** is a type of price adjustment that raises the price of merchandise already in stock. It increases the original retail price placed on the merchandise. It is taken after and in addition to the original (initial) markup. Although it is not a common type of adjustment, a provision must be made when an upward change of the retail prices of existing inventories is necessary. For example, an upward change of wholesale costs might necessitate the immediate upward revision of retail prices on existing inventory.

D. Markup Cancellation

Markup cancellation is a downward price adjustment that offsets an original inflated markup to a markup that is more normal. It is used to adjust the markup on a purchase in accordance with the original intent and is not used to manipulate stock values. Currently, it is controlled by law, which dictates the time period allowed from receipt to reduction of the purchase as well as the size of the markup resulting from this practice. It is justified when quoting "comparable value" prices used in promoting goods. For example, a resource offers a retailer gloves at $7, which is lower than the normal cost of $10. This item may be presently in stock and retailing for $22. During the permitted time, the gloves costing $7, which originally retailed at $22, are reduced to $14. This lowered price appears to the public as a markdown, yet results in a markup that is close to normal. The $8 difference between $22 and $14 is the markup cancellation.

E. Price Change Procedures

An efficient system of reporting and recording price changes is important for the following three reasons:

- Facilitation of the review of price adjustments.
- Accurate calculation of inventory records.
- Identification of shortages.

Figure 11. Price Change

Run Date: 02/28/00 Run Time: 22:29:30	Price Change	Report No: Page: 12

BUYER: 02   DEPT NO: 02

P/C NO: 2331916   P/C TYPE: 01 MARKDOWN-PERMANENT, TOTAL STYLE   ORIGINATING LOCATION: 02 ENTRY DATE: 02-27-00

EFFECTIVE DATE: 03/04/00   REASON: 02 REPRICING CLEARANCE

DOCUMENT NO:

APPLICABLE LOCATIONS 01 02 03 05 07 08 09 11 12 13 14 15 16 17 18 19 20 21 23 24 25 26
SPECIAL INSTRUCTIONS: REPRICING

CLASS	VENDOR	STYLE	UPC	OLD RETAIL	NEW RETAIL	CURR TKT RETAIL	NEW TKT RETAIL		DESCRIPTION
41	1	6028	400100964255	11.00	7.00	11.00	7.00 (	)	LG CIRCULAR STRETC
41	1	6140	400101350996	6.00	4.00	6.00	4.00 (	)	CHANNEL CIRCLE STR
41	1	6143	400101365136	6.00	4.00	6.00	4.00 (	)	STRETCH MATTE META
41	1	9106	400101338239	11.00	7.00	11.00	7.00 (	)	1/2" MESH
41	1	9107	400101109839	14.00	9.00	14.00	9.00 (	)	MESH BELTS
41	1	9115	400101338246	13.00	9.00	13.00	9.00 (	)	ROLLED MESH
41	28	1602	400101479789	10.00	7.00	10.00	7.00 (	)	STUD BELT
41	28	1730	400101479796	10.00	7.00	10.00	7.00 (	)	STUD BELT
41	117	1305	400101271024	9.00	6.00	9.00	6.00 (	)	1 1/4" W/SILVER 3
41	117	1359	400101207726	5.00	3.00	5.00	3.00 (	)	3/4" CROCO SILVER

Figure 11 illustrates a computer printout of a buyer authorized price change.[4] It instructs the individual stores to change the retails on certain merchandise, where to change them (i.e., store location), if the change is permanent or temporary, what the new retails should be, and the reason for repricing. Presently, most systems do not require that the store count the merchandise, but require only remarking it, because, financially the perpetual inventory system[5] has made the adjustment.

F. The Relationship of Repricing to Profit

Every price change has an impact on gross margin and net profits. Because the elimination of price adjustments in retailing is impossible, stores must classify each type of adjustment separately so that they can be analyzed, planned, and controlled. Markdowns, the major type of price changes, reduce the retail price, causing a decrease in gross margin that is further reflected in a decrease and/or elimination of profit. With certain merchandise or classifications, the markdown risk is frequently anticipated. It is offset by planning a higher initial (original) markup. Unfortunately, profit cannot always be preplanned because there are

---

[4]Price change forms are also shown in Unit IV.

[5]Perpetual inventory is discussed further in Unit IV.

business forces that do not permit easy solutions to problems (e.g., nonacceptance of a newly introduced fashion or style, change in competition, etc.). However, it is important for the retailer to realize the effect of price adjustments on gross margin and profit as illustrated by the following example:

Initial retail value of new purchase	$105,000	=	100.0%
− Cost of goods sold	− 49,980	=	− 47.6%
Gross margin	$ 55,020	=	52.4%
− Operating expenses	− 45,990	=	− 43.8%
Net profit	$ 9,030	=	8.6%

The total retail reductions for the period are $5,000:

Net sales	$100,000	=	100.0%
− Cost of goods sold	− 49,980	=	− 50.0%
Gross margin	$ 50,020	=	50.0%
Operating expenses	− 45,990	=	− 46.0%
Net Profit	$ 4,030	=	4.0%

PRACTICE PROBLEMS

Repricing of Merchandise

29. The Merchandise Manager of the Fashion-Rite Stores approved the following reductions. Complete the price change form for the reductions taken.

In Department 32, a group of 75 wool sweaters, style #203, vendor #16, priced at $55 each, were selling slowly. Because it was late in the season, the buyer felt a markdown was needed to stimulate sales of these sweaters and reduced them to $42 each. What was the amount of the markdown per piece? What was the total markdown amount? Record the markdown on the price change form.

(X) TO SHOW TYPE		PRICE CHANGE			DEPT. NO.	PART 1	B				
MARK-DOWN		ISSUED AT: ☐ Paramus									
CANCELLATION OF MARK-DOWN		☐ Danbury		CLASS	DATE _____ ISSUE SEPARATE SHEETS FOR MARK-DOWN, CANCELLATION, MARK-UP, STOLEN, AND SALVAGE ITEMS						
MARK-UP		☐ Hartford									

Show Reason By Letter	↓	Item Description Vendor — Style — Name	Quantity	SEA. LET.	Verified Quantity	Old Retail	New Retail	Difference	Amount
A. PROMOTIONAL PURCHASE REMAINDERS									
B. SLOW MOVING OR INACTIVE STOCK									
C. SPECIAL SALES FROM STOCK									
D. PRICE ADJUSTMENTS									
E. BROKEN ASSORTMENTS AND REMNANTS									
F. SHOPWORN, SOILED OR DAMAGED									
G. ALLOWANCE TO CUSTOMER									
H. STOLEN									
J. SALVAGE									

DO NOT ENTER ANY PRICE CHANGES BELOW THIS LINE			
DEPT. MGR'S SIGNATURE DATE	MDSE. V.P. OR MGR'S SIGNATURE DATE	MARKER'S SIGNATURE DATE	TOTAL DO NOT CARRY THIS TOTAL FORWARD
SEND PART 1 TO STATISTICAL, PART 2 TO NEW YORK STORE DEPT. MGR; LEAVE PART 3 IN BOOK			FOR STATISTICAL DEPT. USE ONLY

30. On Columbus Day, the suit buyer in Department 25 offered a "30% off" for an unadvertised special. On that special sale day, 50 suits, style #1000, vendor #39, originally priced at $100 each were sold. Calculate the total dollar markdown taken. Record the markdown on this price change form.

(X) TO SHOW TYPE		PRICE CHANGE		DEPT. NO.	PART 1	B
	MARK-DOWN	ISSUED AT: ☐ Paramus				
	CANCELLATION OF MARK-DOWN	☐ Danbury		CLASS	DATE _____	
	MARK-UP	☐ Hartford			ISSUE SEPARATE SHEETS FOR MARK-DOWN, CANCELLATION, MARK-UP, STOLEN, AND SALVAGE ITEMS	

Show Reason By Letter	↓	Item Description Vendor — Style — Name	Quantity	SEA. LET.	Verified Quantity	Old Retail	New Retail	Difference	Amount
A. PROMOTIONAL PURCHASE REMAINDERS									
B. SLOW MOVING OR INACTIVE STOCK									
C. SPECIAL SALES FROM STOCK									
D. PRICE ADJUSTMENTS									
E. BROKEN ASSORTMENTS AND REMNANTS									
F. SHOPWORN, SOILED OR DAMAGED									
G. ALLOWANCE TO CUSTOMER									
H. STOLEN									
J. SALVAGE									

DO NOT ENTER ANY PRICE CHANGES BELOW THIS LINE

DEPT. MGR'S SIGNATURE DATE	MDSE. V.P. OR MGR'S SIGNATURE DATE	MARKER'S SIGNATURE DATE	TOTAL DO NOT CARRY THIS TOTAL FORWARD	
SEND PART 1 TO STATISTICAL, PART 2 TO NEW YORK STORE DEPT. MGR; LEAVE PART 3 IN BOOK			FOR STATISTICAL DEPT. USE ONLY	

31. The children's buyer (Department 49) had a group of 150 ski jackets, style #2000, vendor #87, priced at $75 each. The weather was warm, and sales were poor on this particular style. After 25 pieces sold, the buyer decided to reduce them to $68. At this price, 90 pieces sold. The remaining pieces were broken in size and color, so the buyer decided to clear them from stock and further reduced them to $58. What was the total dollar markdown taken? Record the final markdown taken on the price change form.

(X) TO SHOW TYPE	PRICE CHANGE				DEPT. NO.	PART 1	B		

	MARK-DOWN
	CANCELLATION OF MARK-DOWN
	MARK-UP

ISSUED AT:
☐ Paramus
☐ Danbury
☐ Hartford

CLASS

DATE _____
ISSUE SEPARATE SHEETS FOR MARK-DOWN, CANCELLATION, MARK-UP, STOLEN, AND SALVAGE ITEMS

Show Reason By Letter	Item Description Vendor — Style — Name	Quantity	SEA. LET.	Verified Quantity	Old Retail	New Retail	Difference		Amount
A. PROMOTIONAL PURCHASE REMAINDERS									
B. SLOW MOVING OR INACTIVE STOCK									
C. SPECIAL SALES FROM STOCK									
D. PRICE ADJUSTMENTS									
E. BROKEN ASSORTMENTS AND REMNANTS									
F. SHOPWORN, SOILED OR DAMAGED									
G. ALLOWANCE TO CUSTOMER									
H. STOLEN									
J. SALVAGE									

DO NOT ENTER ANY PRICE CHANGES BELOW THIS LINE

DEPT. MGR'S SIGNATURE	DATE	MDSE. V.P. OR MGR'S SIGNATURE	DATE	MARKER'S SIGNATURE	DATE	TOTAL DO NOT CARRY THIS TOTAL FORWARD

SEND PART 1 TO STATISTICAL, PART 2 TO NEW YORK STORE DEPT. MGR; LEAVE PART 3 IN BOOK

FOR STATISTICAL DEPT. USE ONLY

32. The junior sportswear buyer planned sales for the month amounting to $700,000. The markdown percentage was estimated at 12%. How much dollar markdown could be taken?

33. A children's buyer took markdowns in the month of July totaling $2,000. During this month, the net sales for the department were $18,000. If the original markdown plan for this month called for 14% markdowns, was the actual markdown over or under the original plan, and by how much in dollars?

34. For the month of November, a suit buyer took markdowns totaling $1,600. During this month, the net sales for the department amounted to $50,000. What was the markdown percentage for this month?

35. In the month of July, a domestics buyer took markdowns totaling $1,800. During this month, the net sales for the department were $25,000. If the original markdown plan for this month called for 8% markdowns, was the actual markdown over or under the original plan, and by how much in dollars? What was the actual markdown percentage?

36. The seasonal plan for a shoe department shows sales of $153,000, with planned markdowns of 6.4%.

      (a) What is the planned dollar amount of markdowns?

      (b) If the actual markdowns are $7,200, how does the real percentage compare with the plan? Is the actual percentage more or less than planned? By how much?

37. A buyer reduces 75 jackets from $39.50 to $32.95 for a sale. A short while after the sale, the remaining 30 jackets are reduced further to $27. At that price, they all sold out. Find the total markdown amount taken.

38. A coat department had sales of $60,000 for the month of November. During the month, the buyer reduced 50 coats from $60 to $40 and another 100 coats from $80 to $60.

    (a) What was the total markdown for the month?

    (b) Find the markdown percentage for the month.

39. A buyer had 400 pocket calculators in stock at $25 each. They were on sale for $18 each for a one day special event. At the end of the day, 210 remained unsold and were sold eventually at their original price.

    (a) What was the total markdown in dollars?

    (b) What was the markdown percentage on this purchase?

40. A retailer purchased some terry slippers from a new resource. In evaluating the purchase, the records indicated that the total purchase of 360 pairs of slippers as originally retailed for $9.50 per pair. At this price, 290 pairs were sold. The first markdown to $7 resulted in the sale of another 50 pairs. A second markdown to $5 was required on the balance of the merchandise to sell the remaining broken sizes. What were the retailer's total reductions in dollars?

41. For Columbus Day, the buyer advertised all suede coats at 35% off. The records indicated sales of:

- 50 pieces with original retail of $275 each.
- 30 pieces with original retail of $195 each.
- 10 pieces with original retail of $150 each.

(a) What was the total markdown in dollars?

(b) If sales for October were planned at $80,270, with estimated markdowns of 9%, did the buyer have more markdown money to spend for the month? If so, how much? If not, why not?

42. If the markdowns in Problem 41 were the only ones taken for the month, what was the markdown percentage for the month of October?

43. A buyer bought 300 leather belts that were retailed at $18 each. At the end of the season, 25 unsold belts were cleared at $10 each and sold immediately. What was the markdown percentage on this purchase?

44. The lingerie department's estimated sales for the entire Spring season were $750,000, with anticipated markdowns of 11.5%. At the end of the season, the buyer had taken $67,500 in markdowns. Were the actual dollar markdowns taken more or less than planned? Compare the estimated markdowns to the actual markdowns in both dollars and percentage.

Practice Problems for Review

45. A buyer wants to sell sleds at $39.95 each. The markup is 48.5%. How much can the buyer afford to pay for each sled?

46. If a manufacturer suggests a retail price of $12.50 for a line of totebags costing $84.00 per dozen, what is the suggested markup percentage?

47. A manufacturer offered woven belts at $54 per dozen. If a buyer were to take a 47.5% markup, at what retail price would each belt sell?

48. A buyer purchased 1,500 pairs of men's lounging pajamas at $10 each for a Father's Day sale. The advertised price was $20 retail, and 1,000 pairs were sold at this price. After Father's Day, the remaining pieces of this special purchase were integrated into stock at $25 each. Between July 1 and September 1, all but 50 pairs were sold at this price. The remainder was then cut to $12 each, and all sold at that price except 10 pairs that were too damaged and soiled to sell at any price, and therefore were salvaged.[6] What is the markup percentage on this purchase?

---

[6]Goods unfit for resale and, therefore, were reduced to zero value.

49. Find the markup percentage on the following handbag purchases:

- 36 bags costing $22, with a retail of $45.
- 24 bags costing $28, with a retail of $55.
- 12 bags costing $41, with a retail of $75.
- 12 bags costing $53, with a retail of $95.

50. Down quilts costing $82 per unit were promoted at an advertised retail price of $160 each. Of the 800 pieces purchased, 600 sold at full price, and another 140 sold at a one-day special mid-season sale at $125 each. An additional 35 were cleared at $90 in the markdown corner. The 25 soiled counter samples were salvaged. What markup percentage was yielded on this purchase?

51. A purchase of 350 exercise bikes was made at a cost of $106 each and was unit priced at $200. They sold well at the regular price for a time, but ultimately, the last 45 pieces were reduced and sold at $155 each.

(a) What was the markup percentage on this purchase when the order was written?

(b) What was the markdown percentage on the sale of the 350 machines?

52. A job lot of 650 formal bow ties costs $1,950. If 400 are priced at $6 and the remainder at $7.50, what markup percentage is achieved?

53. A junior sportswear department took the following markdowns for August:

- 160 tops from $28 to $21.
- 230 tops from $25 to $17.
- 170 tops from $20 to $14.

Gross sales for the month in this department were $76,500 and customer returns totaled 6%. What were the departmental markdown percentages for the month?

54. For a Veteran's Day sale, a buyer reduced 95 jackets from $95 to $69 each. The following day the buyer marked 59 additional coats from $125 to $95. What was the total dollar markdown taken?

55. A buyer had 96 suitcases in stock at a retail price of $85 each. For a special sale, they were marked down to $55. The markdowns for this month were planned at 6%, with sales for the month estimated at $90,000. After this event, did the buyer have more markdown money to spend? If so, how much more? If not, why not?

56. A lamp retailing for $97 was advertised at 30% off. What was the new selling price of the lamp after the markdown was taken?

57. In May, markdowns taken in a children's department were:

- 60 jackets from $18 to $15.
- 30 sweatshirts from $15 to $12.
- 70 T-shirts from $10 to $7.

Gross sales for the month in this department were $85,000 and customer returns totaled 6%. What was the departmental markdown percentage for the month?

58. The seasonal plan for a swimwear department showed planned sales of $650,000 and planned markdowns of 18%.

  (a) What was the amount of planned markdown dollars?
  (b) If the markdowns amounted to $120,000, was the actual markdown percentage more or less than the planned percentage and by how much?

59. For Valentine's Day, the candy department buyer purchased a special offering of 150 heart-shaped boxes of candy that cost $6 each. There were two assortments, and the buyer decided to retail 75 boxes at $15 each and 75 boxes at $10 each. On February 15, the remaining $15 assortments were reduced to $9, taking total markdowns of $144, and the balance of the $10 assortment were reduced to $6 each, with these markdowns amounting to $72. Six of the $15 hearts that did not sell at $9 were reduced to $5 and were cleared out. Four of the $10 hearts were reduced to $3 and sold out at that price. The net sales of the department for February were $9,750.

  (a) Determine the markup percentage on the original order.
  (b) What was the markdown percentage on this purchase?
  (c) What was the markdown percentage for the month if these were the only markdowns taken?
  (d) What was the markup percentage achieved on this purchase?

60. Discussion Problem: "Markdowns are a normal and positive element of merchandise planning. The markdown factor may be used advantageously by a buyer in an effective departmental operation."

Case Study 1   PRICING IN MERCHANDISING

At the end of October, a key resource offered a department store buyer a group of acrylic knit tops that are promotionally priced at $96 per dozen. The resource, who owns 60 dozen pieces, quoted this low price providing the purchaser bought the entire group. These tops are comparable in quality and styling to similar merchandise purchased from this vendor at $144 per dozen that sold well at $25 each earlier in the season with the normal department markup. The group now being offered by the resource consists of three different styles currently in demand. Group A has 30 dozen pieces, Group B consists of 20 dozen pieces, and Group C is 10 dozen pieces. As a combined offering, the sizes are well balanced and the colors are "fashion" for this season. Group A is a "staple" in styling, Group B reflects this season's "hot seller," and Group C is considered "avant garde" in both color and silhouette. Because sales are sluggish, the buyer wants to stimulate selling for Election Day by retailing these tops with only a 50% markup. By taking a lower than normal markup, the buyer hopes this purchase will result in additional sales and be a total "sellout."

As the buyer reviews the stock condition of the department, it seems the inventory is higher than planned and the report shows that:

(a) 55% of the inventory is current and salable.
(b) 150 pieces remain from a recent promotion, currently priced at $19 each, and are broken in size and color.
(c) A group of 75 pieces, all one style, priced at $22.50 each, are selling very slowly.
(d) 15 pieces are badly soiled and are marked $25 each.

The buyer also noted that there is $1,000 of markdown money available in November.

The buyer feels the purchase would be ultimately advantageous because increased departmental activity will lead to improved sales. To assure this high volume day, the proper pricing of this purchase, plus an accurate count of the current inventory is essential.

To make the correct decisions, the following questions must be answered:

(a) If this group purchase were to be retailed at the normal markup, what would be the retail per piece? What degree of excitement would this produce by quoting a higher "comparable value?"
(b) Determine the markup percentage achieved if the three groups are retailed as follows:
   ■ Group A at $16 each.
   ■ Group B at $18 each.
   ■ Group C at $20 each.

The last group seems to represent particularly good value.

(c) Should the available November markdown money ($1,000) be used now to clear the present inventory, by reducing the three groups all to $16 and using their comparable value prices? Or should the buyer defer these reductions (which seem inevitable), until the store-wide clearance in December?

Decide what course of action the buyer should pursue and mathematically justify your suggestions as you apply the principles in pricing and repricing.

The Justification of the Pricing Strategy

You are a glove buyer for a major specialty store. On November 1, one of your occasionally used importers offers immediate delivery on a group of men's cape-skin gloves made in the Philippines that are 100% wool lined. The vendor offers 1200 dozen pairs of gloves at $228 per dozen if the entire quantity is purchased. If not, the cost is $264 per dozen. To properly assess this offering, you must consider the factors that will be helpful in making the proper decision. They are:

1. There is only one style in this group, but it is similar to a fast-selling number at a higher price line from another resource.
2. The size range is complete and the staple seasonal colors are represented.
3. This classification (men's leather gloves) has enjoyed stronger sales this season than in previous years. The "healthy" position of this classification is such that this offering could contribute to an unexpected sales increase for the entire department.
4. An analysis of the selling reports and the "on order" of this category shows the condition of the present inventory is inadequate to cover the conservative, realistic anticipated sales for November and December.
5. Currently the market is not flooded with desirable merchandise.

Because of the strong sales of this classification and market conditions, the buyer would like to take advantage of this offering and use a strategy in pricing this group that will generate a markup above the required departmental 52.5% to afford a successful post-Christmas clearance sale. The buyer begins to do more basic calculations and considerations that will justify the final course of action to be taken.

Plan 1. If the normal department 52.5% markup were applied in pricing this group, what would be the retail price per pair with a cost of $228 per dozen?

Usually the gloves that cost $264 per dozen carry a 50% markup. Using this as a guideline, what would be the retail price per pair?

Plan 2. What would be the markup realized if the entire group was purchased and integrated into the $44 price line?

Plan 3. There is a GIFT FOR CHRISTMAS ad planned for December 1 that features women's fine Italian kidskin leather gloves priced at $39. This merchandise represents exceptionally good value and quality. Should the men's gloves be combined with this particular promotion?

Plan 4. Immediately upon delivery, should you integrate half of the entire amount of gloves into the $44 price line assortment, and include the balance in the December 1 ad?

State the possible negative and/or positive results for each suggested option. Recommend or develop a pricing strategy and justify mathematically your recommendations.

Unit III

The Relationship of Markup to Profit

Objectives

- Identification of the types of markups and the use of each in making merchandise decisions.
- Calculation of initial markups, cumulative markups, and maintained markups.
- Recognition of the need to balance markups among different items of merchandise.
- Balance of markups for diverse situations.
- Recognition and understanding of both the dollar amounts and percentages of markup needed to evaluate the impact of merchandising decisions.

Key Terms

average cost
average retail
averaging markups
cumulative markup
final selling price

initial or original markup
initial or original retail
maintained markup
retail reductions
vendor analysis

nit II examined the significance of pricing and repricing, as well as factors that influence the retailer when setting retail prices. Thus, the retail prices of merchandise should be based on the markup deemed appropriate by the merchandiser. Markup, which is simply the difference between retail prices placed on merchandise and the cost of this merchandise, has an effect on:

- Sales volume it can generate.
- Markdowns it can cause.
- Gross margin it can achieve.
- Profits it can produce.

As a result, markup must be estimated, always controlled, and, if necessary, adjusted. Because basic markup calculations in both dollars and percentages are used in buying decisions as they relate to a single item or a group of items, the buyer responsible for a particular department is involved with the markups planned and obtained. These markups are constantly monitored because the desired gross margin depends on how successfully they are achieved.

To better understand the various markups indigenous to the retailing business, the term "retail price" must be clarified. The first price placed on merchandise for resale is the **initial or original retail.** The price received when an item sells (which may be different), is the **final selling price.** The original, initial, or first retail placed on merchandise is the price the retailer hopes to realize, and the final selling price is the price actually received for the merchandise (e.g., a raincoat costing $55 is retailed at $120 when received in the store, but eventually sells for only $100). The initial retail price is often higher than the price at which the merchandise ultimately sells, because price reductions may be necessary before the goods are sold.

I. TYPES OF MARKUP

A. Initial Markup

Initial markup[1] is the difference between the billed cost of merchandise and the original or first retail price placed on a given item or group of items. When freight charges are known, they are added to the billed cost when calculating initial markup. Certain vital factors and common practices must be considered in determining the initial markup; the following considerations cannot be ignored.

---

[1]Initial markup is also known as "markon" and **"original markup."**

- Plan, in advance, an initial markup on merchandise when it is received in the store to ensure a favorable gross margin figure that will cover expenses and provide a reasonable profit.
- Forecast an initial markup percentage that will be required on all the merchandise handled during a particular period (i.e., a six-month season), because it is virtually impossible to have available all the data necessary for the calculation of each purchase.
- Recognize that the gross margin figure can fluctuate because it is the result of many merchandising decisions.
- Understand that the initial markup placed on new purchases will be reduced by markdowns, shortages, and employee discounts.
- Be aware of and act on cash discounts offered retailers in the purchase of goods, as well as estimated alteration costs.

For a department, an initial markup planned on a seasonal and/or annual basis can be expressed in either dollar figures or percentages and usually is calculated for both. In most large retail stores, the buyer and/or divisional merchandise manager (under the guidance and supervision of the control division), establishes this initial markup as a guide to check against aggregate markups obtained in pricing new merchandise purchases. In addition, it is essential to know that the initial markup planned for a season must take into consideration the markups on the new purchases and the effect they have on the markup of the merchandise inherited from the last season, because the gross margin figure for the period depends on the markups achieved on all the inventory available for sale. Thus, in planning an initial markup, probable expenses, the profit goal, probable reductions, estimated alteration costs, and anticipated sales must be projected first.

An initial markup is expressed as a percentage of the aggregate original retail price placed on the merchandise, not on the price at which the merchandise sold. The price at which the merchandise sold is expressed as sales plus reductions. For example, if sales are planned at $1,000,000 and all retail reductions at $150,000, the goods that eventually sell at $1,000,000 must be introduced into stock at $1,150,000 with the desired markup expressed as a percentage of this total. This seasonal planned markup percentage can be calculated, and the concept can be expressed by a formula.

Establishing an Initial Markup

To better appreciate the establishment of an initial markup, examine the methods commonly used to institute a seasonal markup, and the calculations (in both dollars and percentages) as they appear in the chart and steps below. (The figures listed in the chart are for illustration only; they do not represent actual retail figures.)

GIVEN:

	Dollars	Percentages
Planned sales	$1,000,000	100.0%
Estimated expenses	393,000	39.3
Price reductions	150,000	15.0
Profit	50,000	5.0

METHOD:

1. Forecast the total sales for the season or the year ($1,000,000).
2. Estimate the required expenses ($393,000) and price reductions ($150,000) needed to reach the sales plan.
3. Set a profit goal-operating profit or department contribution ($50,000).
4. Add the estimated expenses ($393,000) to the price reductions ($150,000) and profit ($50,000) to determine the dollar markup ($593,000).

	Dollars	Percentages
Estimated expenses	$393,000	39.3%
+ Price reductions	+ 150,000	+ 15.0
+ Profit	+ 50,000	+ 5.0
Dollar markup	= $593,000	= 59.3%

5. Determine the original retail price ($1,150,000) by adding the planned reductions ($150,000) to the planned sales ($1,000,000).

	Dollars	Percentages
Planned sales	$1,000,000	100.0%
+ Price reductions	+ 150,000	+ 15.0
Original retail price	= $1,150,000	= 115.0%

6. Compute the markup percentage (51.6%) by dividing the dollar markup $593,000) found in step 4 by the original price ($1,150,000).

	Dollars	Percentages
Markup	$ 593,000	59.3%
÷ Original retail price	÷ 1,150,000	÷ 115.0
Initial markup	= 51.6%	= 51.6%

Calculating the Initial Markup

The formula for calculating an initial markup percentage on goods purchased shows the amount of markup necessary to achieve a desire profit. As already discussed, this markup should cover expenses, reductions, and profits. These projections can be based on past results or calculated mathematically on the basis of anticipated sales, reductions, and expenses. The equation to determine an initial markup percentage can spell out each factor (i.e., expenses + profits + markdowns + stock shortages + employee discounts), or it can be simplified (i.e., expenses + profits = gross margin and markdowns + stock shortages + employee discounts = **retail reductions**). Because gross margin and retail reduction figures are more significant in planning than the analysis of expenses, shortages, and other factors, the second, simplified equation is more often used.

Finding Initial MU Percentages When Gross Margin Percentage and Retail Reduction Percentage Are Known

CONCEPT:

$$\text{Initial markup \%} = \frac{\text{Gross margin \%} + \text{Retail Reductions \%}}{100\% \text{ (Sales)} + \text{Retail Reductions \%}}$$

PROBLEM:

A store has a gross margin of 42.3% (39.3% expenses + 3% profit) and retail reductions (markdowns, shortages, and employee discounts) of 15%. What is the initial markup percentage?

SOLUTION:

$$\text{Initial MU \%} = \frac{\begin{array}{l} 42.3\% \text{ G.M. } (39.3\% \text{ Exp. } + 3.0\% \text{ Profit}) \\ + \ 15.0\% \text{ Retail reductions (markdowns, shortages,} \\ \qquad\qquad\qquad\qquad\qquad\qquad\qquad \text{employee discounts)} \end{array}}{100\% \text{ Sales } + \ 15\% \text{ Retail reductions}}$$

$$= \frac{57.3\%}{115.0\%}$$

Initial markup % = 49.8%

Finding Initial MU Percentage When Gross Margin and Retail Reductions in Dollars Are Known

CONCEPT:

$$\text{Initial markup \%} = \frac{\$ \text{ Gross margin} + \text{Retail reductions}}{\$ \text{ Sales} + \$ \text{ Retail reductions}}$$

PROBLEM:

A store plans sales of $1,000,000, retail reductions of $150,000, and requires a gross margin of $423,000 (i.e., expenses $393,000, profit $30,000). What should be the initial markup percentage?

SOLUTION:

Initial MU % $= \dfrac{\$\ 423,000\ (GM)\ +\ \$150,000\ (Retail\ reductions)}{\$1,000,000\ (Sales)\ +\ \$150,000\ (Retail\ reductions)}$

$= \dfrac{\$\ 573,000}{\$1,150,000}$

Initial MU % = 49.8%

Finding Initial MU Percentage When Cash Discounts and Alteration Costs Are Known

As shown in Unit I, the cost of goods sold is adjusted by alteration and work-room costs and cash discounts. Therefore, these factors (if and when they exist) are essential in calculating retail markups. Because markup covers alteration and workroom costs, these factors are added to gross margin. Because cash discounts reduce the cost of goods sold, which affects the final markup obtained, they are subtracted from gross margin.

CONCEPT:

Initial markup % $= \dfrac{GM\ \%\ +\ Alteration\ costs\ \%\ -\ Cost\ discount\ earned\ \%\ +\ Retail\ reductions\ \%}{Sales\ (100\%)\ +\ Retail\ reductions\ \%}$

PROBLEM:

The desired gross margin of a store is 42.3%, the retail reductions are 15%; the cash discounts earned are 3%, and the alteration costs are 2%.

SOLUTION:

Initial markup % $= \dfrac{42.3\%\ GM\ +\ 2\%\ Alteration\ costs\ -\ 3.0\%\ Cash\ discounts\ +\ 15\%\ Retail\ reductions}{100\%\ (Sales)\ +\ 15\%\ Retail\ reductions}$

$= \dfrac{56.3\%}{115.0\%}$

$= 48.96\%$

Initial MU % = 49%

For assignments for the previous section, see practice problems 1–10.

B. Cumulative Markup

Although an initial markup may be calculated for individual items, the initial markup on merchandise received is more commonly reported for season-to-date, or for the year. Over any such extended period, an initial markup is called cumulative markup, which is the markup percentage figure generally used by retailers to compare merchandising performance and information with other stores. **Cumulative markup** is the markup percentage achieved on all goods available for sale from the beginning of a given period. It is an average markup because it is the markup percentage obtained on the accumulated inventory at the beginning of the given period, plus the markup of all the new purchases received season-to-date. The cumulative markup in dollars equals the difference between the invoiced cost of the merchandise (including transportation) before cash discounts have been adjusted and the cumulative original retail prices of all merchandise handled (opening inventory + net purchases) during a given period of time. Markdowns do not enter into the calculation of the cumulative markup percentage. The concept is simply stated by saying:

CONCEPT:

$$\text{Cumulative markup percent} = \frac{\text{Cumulative markup dollars}}{\text{Cumulative retail dollars}}$$

PROBLEM:

On February 1, a boys' clothing department has an opening inventory of $200,000 at retail with markup of 49.0%. On July 31, the new purchases season-to-date amounted to $1,350,000 at retail with a 49.9% markup. Find the cumulative markup percentage achieved.

SOLUTION:

Given information is in bold, and the other items are calculated from the basic markup formulas; each calculation is identified with the steps of the procedure.

	Cost	Retail	MU%
Opening inventory	$102,000	**$ 200,000**	**49.0%**
+ Purchases STD	+676,350	**+1,350,000**	**49.9%**
Total merchandise handled	$778,350	$ 1,550,000	49.8%

Step 1: Find the cost value of the retail opening inventory.

$C = R \times (100\% - MU\%)$

$C = \mathbf{\$200{,}000}\ (100\% - \mathbf{49.0\%})$

$C = \mathbf{\$200{,}000} \times \mathbf{51\%}$

$C = \$102{,}000$

Step 2: Find the total cost value of all purchases season-to-date.

C = R × (100% = MU%)

C = **$1,350,000** (100% − **49.9%)**

C = **$1,350,000** × **50.1%**

C = $ 676,350

Step 3: Find the total retail value of total merchandise handled.
$200,000 + $1,350,000 = $1,550,000

Step 4: Find the total cost value of total merchandise handled.
$102,000 + $676,350 = $778,350

Step 5: Find the cumulative markup on total merchandise handled.

$1,550,000 Cumulative retail

−   778,350 Cumulative cost

= $ 771,650 Cumulative markup

$ 771,650 (Cumulative markup) ÷ $1,550,000 (Cumulative retail) = 49.8%

Cumulative markup % = 49.8%

The new purchases required a 49.9% markup to achieve a 49.8% cumulative markup, because the merchandise of the opening inventory came into the period with only a 49% markup.

At this point, it must be understood that both the intial and cumulative markup are on merchandise purchased. Initial markup percentage refers to those markups obtained when pricing new merchandise purchases. Cumulative markup percentage is the amount of markup on all the merchandise available for sale, whether it is new purchases or stock-on-hand at the beginning of the period. The cumulative markup percentage is the initial markup percentage calculated from the beginning of the season to any given later date (e.g., the end of the season or year).

For assignments for the previous section, see practice problems 11–15.

C. Maintained Markup

Before maintained markup is explained, it is essential to know that although gross margin and a maintained markup are related, they are not identical. Gross margin is the difference between net sales and the cost of merchandise sold, adjusted by subtracting cash discounts and adding alteration/workroom costs (i.e., total cost of merchandise sold). **Maintained Markup** (MMU) is the difference between net sales and the cost of merchandise sold without the credits of cash discounts and without adding alteration/workroom costs (i.e., gross cost of merchandise sold). If these differences are not considered in calculations, the gross margin and maintained markup figures will be the same. For both, the net sales figure reflects the final selling prices received for the goods sold, and the margin actually realized when the goods are sold. They are both markup on sales. The relationship between gross margin and maintained markup is revealed clearly in the following example:

Net sales		$1,000,000
Cost of goods sold	$ 220,000	
+ New purchases	+ 645,000	
+ Inward freight	+ 14,000	
Total merchandise handled	$ 879,000	
− Closing inventory	− 280,000	
Gross cost of merchandise	$ 599,000	
− Cash discounts earned	− 32,000	
Net cost of merchandise sold	$ 567,000	
+ Alteration/workroom costs	+ 10,000	
Total cost of merchandise sold		− 577,000
Gross margin	=	$ 423,000

CONCEPT:

GM % = Net sales − Total cost of goods sold

= $1,000,000 (Sales) − $577,000 (Total cost of goods sold)

$$= \frac{\$423,000 \text{ Gross margin}}{\$1,000,000 \text{ Net sales}}$$

GM % = 42.3%

While

CONCEPT:

MMU % = Net sales − Gross cost of goods sold

= $1,000,000 Net sales − $599,000 (Gross cost of goods)

$$= \frac{\$401,000 \text{ Maintained margin}}{\$1,000,000 \text{ Net sales}}$$

MMU % = 40.1%

Because the differences between gross margin and maintained markup is the amount of cash discounts and alteration/workroom costs, this relationship can also be expressed (using the same figure) as the following concept.

CONCEPT:

$$\text{GM \%} = \frac{\text{Maintained markup} + \text{Cash discounts} - \text{Alteration costs}}{\text{Net Sales}}$$

$$= \frac{\$401,000 \text{ MMU} + \$32,000 \text{ Cash discounts} - \$10,000 \text{ Alteration costs}}{\$1,000,000 \text{ Sales}}$$

$$= \frac{\$\ 423,000}{1,000,000}$$

$$\text{GM \%} = 42.3\%$$

While

CONCEPT:

$$\text{MMU \%} = \frac{\text{Gross margin} - \text{Cash discounts} + \text{Alteration costs}}{\text{Net sales}}$$

$$= \frac{\$423,000 \text{ Gross margin} - \$32,000 \text{ Cash discounts} + \$10,000 \text{ Alteration costs}}{\$1,000,000 \text{ Sales}}$$

$$= \frac{\$\ 401,000}{1,000,000}$$

MMU % = 40.1%

Maintained markup is the markup actually achieved on the sale of the merchandise and is generally calculated for a department or, when desired, for a **vendor analysis,** which is an investigation of the profitability of each vendor's products sold by a retailer. It is not customary to plan a maintained markup, because it is the result of merchandising activities. The initial markup must be planned in advance so that the desired final or maintained markup goal is achieved. In addition, maintained markup must be large enough to cover expenses and provide a profit while, as previously explained, the initial markup must be high enough to anticipate and also cover all possible retail reductions (i.e., markdowns, shortages, and employee discounts). However, once the initial markup and retail reductions are planned, the probable maintained markup can be projected.

Finding Maintained Markup When Initial Markup and Retail Reductions Are Known

CONCEPT:

MMU % = Intial MU % − Retail reduction % × (100% − Initital MU %)

PROBLEM:

A department planned an initial markup of 49.8% and retail reductions of 15%. What is the maintained markup?

SOLUTION:

$$
\begin{aligned}
\text{MMMU \%} &= 49.8\% - 15\% \times (100\% - 49.8) \\
&= 49.8\% - 15\% \times 50.2\% \\
&= 49.8\% - 7.53\% \\
\text{MMU \%} &= 42.27 \text{ or } 42.3\%
\end{aligned}
$$

Finding Retail Reductions When Initial Markup and Maintained Markup Are Known

CONCEPT:

$$
\text{Reduction \%} = \frac{\text{Initial markup \% − MMU \%}}{\text{Sales (100\%) − Initial markup \%}}
$$

PROBLEM:

The department planned an initial markup of 49.8% and wanted to achieve a maintained markup of 42.3%. What should be the amount of retail reductions?

SOLUTION:

$$
\text{Reduction \%} = \frac{49.8\% \text{ Init. MU} - 42.27 \text{ MMU \%}}{\text{Sales (100\%)} - 49.8\% \text{ Initial MU}}
$$

$$
= \frac{7.53\%}{50.2\%}
$$

Reduction % = 15.0%

The same factors have been used deliberately to show the calculations of both initial and maintained markups, so that the relationship can be fully appreciated. The maintained markup concepts can also be expressed in dollars, and the procedure for calculation is identical. A particular merchandising situation, however, may require the focus to be on dollars rather than percentages (e.g., merchandising fast-turnover goods).

For assignments for the previous section, see practice problems 16–22.

Notes

PRACTICE PROBLEMS

Initial Markup

1. A lingerie buyer determines that the department has net sales of $750,000, expenses of $315,000, and total reduction of $75,000. This buyer also wants to attain a net contribution of 4.5%. Find the initial markup percentage.

2. A department shows a gross margin of 41% (37.9% expenses + 3.1% profit) and lists retail reductions (i.e., markdowns, shortages, and employee discounts) of 13%. What is the initial markup percentage?

3. A chain of specialty shops plans sales of $1,500,000 and retail reductions of $260,000. It needs a gross margin of $605,000 (i.e., expenses $550,000, profit $55,000). What should be the initial markup percentage?

4. In a small leather goods department, the markdowns, including employee discounts, were 18.7%, stock shortage was 3.8%, and the gross margin was 46.6%. Determine the initial markup percentage.

5. A retailer in a boutique jewelry store has estimated expenses of 39%, markdowns at 15%, and stock shortage at 6.3%. A profit of 4% is desired. Calculate the initial markup percentage required.

6. The intimate apparel buyer wants to determine an initial markup percentage for the robe classification. The buyer knows that the gross margin is 44.0%, markdowns are at 31.4%, and shortages are at .6%. Calculate the initial markup percentage.

7. A gross margin of 49.4% is targeted by a gift department. Retail reductions are 16% and cash discounts are 4%, with alteration costs of 1%. Find the initial markup percentage.

8. A buyer plans, for the period, net sales of $1,500,000 with a 49% gross margin. The acceptable markdowns are 12%, with employee discounts at 1%, and planned shortages of 2.5%. Cash discounts to be earned are estimated at 6%, and alteration costs are 0.5%. What initial markup percentage is needed to achieve the desired results?

9. Determine the initial markup percentage from the following data:

Gross margin	=	46.8%
Markdowns	=	10.0%
Employee discounts	=	1.5%
Cash discounts to be earned	=	5.0%
Alteration costs	=	.5%

10. The petite sportswear buyer plans seasonal net sales of $2,000,000 with a gross margin of 48%, markdowns (including employee discounts) estimated at 32.9%, planned shortages to be 2.1%, cash discounts to be earned planned at 6%, and alteration costs at 1%. Calculate the planned initial markup percentage.

Cumulative Markup

11. A hosiery buyer has an opening stock figure of $180,000, at retail, which carries a 52% markup. On March 31, new purchases since the start of the period were $990,000 at retail, carrying a 54% markup. Find the cumulative markup percentage on merchandise handled in this department to date.

12. The slipper department showed an opening inventory of $80,000 at retail with a markup of 48%. The purchases for that month amounted to $30,000 at cost, which were marked in at 52%. The initial markup planned for this department was 50.5%.

    (a) Determine the season-to-date cumulative markup percentage for the department.

    (b) Was the department markup achieved on target? If not, what factors caused a deviation?

13. A belt department had an opening inventory of $95,000 at retail, with a 55.8% markup. Purchases during November were $64,000 at cost, and $142,000 at retail. Determine:

    (a) The cumulative markup percentage.

    (b) The markup percentage on the new purchases.

14. During the fall season, a retailer determined that the total amount of merchandise required next season to meet planned sales was $360,000, at retail, with an initial markup goal of 52%. At the beginning of the next season, the merchandise on hand (opening inventory) came to $80,000 at retail, with a cumulative markup of 49% on these goods. For the coming season, what initial markup percentage does the buyer need to achieve on any new purchases.

15. In preparation for a foreign buying trip, a buyer determines that a 55.4% markup is required on purchases that will amount to $560,000 at retail. While on this trip the following purchases are made:

	Cost	Retail
Resource A	$20,000	$ 45,000
Resource B	50,000	125,000
Resource C	70,000	170,000

What markup percentage is needed on the balance of the purchases?

Maintained Markup

16. A men's shop with an initial markup of 53% had markdowns of 12%, employee discounts of 2.5%, and shortages of 1.5%. What was the maintained markup percentage?

17. A sporting goods store has an initial markup of 44.5%. The expenses are 31%, markdowns are 12%, cost of assembling bicycles, etc. (i.e., workroom costs), are 6%, and shortages are 1%. What was the maintained markup percentage?

18. The Closet Shop had the following operational results:

Net sales	=	$125,000
Billed cost of new purchases	=	64,000
Inward freight	=	1,000
Alteration costs	=	2,000
Cash discounts	=	7,000

Find:

(a) The maintained markup in dollars and percentages.
(b) The gross margin in dollars and percentages.

19. The jewelry department has an initial markup of 55.6%, with total retail reductions of 15%. There are no alteration costs or cash discounts. What is the maintained markup percentage and the gross margin percentage?

20. A children's store has sales of $500,000, with markdowns of 14.5% and shortages of 2%. The initial markup was 51.7%. What was the maintained markup percentage?

21. The T-shirt department buyer determined that the department's initial markup should be 51.5%. The buyer also wanted to attain a maintained markup of 45%. Under this plan, what retail reductions (in percentages) would be allowed?

22. A boutique had planned a gross margin of 49%, with total retail reductions of 18%. At the end of the period, the maintained markup attained was actually 48.8%.

(a) Find the initial markup percentage needed to achieve the planned gross margin of 49%, with total retail reductions of 18%.

(b) Find the actual amount of markdowns (in percentages) taken.

(c) Prove your calculations and explain your findings. What may have caused the maintained markup percentage to vary from the planned gross margin target?

II. Averaging or Balancing Markup

A buyer's skill is truly tested by the ability not only to buy "the right goods, at the right time, in the right amounts," but a buyer must also be able to achieve a predetermined markup percentage over a season or year. Failure to reach this goal can have an adverse effect on profits, and sometimes can determine whether or not a profit is generated at all. Ultimately, as short-term buying decisions are made, the merchandiser must know how any deviations from the markup objective will affect the long-term performance.

In the actual pricing of goods in retailing, it is seldom possible to obtain the same markup on all lines of merchandise, all classifications, all price lines, or all items carried within a particular department. In the real world of retailing, deviations from the planned seasonal markup will occur. These differences can be the result of competition, variations in special promotional merchandise offered by resources, special buying arrangements, private brands, imports, and other factors that rely on the buyer's judgment. Thus, to realize the planned markup necessary for a profitable operation, below-average markups should be balanced by above-average markups. **Averaging markups** means adjusting the proportions of goods purchased at different markups, to achieve the desired aggregate markup, either for an individual purchase or for a certain period. In merchandising the purchases, the buyer builds a "cushion" or lowers the markup depending on the situation. This practice is prevalent in the fashion and fashion-related industries.

There are diverse pricing policies that are determined by an industry or by the specific retailer. Some of these factors are odd pricing (i.e., $89.99 instead of $90); multiple unit pricing (i.e., one for $3.25, two for $6); loss leaders, when the item is sold below the retailer's cost; high-low pricing, using high everyday prices combined with "specials" or low leader pricing on featured items advertised weekly. Each retailer must evaluate the usefulness of each type of pricing service. The appropriate cumulative markup originates from effective averaging of many purchases.

When solving problems that illustrate how markups are averaged or balanced, it is helpful to remember that:

- On a day-to-day basis, buyers strive to achieve a projected markup by the averaging process.
- Appropriate cumulative markups result from the effective averaging of many purchases, and the effects of this averaging on the entire inventory.
- Basic markup equations are applied to given information for calculation of the figures required for solutions.

■ Solutions can be calculated readily when:

It is understood what information is missing.

The given information is determined.

The calculations required for the solution (based on the given information) are identified.

The next section's problems and solutions employ the above principles in two ways; that is, the steps necessary for the calculations are listed in sequence, and the results of these calculations are arranged in a diagram. It should be understood that an average markup is always determined by working with a total cost figure and a total retail figure.

A. Averaging Costs When Retail and MU% Are Known

This merchandising technique involves one retail price with two or more costs. It is common to have one retail line that consists of merchandise with varying wholesale costs. The merchandiser must be able to calculate the proportion of merchandise at different cost amounts that can carry the same retail price and still achieve the desired markup percentage. To understand this, it is essential to realize that the merchandiser is attempting to proportion the varying costs to achieve the desired markup percentage, because the aggregate results are the buyer's major concern.

PROBLEM:

For a special sale, a men's sportswear buyer plans to promote a $25 vest. Consequently, the buyer purchases 500 vests, and wants to achieve a 52% markup. An order for 100 vests that cost $10.75 each is also placed by this same buyer. What will be the average cost of the remaining pieces?

SOLUTION:

Given information is in bold, and the other items are calculated from the basic markup formulas; each calculation is identified with the steps of the procedure.

Step 1: Find the total planned retail.
500 pieces × **$25** = $12,500

Step 2: Find the total cost of total planned retail using a planned MU percentage.
C = R × (100% − MU%)
C = $12,500 × (100% − 52%)
C = $12,500 ×   48%
C = $6,000

Step 3: Find the cost of purchases to date.
100 pieces × **$10.75** = $1,075

Step 4: Find purchase balance in units and dollars.
Purchase balance = Total planned figures − Purchases to date.
(500 pieces cost $6,000) − **(100 pieces cost $1,075)** = (400 pieces cost $4,925)

Step 5: Find the average cost of purchase balance. Average cost of purchase
balance = $ Cost on balance of purchase ÷ Purchase balance number of units
= $4,925 ÷ 400 pcs.
= $12.31

	Total Pieces	Total $Cost	Total $Retail	MU%
Total plan	**500** (1)	**$6,000** (2)	**$12,500**	**52%**
− **Purchases to date**	**−100** (3)	**−1,075** (3)		
Purchase balance	400 (4)	$4,925 (4)		

$4,925 ÷ 400 pcs. = $12.31 each is the **average cost** of remaining pieces. (5)

For assignments for the previous section, see practice problems 23–27.

B. Averaging Retail(s) When Costs and MU% Are Known

In merchandising, a buyer must be able to manipulate markups, because purchases may be made that have two or more costs, and the buyer may want to
determine an **average retail** that will achieve the desired markup percentage.
Furthermore, the buyer may make purchases that have not only two or more
costs, but may also have two or more retails. These situations require the
proper proportion of varying retails to achieve the planned markup percentage
because a buyer is always concerned with the aggregate results. The following
problems illustrate the averaging processes.

PROBLEM:
At the end of the season, a swimwear manufacturer offered a retailer 50 two-
piece solid-color suits that cost $16.75 each, 75 nylon tank suits that cost $12.75
each, and 40 one-piece skirted suits that cost $14.75 each. The average retail
price on each unit was based on the buyer's goal of obtaining a 49% markup on
this purchase. What would be the average retail price of each swimsuit?

SOLUTION:

(Given information is in bold, and the other items are calculated from the basic markup formulas; each calculation is identified with the steps from the basic markup formulas; each calculation is identified with the steps of this procedure.)

Step 1: Find the total cost and total units of purchase.

50 suits @ **$16.75** = $ 837.50
75 suits @ **$12.75** = + 956.25
+ **40** suits @ **$14.75** = + 590.00
_____
165 suits = $2,383.75

Step 2: Find the total retail from the planned MU percentage.
R = Cost ÷ (100% − **49%**)
R = $2,383.75 ÷ 51%
R = $4,674.02

Step 3: Find average retail for each piece.
Average retail = Total retail ÷ Total units purchased
= $4,674.02 ÷ 165 pcs.
= $28.33

	Total Pieces	Total $Cost	Total $Retail	MU%
Total Plan	**165**	**$2,383.75**	$4,674.02	**49%**
	(1)	(1)	(2)	

$4,674.02 ÷ 165 = $28.33 retail for each (3)

PROBLEM:

The men's apparel buyer bought 50 plaid sportcoats that cost $32.75 each and 80 check sportcoats that cost $42.75 each. An overall markup of 52.5% is needed. If the buyer retails the plaid sportcoats at $65 each, what must be the average retail price for each check sportcoat to achieve the planned markup percentage?

SOLUTION:

(Given information is in bold, and the other items are calculated from the basic markup formulas; each calculation is identified with the steps of the procedure.)

Step 1: Find the total cost and total units.
50 plaid sportcoats @ **$32.75** = $1,637.50
+ 80 check sportcoats @ **$42.75** = + 3,420.00
_____
130 plaid & check sportcoats = $5,057.50

Step 2: Find the total retail from planned MU percentage
R. = Cost ÷ (100% − **52.5%**)
R. = $ 5,057.50 ÷ (100% − **52.5%**)
R. = $ 5,057.50 ÷ 47.5%
R. = $10,647.37

Step 3: Find the total on established retail.
(50 plaid sportcoats × $65 = $3,250)

Step 4: Find the purchase balance in units and dollars. Purchase balance = Total planned figures (minus) − Total established retail figures

$$
\begin{array}{rl}
130 \text{ pcs. @} & \$10,647.37 \\
- 50 \text{ pcs. @} - & 3,250.00 \\
\hline
80 \text{ pcs.} = & \$ \; 7,397.37
\end{array}
$$

Step 5: Find the average retail of purchase balance. Average retail of purchase balance = Purchase balance $ retail ÷ Purchase balance number of units
= $7397.27 ÷ 80 pcs.
= $92.47

	Total Pieces	Total $Cost	Total $Retail	MU%
Total plan	**130** (1)	**$5,057.50** (1)	$10,647.37 (2)	**52.5%**
− Established retail	− 50 (3)		− 3,250.00 (3)	
Purchase balance	80 (4)		$ 7,397.37 (4)	

$7,397.37 ÷ 80 pcs. = $92.47 each for av. retail of remaining pieces. (5)

For assignments for the previous section, see practice problems 28–29.

C. Averaging MU% When Retail and Planned MU% Are Known

Realistically, a profit goal can be realized only when a buyer is able to determine the markup percentage that must be obtained on present or future purchases to balance out the markup percentage that has already been achieved on past purchases. This involves the proportioning of markup percentages on goods so that the aggregate results produce the desired, planned markup percentage.

PROBLEM:

A coat buyer plans to buy $5,000 (retail) worth of merchandise. This same buyer requires a 49% MU. The first purchase is 50 coats costing $31.75, with a planned retail of $55. What MU percentage should the buyer obtain on the balance to attain the planned MU goal of 49%?

SOLUTION:

Given information is in bold, and the other items are calculated from the basic markup formulas; each calculation is identified with the steps of the procedure.

Step 1: Find the total cost of total planned retail from planned MU%.
C = R × (100% − MU%)
C = **$5,000** × (100% − **49%**)
C = **$5,000** × 51%
C = $2,550

Step 2: Find the total cost and retail of purchases to date.
50 suits @ **$31.75** = $1,587.50 Total cost
50 suits @ **$55.00** = $2,750 Total retail

Step 3: Find purchase balance at cost and at retail.
Purchase balance = Total planned $ cost and $ retail amounts − Respective figures of purchases to date.
$2,550 − $1,587.50 = $962.50
$5,000 − $2,750 = $2,250

Step 4: Find the MU% on purchase balance.
$ MU = R. − C.
$ MU = $2,250 − $962.50
$ MU = $1,287.50
MU % = $ MU ÷ R.
MU % = $1,287.50 ÷ $2,250
MU % = 57.2%

	Total $Cost	Total $Retail	MU%
Total Plan	$2,550	**$5,000**	49%
− Purchases to date	**−1,587.50** (2)	**−2,750.00** (2)	
Purchase balance	$ 962.50 (3)	$2,250.00 (3)	

$1,287.50 ÷ $2,250 = 57.2% on purchase balance (4)

For assignments for the previous section, see practice problems 30–34.

PRACTICE PROBLEMS

Average Costs

23. A hosiery buyer plans to purchase 120 dozen pairs of sox for a pre-Christmas sale. The unit retail price is planned at $17.50, and the markup goal for the purchase is 48%. Forty dozen pairs are purchased at the Slimline Company showroom, at $110 per dozen.

      (a) What is the most the buyer can pay for the balance of the total purchase?

      (b) What will be the average cost per dozen for the sox (80 dozen) yet to be purchased?

24. A separates buyer—who operates on a 51% markup—needs 300 skirts to retail at $32 each and 180 sweater vests to retail at $25 each. If this buyer pays $11.75 for each sweater vest, how much can be spent for each skirt, without deviating from the target markup percentage?

25. A buyer who needs $10,000 worth of merchandise at retail for a housewares department has written orders for $2,875.50 at cost. The planned departmental MU percentage is 53.5%. How much (in dollars) is left to spend at cost?

26. A December promotion of 1,500 crystal bud vases to retail at $40 each is planned. The buyer requires a 48.5% average markup and has made an initial purchase consisting of 1,200 units costing $23 each. What is the cost to be paid on each remaining unit? Comment on the buyer's "predicament" if you detect one.

27. A buyer for the exclusive Britique Shop purchased 100 cashmere pullover sweaters at $41 each and priced them at $90 retail. Also planned is a purchase of 72 shetland/mohair blend bulk knit pullovers to retail at $50 each. Departmental goal markup is 51.8%. How much can be paid for each shetland/mohair pullover?

Average Retails

28. A buyer purchases a job lot of 400 pairs of men's jeans, 280 pairs costing $14 each and 120 pairs costing $9 each. If a 51% markup is targeted, what would be the average unit retail price on the lot?

29. A buyer purchased 120 maillot swim suits at $32 cost and placed a $65 retail on them. Sixty string bikinis are also purchased at $14 each. What would be the retail price on the bikinis if a 50% markup is desired on the combined purchase?

Average Markup Percentage

30. A buyer plans to purchase jackets at a 48% markup with a retail value of $18,500. If the buyer acquires 100 jackets at $69.75 each and retails them at $125 each, what markup percentage must now be obtained on the balance of the purchases to achieve the desired markup percentage?

31. A buyer, who needs $23,000 worth of goods at retail for May, has a planned markup of 49.5%. On May 10, the orders to date total $5,500 at cost and $9,800 at retail. What markup percentage must now be obtained on the balance of the purchases for May to achieve the planned markup percentage for the month?

32. The men's outerwear buyer, who needs a 51% average markup for this department, is planning to buy $9,500 worth of merchandise at retail for the month of January. To date, 100 imported raincoats costing $21.75 each have been purchased, with a plan to retail them at 48% markup. What markup percentage is needed on the balance of the purchase to attain the average markup percentage?

33. A suit buyer who plans sales of $75,000 at retail during April, has an average markup goal of 49%. An order is placed with the B&C Sportswear Company for April delivery in the amount of $5,975 at cost and $11,000 at retail. What markup must be made on the balance of the April purchases to achieve the planned markup?

34. A housewares buyer plans a $15,000 promotion of decorative stepstools to retail at $25 each at a 48% markup. A local manufacturer supplies 500 stools for $14 each. What markup percentage must be obtained on the remainder of the planned purchase to reach the markup goal?

III. LIMITATIONS OF THE MARKUP PERCENTAGE AS A GUIDE TO PROFITS

From the discussions on markup and its relationship to profit, it is understood that markup can be calculated in both dollars and percentages. A markup percentage is a useful guideline in establishing a markup high enough to cover expenses, provide for reductions, and still realize a profit.

In the calculation of all types of markup, the focal point is generally on the markup percentage because it is particularly meaningful for analysis and comparison. However, under certain conditions, attention must be given to the dollar markup. Expenses are paid in dollars and profit is invested, reinvested, or taken to the bank in dollars. During periods of declining sales, a markup percentage initially deemed appropriate, may be insufficient for a profit because a certain markup percentage is based on a specific estimated sales figure. There is a correlation between these two figures. For example, a buyer achieves sales of $300,000 and attains the required initial markup of 52% that would be large enough to cover expenses of $136,000 and markdowns of $12,000, and allow a profit of $8,000. In dollars and percentages this calculation would be:

		Dollars	*Percentages*
Sales		$300,000	100%
− Cost of goods sold		− 144,000	− 48
Initial markup		= 156,000	= 52%
Expenses − $136,000 Markdowns + 12,000		− 148,000	− 49.3
Total Profit		= $ 8,000	2.7%

If sales declined 10% to $270,000, the 52% markup may not yield a profit. As sales decline, the fixed nature of expenses will not decline proportionately to the sales, if at all, and it is not always possible to lower markdown reductions, which may increase to stimulate lagging sales. This type of situation can result in a loss despite the establishment of what seemed a satisfactory markup percentage.

The results are illustrated in the following example:

With the same 52% markup, only $140,000 would be available to cover the expenses of the $136,000 and the markdowns of $12,000.

	Dollars	Percentages
Sales	$270,000	100%
− Cost of goods sold	− 129,600	− 48
Initial markup	= $140,400	52%
Expenses − $136,000 ⎱		
Markdowns + 12,000 ⎰	− 148,000	54.8%
	= − $ 7,600 (Loss)	2.8%

Conversely, as sales increase, the markup percentage can decline even though the dollar markup is maintained at an adequate level. The astute retailer recognizes that the dollar markup figure cannot be ignored while attempting to achieve a fixed markup percentage.

Practice Problems for Review

35. Determine the initial markup for a designer boutique that has the following projections for the next season:

Planned sales	=	$4,000,000
Markdowns	= $	600,000
Expenses	=	38%
Cash discounts	=	4%
Shortages	= $	20,000
Profit	=	5%

36. What is the cumulative markup to date for an accessories department whose figures are:

	Cost	Retail
Opening inventory	$360,000	$780,000
Purchases resource X	60,700	120,500
Purchases resource Y	120,000	245,000
Purchases resource Z	150,000	325,000

37. A shoe department with an initial markup of 53.2% had total retail reductions of 12%. What maintained markup was achieved in this department?

38. A men's outerwear department, with an initial markup of 54%, needs to maintain a markup of 48%. How much can be allowed for reductions?

39. Determine if the maintained markup of 48% would be obtained using the reduction percentage calculated in Problem 38.

40. The owner of a children's store wishes to increase annual profits (which were 2.5% of net sales) from $5,000 to $15,000. The operating expenses are anticipated to increase from 30% to 32% because of increased promotional events. The total retail reductions are planned at 15.5%, the same as last year, and there are no cash discounts or alteration costs.

    (a) What was last year's initial markup percentage?
    (b) To achieve the owner's increased profit on the same sales volume, what initial markup should be planned for this year?

41. A buyer wishes to buy 3,500 novelty scarves for a special import promotion. The item is to retail at $16.95 each with a planned markup of 54%. If the cost for each of 2,100 scarves is $8.75, how much may be paid for each scarf not yet purchased?

42. A luggage buyer plans a European buying trip to purchase $250,000 (cost value) of assorted travel packs. On the first stop in London, orders are placed for $92,000 (at cost) for an assortment of leather luggage, which will be priced at $180,000 retail. If the average markup is targeted at 52%, what markup percentage should now be taken on the balance of the European orders?

43. A men's furnishings buyer purchases a closeout of 1,500 velour shirts offered at $9.85 each and 950 knit shirts at $5.80 each. The planned markup on the purchase is 49.5%. If a unit retail of $17.95 is placed on the velour shirts, what is the lowest possible retail price that the knit shirts may be marked, to remain within the markup framework indicated?

44. A buyer, who has a departmental markup of 49%, wants $40,000 (retail) worth of men's casual shirts for next season. An order for turtlenecks is placed in the amount of $6,400 at cost and $11,000 at retail. What markup percentage must now be achieved on the balance of the purchases?

45. A lingerie department made a purchase of 100 dozen nylon briefs costing $36/dozen, 75 dozen stretch bras costing $54/dozen, and 12 dozen teddies at $84/dozen. if the briefs are retailed at $6 each, and the bras at $9 each, at what retail price should the teddies be marked to attain a 53% markup?

46. The buyer of decorative pillows needs a markup of 50%, and plans to purchase $5,000 worth of goods (retail value) during the month of November. At the middle of the month, the total of the invoices for the purchases to date (at both cost and retail) for the month to date amount to $2,000 at cost and $3,700 at retail. What markup in dollars and percentage must be obtained on the balance of the purchases?

47. A buyer needs 5,000 umbrellas for the 37th annual storewide "April Showers" promotional event, to retail at $14 each. The planned markup is 49%. If 3,500 units are bought at one resource for $7.70 each, how much can the buyer afford to pay for each of the remaining 1,500 units?

48. A children's apparel buyer is offered a lot of denim jackets consisting of 125 toddler boys' jackets at $20 each and 160 toddler girls' jackets at $23 each. All the jackets will be sold at the same retail price. If the buyer is to make a 54% markup on the entire transaction, at what price must each jacket be retailed?

49. A men's accessories buyer purchases 10,000 neckties from a manufacturer—who is relocating—at a cost price of $10 per tie. Noticing that the ties are of two types, 6,200 solids and 3,800 stripes, the buyer decides to attempt some creative merchandising. If each solid tie is retailed at $18, what retail price should be placed on each striped tie if an average markup of 51% is desired?

50. An outerwear buyer confirms an order reading as follows:

145 tailored raincoats costing $47 each.

75 three-quarter-length rainjackets costing $26 each.

If a retail price of $85 is placed on the tailored coats, and a markup average of 48% is sought, what retail price must the rainjackets carry?

51. The boyswear buyer purchases 20 dozen pairs of jeans at $108/dozen and 15 dozen flannel shirts at $96/dozen. The departmental markup is planned at 52%. If the jeans are priced at $18, what price must be put on the shirts to reach goal markup?

52. A buyer purchases a closeout of 1,000 fleece coats at a cost of $46 each, which are divided into two groups: 425 belted coats and 575 unbelted. If the desired average markup is 49%, what retail price should be placed on each of the unbelted coats if the belted ones are priced at $95 each?

53. A junior sportswear department shows an opening stock figure of $540,000 at retail, owned at a 48% markup. To date, since the last stock determination, new purchases were $1,700,000 at retail, with a 50% markup. Find the cumulative markup percentage on total merchandise handled in this department to date.

54. The gross margin in a handbag department is 42.7% (40% expenses + 2.7% profit), which shows reductions (total of markdowns, shortages, and employee discounts) of 14.5%. State the initial markup percentage.

55. The planned gross margin in a young men's sportswear department is 46%, with reductions of 15%, cash discounts earned equalling 6%, and alteration costs amounting to 2%. What is the initial markup percentage?

56. A men's apparel department planned an initial markup of 49% and reductions of 16%. Find the maintained markup.

57. For a Columbus Day event, a buyer plans to purchase 250 knit dresses to retail for $75 each. A 47% markup is needed on the total purchase. From one of the buyer's best resources, 110 dresses were purchased that cost $33.75 each. The buyer knows, however, that the costs will have to be averaged on the balance of other purchases from alternate resources in order to achieve a 47% markup on the entire group.

    (a) What must be the average cost per dress on the balance of the purchases if the buyer is to attain the planned MU percentage?

    (b) What MU percentage did the buyer attain on the first purchase of 110 dresses?

    (c) What MU percentage did the buyer have to get on the balance of the purchases to realize the overall needed MU?

58. For the month of July, a sporting goods department had net sales of $250,000. The billed cost of the goods, including transportation, was $120,000. Cash discounts amounted to $9,600 and there were alteration costs of $400. Calculate (in dollars):

    (a) The maintained markup.

    (b) The gross margin.

Targeting Gross Profit

Miss Jay Tee is the shoe buyer for a fashion specialty store located in the trendy "Near-North Side" of Chicago. It is October 1, and she is scheduled for a European buying trip on October 25, during which she will place orders for Spring delivery. Her Spring six-month plans are complete and have been approved by management.

Before leaving on her buying trip, she reviews her current operational figures to evaluate her position for the forthcoming last quarter of the year (i.e., November, December, January). They are:

- Merchandise on hand (BOM) November 1: $1,300,000 with a 51.5% cumulative markup.
- Closing inventory (BOM) February 1: $400,000.
- Planned sales:

	November	December	January	Total Sales
	$500,000	$550,000	$250,000	$1,300,000

- Planned markdown to be taken in November, December, January: $80,000 or 6.2%.
- Estimated shortages are 2.0% for this period.
- Gross margin (no cash discounts or alteration costs): 48.1%.

Based on this information, Miss Tee did some calculations and determined that she still had $506,000, at retail, to spend for this quarter.

It is customary for Miss Tee to devote several days at the beginning of her trip to scout the market to obtain extremely desirable current seasonal goods, available for immediate shipment, at advantageous prices that will stimulate pre-Christmas sales and furthermore, will generate sales in the slow-selling month of January, traditionally associated with only clearance and/or highly competitively priced merchandise.

On October 25, she arrives in Florence, Italy, and as she covers the boot resources, she finds there is an abundance of the current season's merchandise—available for immediate shipment—because of cancellations by importers and retailers. This situation has been caused by sluggish economic and business conditions. One of her best key resources has in stock 4,000 pairs of leather boots in this season's avant garde styling with balanced sizes and colors. Fifty percent of the resource's offering are the same styles as 500 pairs currently in stock, selling reasonably well at $200 retail. Providing she agrees to buy the complete group, the final landed cost negotiated is $50 per pair. Despite the fact that she considers this merchandise to be superb value at this sensational cost, she is hesitant about buying such a large quantity so late in the selling season. However, she receives a fax from her assistant informing her that the boots are moving quickly and sales have increased due to very cold, wintery weather conditions. She decides to buy this offering before a competitor has an opportunity to do so. Her strategy considerations are:

- Retailing the group.
- Shipping for present selling.
- Integrating this purchase with present stock.
- Obtaining the necessary markup percentage.

She commits herself to the purchase, returns to her hotel and diligently works to map out the delivery and pricing factors. Her first decision is to start shipping some of these goods so they are available, as soon as possible, for November selling. Therefore, despite the expense, she immediately sends 1,000 pairs by air because it is fast and it serves her purpose. This mode of transportation increases the delivered cost of the 1,000 pairs form $50 to $55 a pair, and the retail is set at $150.

After making this decision, she turns her attention to the 500 pairs in stock currently selling at $200 a pair. Because markdown money is available, Miss Tee wants to begin to reduce the higher-priced boots while there is traffic. She can afford to reduce these 500 pairs from $200 to $150, taking a larger than usual first markdown, because the markup of the 1,000 pairs (that will sell simultaneously) is so above average.

On the balance of the 3000 pairs, she divides half for December selling and retails them for $125. The remaining 1500 pairs she reserves for her annual Blizzard Promotion scheduled in January. For this event, her boot sales rely solely on merchandise that create "riots." She did not yet set a retail price on the 2,500 pairs for the January sale because she would like to price them at levels that are somewhat low, but will not kill the required markup for the season. However, she calculated that a 54.4% markup was needed on the entire purchase so that her seasonal markup target will be met.

Prepare a merchandising plan for class discussion and, in doing so, consider the following:

- Do you agree with the merchandising techniques Miss Tee used in this particular purchase? If so, why? If not, why? Justify your position mathematically.
- Advise Miss Tee of the retail price you would establish on the 1500 pairs of boots targeted for the January promotion, keeping in mind that all of her objectives should be satisfied.

ASSURING FAVORABLE GROSS MARGINS

You have been hired by a group of investors to buy and merchandise accessories for their small chain (4 stores) of infant apparel shops. This new classification is to complement and reflect their prestigious, unique merchandise assortments which are targeted for the young, upper income mother and/or grandparents looking for the "unusual." This new classification was introduced in the Fall/Winter period and was well received by their clientele. Although the projected sales goal was met, the profit performance was more than disappointing.

After analysis of each market segment and location, your focus will be on the combined merchandise selection factors that form the basis of your ultimate selections suitable for your particular customer group.

The pricing factor is one the elements that is of major importance and is not only significant, but also observable. Because of the relationship of pricing to gross margin, management has planned and set certain gross margin guidelines and limitations to assure achieving a more satisfactory gross margin. These figures are to be achieved while accomplishing the projected sales. As an incentive, you have been promised an additional bonus if you provide gross margin results that are an improvement over the following expected guidelines:

Gross Margin	47.4%	(43.4% expenses, 4% profit)
Sales	$600,000	
Markdowns	$ 60,000	(10%)
Shortages	$ 12,000	(2%)
Opening Inventory	$150,000	
Closing Inventory	$200,000	

You are confident that with appropriate planning and forecasting you will be able to attain the results management wants, and the phantom bonus mentioned could become a reality for you.

Situation 1. A key factor in gross margin control is the pricing of merchandise. Since management already established a 47.4% gross margin, will advance planning of an initial markup help assure a favorable gross margin? Yes or No? Why? Should you be able to determine the gross margin or maintained markup having calculated the initial markup? What is to be gained by determining these two figures?

Situation 2. During the course of the season, you know the cumulative MU% is another important profit factor because it represents the markup on the merchandise on hand at the beginning of the season, as well as the purchases during this period. You notice that the opening inventory of $150,000 carried a 52.0% markup. What, if any, effect will this have on the markup percentage required of the new purchases in order to achieve for the season the cumulative markup of 53%.

Situation 3. Although you will focus on obtaining the desired markup percentage, you will also have to pay attention to the markup dollar. Why? Because these (sales, markdowns, shortages) are projections (which could prove erroneous),compute and compare how the dollar markup could give different results if the actual reductions increased to 13%. Should you aim at a higher initial markup in order to build "a cushion" to satisfy the unpredictable?

Spreadsheet Analysis: Balancing of Markup

In preparation for a foreign buying trip, a buyer determined a 54% markup was required on all purchases which amounted to $750,000 at retail.

Upon completion of the trip, the buyer reviewed the orders placed.

At the end of the season, a vendor analysis revealed the sales results shown below:

	Cost	Initial Retail	Final Retail
Resource A	$ 25,000	$ 50,000	$ 50,000
Resource B	40,000	85,000	83,000
Resource C	60,000	135,000	130,000
Resource D	55,000	135,000	135,000
Resource E	75,000	170,000	167,000
Resource F	90,000	175,000	165,000
Total	$345,000	$750,000	$730,000

Compute the following:

(a) Initial markup percentage for each resource.
(b) Final markup percentage achieved for each resource.
(c) Compare the anticipated markup percentage of the entire purchase with the actual markup percentage achieved.
(d) Which vendor(s) markup percentage performance was superior to the overall markup percentage and by how much?

Notes

Unit IV

THE RETAIL METHOD OF INVENTORY

Objectives

- Knowledge and understanding of the retail method of inventory.
- Differentiation between physical inventory and book inventory.
- Identification and recognition of procedures necessary to implement the retail method of inventory.
- Calculation of book inventory figures at cost.
- Identification and description of the forms used in the retail method of inventory.
- Recognition and identification of the causes of overages and shortages.
- Calculation of overages and shortages based on inventory figures.
- Evaluation of the advantages and limitations of the retail method of inventory.

Key Terms

book inventory

charge-back to vendors

closing book inventory

closing physical stock

debit memo form

journal or purchase record

opening book inventory

overage

perpetual inventory

physical inventory

price change form

retail method of inventory

return to vendor

running book inventory

shortage

transfer

To control and guide the operations of a retail organization, it is essential to keep records. Records are the working tools that provide information on the profitability of a business or for making everyday decisions (e.g., what types of merchandise are needed, when and how much is needed, etc.). Of particular concern to management and buyers is inventory control.

Successful merchandising requires that the size of stocks offered the consumer be large enough to satisfy demand, but that the dollar investment be kept as low as possible. This can be accomplished only by having a frequent indication of stock on hand. The retail merchandiser who is concerned with the question "How much can I sell?" must know how much to buy to maintain this satisfactory relationship between the amount of sales volume and the size of stocks carried. In recent years, the increased use of computer information systems by department stores, small retail businesses, and most merchandising chains has had a major impact on the management of merchandise inventories and other areas of record-keeping.

In large retail stores, it would be inconvenient and prohibitive in terms of cost to constantly determine the value of the amount of stock on hand by taking an actual count. However, because this balance of sales to stocks is vital, a system of accounting that determines the probable amount of stock-on-hand at any given time—without physically counting the goods—has been devised. This retail system of accounting that values merchandise at current retail prices that can be converted by markup formula to cost value is called the **retail method of inventory.** Although the computer turns available information into electronic documents, for illustrative purposes, in the study of the retail method of inventory, the actual types of records connected with this method are shown here in order to appreciate the data required by this accounting system. The information required is critical, not the means of collection.

The retail method of inventory is a method of averages, with the retail stock figure at the end of an accounting period providing the basis for determining the cost value of stock. The conversion of the closing inventory at retail to a cost figure is calculated by the determination of the cumulative markup percentage on the total merchandise handled as described in Unit III. To understand the retail method of inventory, it is vital to realize that it operates on the theory that the merchandise in stock is always representative of the total merchandise handled to date (i.e., stock plus new purchases). It allows an acceptable cost value of the book inventory to be established so that gross margin can be determined periodically.

It is common practice for large stores to "think at retail" because net sales (100%) are primarily the basis for the analysis of all the relationships of expenses to sales and are the ultimate determining factors that show whether the merchandising endeavors result in a profit or a loss. Gross margin, which is the difference between the cost of goods sold and the income received from this merchandise (i.e., net sales) is also expressed as a percentage of net sales. Consequently, the danger of failing to make the correct percentage comparisons is eliminated because these percentages are all calculated on the same base (i.e., net sales), which is a retail figure. The dollar value of the inventory owned must also be expressed as a retail figure to predetermine the desired relationship of these two factors (i.e., sales to stocks; see Unit I). In the process of buying and selling to yield a more satisfactory profit, retailers can contrast and compare their merchandising operations with that of other retailers. They compare such factors as net sales produced (a retail figure); the relationship of retail stock to net sales (figures used to attain the needed proportion); the pricing of merchandise expressed as a percentage based on the retail, and the percentage of reductions (figures needed to revise prices originally set on merchandise). Finally, when filing income taxes, insurance claims, and so on, the current retail price of the merchandise is the significant valuation.

These three examples illustrate the importance of the maintenance of a perpetual retail inventory figure. Though inventory figures are not always perpetually derived, they can be obtained as often as is desirable, usually every week or month.

I. Explanation of the Retail Method of Inventory

The retail system of merchandise accounting permits the retailer to determine the value (at retail) of the stock-on-hand at frequent and periodic intervals without taking constant physical counts. However, it must be noted that periodic—generally semiannual—physical counts (i.e., inventories) are taken at the current retail prices of the merchandise on hand. To control stocks and determine the profitability of individual departments, the retail method of accounting is applied separately for each department. The retail method of inventory valuation involves:

- Taking a physical inventory count to determine the total retail value of a particular department.
- Determining the cumulative markup percentage on the total merchandise handled.
- Deriving the cost value of the closing inventory from the retail by using the cumulative markup percentage achieved on the total merchandise handled. Subsequently, this valuation is used to find the cost of goods sold to establish the gross margin.

This system requires the collection and analysis of data pertaining to any movement of merchandise from the time it is bought until it is sold to the consumer. The retail method of inventory requires maintaining a book inventory at retail, as well as other records that permit the calculation of the cost of total merchandise handled during the period. This, in turn, allows constant calculation of the gross margin amount, including the possible protection of profitability. All additions to and deductions from stock must be recorded in dollar values. The computation from "statistical records" or book figures of the amount of merchandise that should be on hand, at retail, is called a **book inventory.** At the beginning of the accounting period under consideration, a **physical inventory** count is taken at the current retail price of the goods owned. It is common that when large stores take a semiannual physical count of stocks and record the value at retail, that date of receipt of merchandise into stock is also recorded. For example, Figure 12 illustrates the information generally recorded during a physical inventory count.

When taking a physical inventory using this method, it is not necessary to list the cost price of each individual item. The physical count of each individual item, at the retail price stated on its ticket, is recorded and the total retail figure (e.g., $100,000) is the actual amount of goods accounted for at the time the semiannual count is made. If warranted, this count can be made more often. This actual physical count figure is then used as the closing physical stock figure for that accounting period. If the physical inventory value is less than the book inventory, the difference is called a **shortage.** When the physical inventory value exceeds the book inventory, that difference is called an **overage.**

Figure 12. Physical Inventory Count Sheet

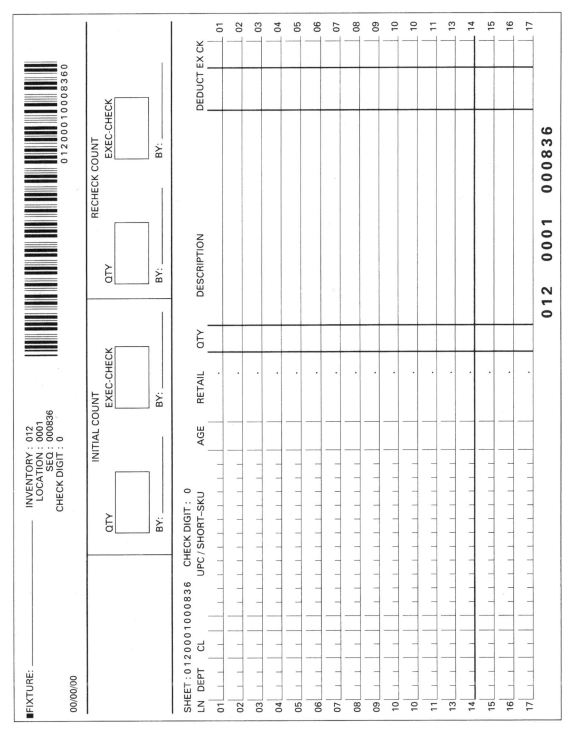

II. GENERAL PROCEDURES FOR IMPLEMENTING THE RETAIL METHOD OF INVENTORY

A. Finding an Opening Book Inventory Figure

When the "retail method" system is first installed, a complete physical count, at retail (see Figure 12), is taken for each merchandising department. (Please note that this physical count reflects the retail value of the inventory at aggregate retail prices.) The retail value of the goods counted is used as the **opening book inventory** figure. This is the same figure as the **closing physical stock** figure of the previous accounting period. Inventory counts continue to be taken semi-annually at the current retail prices of the goods. (Remember, closing physical inventory equals the opening book inventory for the next period.)

B. Maintaining a Perpetual Book Inventory Figure

A book inventory indicates the amount of stock in dollars that has been determined from records rather than from an actual count. During the time period between the semiannual physical counts just described, many other merchandising transactions occur, such as:

- Goods are sold to customers.
- Merchandise is purchased and received from resources.
- Customers return merchandise.
- Merchandise is marked down.
- Goods are transferred to other departments in the same store for resale.
- Merchandise is transferred to other stores.
- Merchandise is returned to vendors occasionally.

Every such transaction and any other kind of merchandise movement is accompanied by paperwork in the form of saleschecks, return-to-vendor forms, orders, and so on. The retail organization's statistical department or the accounting division records every transaction and adds to or reduces the "book stock" accordingly. For example, sales to customers or transfers to other departments reduce the "book stock" (also known as **perpetual or running book inventory**) by the dollar amount corresponding to the retail value of the goods sold or transferred. The records must be current and accurate so that a retail book inventory figure is always available during an accounting period. Any additions to or deductions from stock must be recorded as the current retail prices and reported to the statistical department. In other words, every change that affects the stock value must be recorded.

In a multistore operation, a constant inventory figure is maintained for the particular department in each store. This inventory figure is evaluated, not only on an individual store basis, but also on a department's overall operation. The main reasons for calculating a physical book inventory are:

- The determination of stock shortage whenever physical inventory is taken can prevent or lessen losses by prompt action.
- The accurate determination of stock on hand periodically maintains the proper relationship between sales and stock as merchandise purchases are controlled in ratio to ample stocks.
- The estimation of profits at any given time allows the timely correction of any adverse conditions.
- The maximization of possible insurance claims by providing acceptable, accurate records of inventory validation.

The following is an example of a department for a branch store, which should serve to illustrate the "addition or deduction" of the value of the merchandise in stock. All these changes must be recorded to ensure accuracy.

EXAMPLE:

Increase of Retail Value		*Decrease of Retail Value*	
Purchases (total retail value of merchandise. received)	$35,000	Net sales	$28,000
+ Transfers in, at retail	+ 5,000	+ Transfers out at retail	2,000
		+ Returns to vendor	3,000
Total stock additions (Total ins)	$40,000	+ Employee discounts	500
		+ MD differences[1]	+ 500
		Total stock deductions (Total outs)	$34,000

Calculating a Book Inventory Figure at Retail

A retail book inventory is determined by:

- Taking a periodic physical count, at retail, to determine a closing physical stock figure.
- Establishing the physical count amount as the opening retail book inventory.
- Adding all new purchases at retail to determine the total merchandise handled at retail.
- Subtracting all retail deductions (e.g., net sales, markdowns, etc.) from the retail total merchandise handled to find the **closing book inventory** at retail.

---

[1]Markdown differences are included in stock deductions because they lower the value of the inventory.

CONCEPT:

Book inventory at retail = Add the opening physical inventory figure to the net retail purchases (total merchandise handled) and any other stock additions; then, (from the resultant sum) subtract net sales, markdown differences, and any other deductions from stock.

PROBLEM:

On January 31, the physical count of the infants' department in Branch #15 revealed an inventory of $20,000. On February 1, the opening retail inventory of this department was $20,000. From February 1 to July 31 retail purchases amounting to $40,000 were received. The net sales for this period were $30,500, the markdowns taken were $2,300, employee discounts were $200, returns to vendors were $350, and transfers out were $750. What was the retail book inventory for this period under consideration?

SOLUTION:

Opening book retail inventory (Feb. 1)		$20,000
+ Retail purchases (Feb. 1–July 31)		+40,000
Total merchandise handled (ins)		$60,000
Net sales	$30,500	
+ Markdown differences	+ 2,300	
+ Employee discounts	+ 200	
+ Returns to vendor	+ 350	
+ Transfers out	+ 750	
Total deductions (outs)	= $34,100	−34,100
Retail Book Inventory		= $25,900

Calculating a Book Inventory at Cost[2]

A book inventory, at cost, is determined by:

- Converting the opening retail book inventory to a cost inventory figure by using the cumulative markup percentage achieved on the stock plus purchases during the previous accounting period.
- Adding all new purchases, at cost,[3] plus freight (on cost only) to the cost opening inventory figure to determine the total merchandise handled at cost.

---

[2]The retail method of inventory assumes that the average markup on the closing inventory is the same as the markup on the total merchandise handled.

[3]Generally, purchases are accumulated over a specific period of time (e.g., a six-month season), not month by month, and they are then added to the opening inventory at cost to find the total merchandise handled at cost.

■ Converting the closing book inventory at retail to a closing book inventory at cost, by using the cumulative markup percentage that has been calculated from the difference between the total merchandise handled at retail and total merchandise handled at cost.

PROBLEM:

Calculate a book inventory at cost, if the markup percentage on the previous season's inventory is 51% and the cost of the new purchases is $19,800. (The same figures are used as in the previous problem illustrating the determination of a book inventory figure at retail.)

SOLUTION:

1. Convert opening book retail inventory figure to cost inventory figure.

Opening cost inventory = $20,000 R × (100% − MU%)

$$= \$20,000 \times (100\% - 51\%)$$

$$= \$20,000 \times \ \ 49\%$$

$$= \$ \ 9,800$$

2. Add all new purchases plus freight to opening inventory at cost. Given:

New purchases, at cost	= $19,800
+ Freight	= + 200
	$20,000

Opening inventory at cost	= 9,800
+ New purchases (including freight) at cost	= +20,000
Total merchandise handled at cost	= $29,800

3. Find cumulative markup percentage on total merchandise handled.

	Cost	Retail
Opening inventory	$ 9,800	$20,000
+ Purchases	+20,000	+40,000
Total merchandise handled	$29,800	$60,000

Markup		
	= $60,000	Retail of total merchandise handled
	−29,800	Cost of total mdse. handled
	$30,200	MU

$$= \frac{\$30,200 \ \text{MU}}{\$60,000 \ \text{Retail}}$$

$$= \$50.3\%$$

4. Convert closing book inventory at retail to closing book inventory at cost by using the cumulative MU percentage.

Closing book inventory at retail = $25,900

$25,900 × (100% − 50.35%)

= $25,900 × 49.7%

Closing Book Inventory at Cost = $12,872.30

For assignments for the previous section, see practice problems 1–10.

C. Forms Used in the Retail Method of Inventory

Today a retailer's records are often supplemented and/or obtained through the store's (or organization's) computer system (e.g., POS markdowns). How the information is recorded is a matter of choice or monetary necessity, but the loss of records or the failure to record the proper information that shows the increase or decrease in the value of the stock will result in an inaccurate stock valuation of the book inventory. There are many forms to help the retailer accurately record this valuable information. Each form serves a particular function, but not all retailers use identical forms. The forms in this section illustrate the function of each record required to appreciate or depreciate the value of a stock. Today, with the widespread use of automated merchandising systems, the information necessary to maintain an accurate recording of transactions is adopted and tailored to each retailer's needs.

Journal or Purchase Record

Figure 13 is a Purchase Record, which provides a record of the billed or invoiced costs, transportation charges, cash discounts, retail amounts, and the percentages of markup for each individual purchase. The names of the vendors, dates of invoices, and the invoice numbers are also entered. Each department checks this record periodically to ensure that the department is being charged or credited with merchandise either entering or leaving a department and that these amounts are only intended for that department. This report also shows the department classification, vendor, style, and price receipts in units for the total store as well as individual branches. The negative units represent returns to vendors or corrections. The purpose of the report is to allow buyers to examine receipts entered into the computer against copies of the purchase order. Discrepancies are then reported so that appropriate adjustments can be made.

Transfer of Goods

A **transfer** of merchandise involves the movement of goods. When the merchandise leaves a department, the transfer is out; conversely, when the merchandise is received, the transfer is in. When merchandise is transferred from one store to another (e.g., a branch), an Outstanding Transfer List Form is used to record the number of units transferred, unit cost, total cost, unit retail, and total retail. Merchandise may also be transferred from one department to an-

Figure 13. Journal of Purchase Record

ST	DEPT. NO.	VENDOR NO.	APRON NO.		INV. NO.	INV. DATE	REC. DATE	RETAIL	INV. AMT.	MU%	TRANS.	DISCOUNT	ANTIC.	VENDOR FRT.	NET
DATE 04/30														PAGE	
DIV 04			VENDOR NAME												
			GREEN & CO.												
2	310100	616920	14020		004803	3/01/0	3/10	115	62.10	46.00	.00	1.86	.00	.00	60.24
8	310100	616920	48049		004805	3/08/0	3/10	126	69.10	45.16	.00	2.07	.00	.00	67.03
8	310100	616920	48049		004806	3/08/0	3/10	76	41.80	45.00	.00	1.25	.00	.00	40.55
8	310100	616920	48049		004807	3/08/0	3/10	773	395.05	48.89	.00	11.85	.00	.00	383.20
2	310100	616920	14936		004984	3/16/0	3/17	360	197.87	45.04	.00	5.94	.00	.00	191.93
2	310100	616920	14936		004985	3/16/0	3/17	619	387.23	37.44	.00	11.62	.00	.00	375.61
3	310100	616920	49226		005069	3/19/0	3/22	317	174.50	44.95	.00	5.24	.00	.00	169.26
3	310100	616920	49226		005070	3/19/0	3/22	417	229.54	44.95	.00	6.89	.00	.00	222.65
2	310100	616920	AJ742	SU	074230	4/05/0			.00		.00	17.65–	.00	.00	17.65
	TOTALS FOR VENDOR 616920							2,603	1,557.19		.00	29.07	.00	.00	1,528.12

Figure 14. Outstanding Transfer List Form

```
                              OUTSTANDING TRANSFER LIST AS OF  OCT 08,YY      DATE  OCT 09,YY         PAGE: 1
                                                                              TIME  5:31 PM
1) BY FROM STORE - WITH DETAILS

FROM    TO     TRANSFER    TRANSFER   SKU      STYLE    COL    SIZE   QUANTITY   PRICE    RETAIL      COST     TRANSFER
STORE   STORE  NUMBER TYPE DATE       NO.      NO.                      —                 AMOUNT      AMOUNT   REASON

001     002    000002  1  OCT 08,YY   0015149  SW10     030    XS       4        22.55    90.20       40.00    001 Slow Moving
                                      0015156  SW10     030    S        4        22.55    90.20       40.00
                                      0015164  SW10     030    M        5        22.55    112.75      50.00
                                      0015172  SW10     030    L        3        22.55    67.65       30.00
                                      0015180  SW10     030    XL       2        22.55    45.10       20.00

003     001    000001  1  OCT 07,YY   0014555  200XT    020    R - 40   3        440.00   1,320.00    825.00   003 Fast Moving
                                      0014563  200XT    020    R - 42   3        440.00   1,320.00    825.00
                                      0014571  200XT    020    R - 44   3        440.00   1,320.00    825.00
                                      0014589  200XT    020    R - 46   3        440.00   1,320.00    825.00
                                      0014662  200BK    020    T - 38   1        440.00   440.00      275.00
                                      0014670  200BK    020    T - 40   1        440.00   440.00      275.00
                                      0014688  200BK    020    T - 42   1        440.00   440.00      275.00
                                      0014696  200BK    020    T - 44   1        440.00   440.00      275.00
                                      0014704  200BK    020    T - 46   1        440.00   440.00      275.00
```

other. This record is used to indicate the change of ownership of merchandise. Figure 14 (Outstanding Transfer List Form) illustrates the detailed information that an automated merchandising system can furnish on interstore transfers (e.g., reasons for transfers, size, color, etc.).

Price Change Forms

All retail price changes that are required to merchandise a department must be recorded. Among the changes necessary to record are:

- The number of units.
- The old retail price per unit.
- The new retail price per unit.
- The difference per unit.
- The total amount of difference.

Figure 15. Buyers Price Change Worksheet

BUYERS PRICE CHANGE WORKSHEET

SYSTEM GENERATED NUMBER	DEPT.	REGION	TYPE	REASON	EFFECTIVE DATE	END DATE	MANUAL DOCUMENT #

01-ALL SELLING LOCATIONS
02-07.22
03-19 ONLY

REFERENCE #

INFO ONLY – ☐ YES OR ☐ NO

(TYPE FOUR PRICE CHANGE ONLY)

SPECIAL INSTRUCTIONS:

CHECK OFF STORE CODE IF PRICE CHANGE IS NOT FOR ALL LOCATIONS

01-NY	06-SH	10-PGA	14-TC	18-N/A
02-BR	07-CP	11-CH	15-N/A	19-WH
04-NA	08-NM	12-WP	16-KP	21-FA
05-BC	09-GC	13-WF	17-WG	

NON-ITEM DEPARTMENTS ALL IN SHADED AREA

LINE #	CLASS #	VENDOR #	MARK STYLE # (NO CHECK DIGIT)	COLOR #	SIZE #	CURRENT OWN RETAIL	NEW OWN RETAIL	ON HAND	ITEM DESCRIPTION
01									
02									
03									
04									
05									
06									
07									
08									
09									
10									

TYPES:
01-MARKDOWN TOTAL STYLE
02-MARKDOWN PARTIAL STYLE
04-PROMOTIONAL MARKDOWN
05-MARKDOWN CANCELLATION
06-MARKUP

REASONS: CLEARANCE
10-FIRST MARKDOWN
11-SECOND MARKDOWN
12-ANY ADDITIONAL MARKDOWN
19-JOB OUT OF STOCK (JOBBER)
20- MARK OUT OF STOCK (SALVAGE)

REASONS: PROMOTIONAL
22-NON POS MD
23-NON POS MDC

REASON CODE 20 (SALVAGE)
WILL NOT UPDATE ITEM OWNED RETAIL, BUT
WILL REDUCE QUANTITY ON HAND AMOUNT

COMPLETE ONLY IF
MD CANCELLATION FOR VENDOR ALLOWANCE

	REASON CODE
VENDOR HOUSE _____	
PRIMARY CLASS _____	
PROMOTIONAL	☐ 21
CLEARANCE	☐ 13
C.C. NUMBER	

C.C. DOCUMENT MUST BE ATTACHED
(NOTE: KEY C C NUMBER IN REFERENCE NUMBER FIELD)

Figure 16. Computer Price Change Entry

```
DATE: OCT 09,YY
                              PRICE CHANGE ENTRY
============================================================================

COMPANY 01  GROUP 0001  TYPE 1  FUNCTION 1  DATE 10/09/YY  EFFECTIVE DATE FR: 10/10/YY
                         (New)    (Price Change)            EFFECTIVE DATE TO: 12/31/YY

 1) AUTHORIZATION   :123456
 2) ENTRY TYPE      :1      MARKDOWN
 3) BUYER NO        :001    Michael Wood
 4) REASON          :001    Slow Moving                          :12/31/YY
 5) EFF. DATE FROM  :10/10/YY        6) EFF. DATE TO             :000
 7) REGION FROM     :000             8) REGION TO                :000
 9) STORE FROM      :000            10) STORE TO                 :Y
11) REM-1: Permanent price change   13) PRODUCE TICKETS (Y/N)    :N
12) REM-2: effective for all stores 14) COUNT INVENTORY

LINE   SEASON DEPT CLS PR  LN COST  PT COOR GR  STYLE  CHANGE    TO RETAIL
                                                       %   AMT   PRICE
001 FROM  L      01                                    10.00
     TO   L      02
EXCLUDE STYLES: 12056        12654      13101      141256
```

Today it is common that temporary price changes (e.g., one-day sale items) are recorded by a cash register at the time of the purchase. As described in Unit II, this is called a point-of-sale markdown (POS). When a consumer pays for a purchase, the preprogrammed cash register records the new or lower retail, which corresponds exactly with the prescribed reduction posted on signs displayed with the merchandise. Only permanent reductions are recorded manually on forms illustrated by Figures 15 to 17. Figure 15 is a worksheet, which requires the listing of any or all price changes. Figure 16 shows the permanent or temporary price change information that has been entered onto a computer screen, and Figure 17 illustrates the form that is used by the individual branches.

Charge-Back to Vendors

A **debit memo form,** shown in Figure 18, records the return of merchandise from the retailer to the vendor, which may occur for a variety of reasons. It displays the number of pieces or units, the name of the item, and both cost and retail prices. Typically, a worksheet, as illustrated by Figure 19, is used to record the **return to vendor** information before it is verified by the person packing the merchandise. This ensures that the actual debit memo is legible and correct.

Figure 17. Branch Price Change

BRANCH PRICE CHANGE

DOCUMENT NUMBER
12899

REASON: [ ] TYPE: [ ]

STORE NO.: [ ]

TOTAL COUNT: [ ][ ][ ][ ]

REF-NBR: _____

EFF-DATE: _____
(DATE KEY ENTERED)

LINE	DPT	CL	VND	MKST (NO CHECK DIGIT)	CC	SIZ	SKU-UPC	CUR-OWN RETAIL	NEW-OWN RETAIL	CNT	DESCRIPTION	PC NUMBER (FROM SCREEN)
01												
02												
03												
04												
05												
06												
07												
08												
09												
10												
11												
12												
13												
14												
15												
16												

REASONS: CLEARANCE
50 - Customer adj
51 - Salvage
49 - Store initiated clearance
42 - Missed markdown

REASONS: PROMOTIONAL
41 - Customer service to
meet competition

TYPES:
01 - Markdown
05 - Markdown Cancellation
06 - Markup

(NOTE: ONLY ONE REASON CODE PER PRICE CHANGE PER FORM)

INPUT BY: DATE:

Figure 18. Debit Memo

DEBIT MEMO
INVOICE

718584

POSTMASTER: RETURN REQUESTED

DATE	DEPT.	VENDOR NO.	STORE

CHARGE (PRINT)	
STREET (PRINT)	
CITY, STATE & ZIP CODE (PRINT)	

SEND (PRINT)
STREET (PRINT)
CITY, STATE & ZIP CODE (PRINT)

REFERENCE	A/P AUTH. NO.

RETURN ARRANGED WITH	PREPARED BY

SPECIAL INSTRUCTIONS

OFFICE APPROVAL	TERMS	FREIGHT
		VENDOR ☐ DEPT ☐

STYLE	ITEM / SKU #	COLOR	CLASS	QUANTITY	UNIT	COST UNIT	COST EXTENSION	RETAIL UNIT	RETAIL EXTENSION

REASON FOR RETURN AND/OR CHARGE:

1	ADVERTISING	4	CREDIT AS AGREED	7	NOT AS ORDERED	10	*STOCK REPAIR
2	CANCELLED ORDER	5	DAMAGED	8	NOT ORDERED	11	**CUST. REPAIR
3	COLOR WRONG	6	DEMO SALARY	9	OVER SHIPPED	12	OTHER _____

HANDLING	
SUB-TOTAL COST	
FREIGHT-IN	
FREIGHT-OUT	
TOTAL COST	

TOTAL RETAIL	

* ISSUE NEW INVOICE TO COVER REPLACEMENT OR STOCK REPAIR.
** VALUE OF MDSE. TO BE CHARGED TO YOU IF NOT RETURNED IN 30 DAYS.

SHIP VIA	IF FREIGHT IS PREPAID ENTER THE AMOUNT HERE $	CARTONS	WEIGHT	PACKED BY	DATE PACKED

NAME OF CARRIER	BILL OF LADING #	NUMBER OF CARTONS	DATE PICKED UP	PICKED UP BY (SIGNATURE)

FREIGHT IN & OUT IS CHARGED TO YOUR ACCOUNT WHEN A SHIPMENT IS MADE CONTRARY TO THE TERMS OF OUR PURCHASE ORDER.

ROUTING INSTRUCTIONS:
WHEN RETURNING MERCHANDISE (UNLESS OTHERWISE SPECIFIED HEREIN), SHIP PER CURRENT ROUTING INSTRUCTIONS.

IF YOU DO NOT HAVE THESE INSTRUCTIONS CONTACT: CORPORATE TRAFFIC OFFICE

WHEN RETURNING MERCHANDISE, ADDRESS SHIPMENT TO THE APPROPRIATE ADDRESS BELOW.
BE SURE TO SHOW OUR STORE #, DEPT. # AND INVOICE # **ON ALL CARTONS AND MEDIA.**

Figure 19. Return to Vendor Authorization and Worksheet

RETURN TO VENDOR AUTHORIZATION AND WORKSHEET   № 627893

Instructions: (Please print legibly)

Department Manager

1) Dept. Mgr. prepares worksheet
2) Complete Worksheet including quantities and extensions
3) Completely prepare D.M. from information on Worksheet except for merchandise quantities, AND extensions. (D.M. Room will do this).
4) Do Not put in cost figures.

DM No. _____

Dept. _____ Store _____ Prepared by _____ Date _____

Mfr. Name _____ Freight paid by dept. _____ vendor _____
                                                          CHECK ONE

Vendor No.   _____

Return arranged with _____ Sticker needed Yes _____ No _____

Special Instructions _____ Terms _____

Reason _____

CHARGE TO:	SEND TO:
Name	Name
Address	Address
City State Zip	City State Zip

Item / SKU No. *	Class	Style	Size	Color	Qty.	Units	Cost Unit	Cost Ext.	Retail Unit	Retail Ext.
Total										

ON DMS OVER $400 RETAIL

COMPLETE THE FOLLOWING:

ACCTS. PAYABLE AUTH. NO. _____

D.M. ROOM COMPLETES

D.M. # _____

Date _____

Total $ Amount _____

Packed by _____

Checked by _____

*IF BSR MERCHANDISE IS INVOLVED, INFORMATION MUST BE PROVIDED TO THE BSR OFFICE BY STYLE, SIZE AND COLOR.

17-930-061 (REV. 6/91)

Sales Reports

Today's automated business systems offer sophisticated reporting for processing and auditing sales. In addition to full accounting sales summaries, Figures 20 and 21 show information that can be provided to improve sales performance. Figure 20, Daily Exception Selling Price Report, highlights daily sales for items sold at prices other than the current retail (e.g., markdown price). Salesperson performance is then analyzed by the use of a Sales and Productivity Report, as illustrated by week in Figure 21.

Figure 20. Daily Exception Selling Price Report

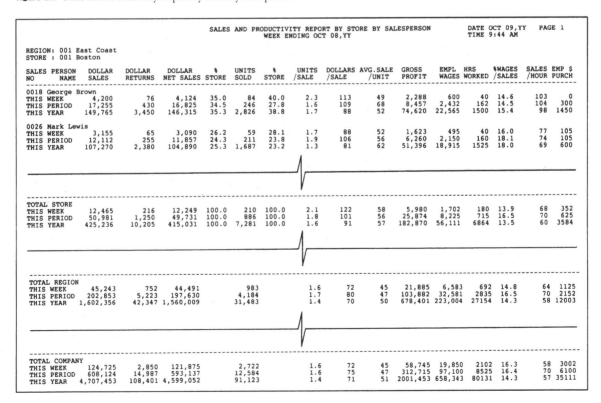

```
                         DAILY EXCEPTION SELLING PRICE REPORT          DATE  OCT 09,YY        PAGE: 1
                                                                       TIME   9.10 AM

 DATE OF SALE: OCT 08, YY
 MINIMUM PRICE DIFFERENCE REQUIRED: 10.00%

 STORE  SALES BILL  CLERK  STYLE  SEASON   DESCRIPTION       COLOR  SIZE  QTY  -- PRICE PER UNIT --   TOTAL EXTENDED    %
 NO.      NUMBER                                                               CURRENT    ACTUAL       DIFFERENCE     M/DOWN
 001     103256     0018   SW50A   M    Cotton V-Neck Sweater  030   -  S   1    45.00     32.00         13.00        29
         103273     0026   SK1715  M    Cotton Pants           030   -  L   2    64.00     50.00         28.00        22
                                                                   STORE DAILY TOTAL                    41.00        24

 002     204312     0042   SC1210  M    Wool Sweater           010   -  M   1    95.00     75.00         20.00        21
         204317     0042   200XT   M    2 Pces Dress Suit      020  R - 40   1   440.00    390.00        50.00        11
                                                                   STORE DAILY TOTAL                    70.00        13


                                                                   APPROVED BY: _____
```

Figure 21. Sales and Productivity Report by Store by Salesperson

```
                          SALES AND PRODUCTIVITY REPORT BY STORE BY SALESPERSON       DATE OCT 09,YY    PAGE 1
                                          WEEK ENDING OCT 08,YY                        TIME 9:44 AM

 REGION: 001 East Coast
 STORE : 001 Boston

 SALES PERSON  DOLLAR   DOLLAR    DOLLAR    %    UNITS   %    UNITS  DOLLARS AVG.SALE  GROSS    EMPL   HRS   %WAGES  SALES EMP $
 NO    NAME    SALES    RETURNS  NET SALES STORE SOLD  STORE /SALE  /SALE   /UNIT    PROFIT   WAGES WORKED /SALES  /HOUR PURCH

 0018 George Brown
 THIS WEEK      4,200       76    4,124   35.0    84  40.0   2.3    113     49     2,288     600    40   14.6    103     0
 THIS PERIOD   17,255      430   16,825   34.5   246  27.8   1.6    109     68     8,457   2,432   162   14.5    104   300
 THIS YEAR    149,765    3,450  146,315   35.3 2,826  38.8   1.7     88     52    74,620  22,565  1500   15.4     98  1450

 0026 Mark Lewis
 THIS WEEK      3,155       65    3,090   26.2    59  28.1   1.7     88     52     1,623     495    40   16.0     77   105
 THIS PERIOD   12,112      255   11,857   24.3   211  23.8   1.9    106     56     6,260   2,150   160   18.1     74   105
 THIS YEAR    107,270    2,380  104,890   25.3 1,687  23.2   1.3     81     62    51,396  18,915  1525   18.0     69   600



 TOTAL STORE
 THIS WEEK     12,465      216   12,249  100.0   210 100.0   2.1    122     58     5,980   1,702   180   13.9     68   352
 THIS PERIOD   50,981    1,250   49,731  100.0   886 100.0   1.8    101     56    25,874   8,225   715   16.5     70   625
 THIS YEAR    425,236   10,205  415,031  100.0 7,281 100.0   1.6     91     57   182,870  56,111  6864   13.5     60  3584



 TOTAL REGION
 THIS WEEK     45,243      752   44,491          983         1.6     72     45    21,885   6,583   692   14.8     64  1125
 THIS PERIOD  202,853    5,223  197,630        4,184         1.7     80     47   103,882  32,581  2835   16.5     70  2152
 THIS YEAR  1,602,356   42,347 1,560,009       31,483        1.4     70     50   678,401 223,004 27154   14.3     58 12003



 TOTAL COMPANY
 THIS WEEK    124,725    2,850  121,875        2,722         1.6     72     45    58,745  19,850  2102   16.3     58  3002
 THIS PERIOD  608,124   14,987  593,137       12,584         1.6     75     47   312,715  97,100  8525   16.4     70  6100
 THIS YEAR  4,707,453  108,401 4,599,052       91,123        1.4     71     51  2001,453 658,343 80131   14.3     57 35111
```

Employee Discounts

As described in Unit II, an employee discount is the common practice in retail stores that allows store employees a percentage off the retail price when making purchases for themselves. It is essential to record the difference between the retail price and the price paid by the employee. The procedure and form of record used for this transaction vary widely from store to store. Typically, employee discounts are listed under "Retail Reduction," but are classified separately from markdowns even though they are reductions in retail price.

PRACTICE PROBLEMS

Maintaining a Perpetual Book Inventory Figure

1. On July 15, a statistical inventory indicates an on hand retail stock of $64,250. A physical count on that date reveals a stock of $62,875. What is the opening retail book inventory figure for the period commencing July 16?

2. Opening inventory at retail for an outerwear department is $175,000. Purchases retail for the following six-month period are $490,000, net sales are $400,000, markdowns are $30,000, returns to vendors are $10,000, transfers (transfers out) to the third floor boutique are $15,000, and employee discounts are $6,000. Find the retail book inventory at the end of this six-month period.

3. Using the following figures from an accessories department, find the closing book stock at retail.

Physical inventory January 15	$ 85,000
Purchases retail January 16 through July 15	165,000
Gross sales	170,000
Returns from customers	30,000
Returns to vendors	5,000
Markdowns	10,000

4. The following figures are from a junior sportswear department:

Markdowns	$ 12,000
Purchases (retail)	315,000
Returns to vendors	20,000
Transfers in (retail)	8,000
Transfers out (retail)	4,000
Net sales	265,000
Opening book inventory (retail)	180,000

(a) Determine the closing book inventory for the period at retail.

(b) How would the opening retail inventory for the coming six-month period be determined?

5. The following figures are from a small boutique, which has a 49% MU:

Opening book inventory at retail	$16,000
Net sales	31,000
Markdowns	2,000
Purchases (retail)	40,000

(a) Determine the retail book inventory for the period.

(b) Convert the closing retail book inventory figure to the cost value.

6. Distinguish between physical inventory and book inventory. Which one is more likely to be affected by human error? Why? Which one has become more accurate since the advent of EDP capability?

7. A lingerie department buyer was given the following data:

	Cost	Retail
Opening inventory	$ 320,000	$ 530,000
Purchases	1,118,000	2,271,000
Net sales		1,400,000
Markdowns (incl. empl. disc.)		90,000

Calculate

    (a) The closing book inventory at retail.

    (b) The closing book inventory at cost.

8. The athletic footwear department had a closing book inventory, at retail, of $400,000 and had achieved a 53.5% markup on total merchandise handled. Determine the closing inventory at cost.

9. Find the closing inventory, at cost, of a furniture department, if:

	Cost	Retail
Net sales		$330,000
Opening inventory	$150,000	325,000
Markdowns		25,000
Returns to vendors	13,000	18,000
Employee discounts		6,500
Gross purchases	200,000	390,000

10. Utilize the following figures to calculate:

    (a) The closing book inventory at retail.

    (b) The cost value of this closing book inventory.

	Cost	Retail
Opening inventory	$390,500	$ 774,000
Gross purchases	690,000	1,360,000
RTV	6,400	12,000
Freight	3,260	
Gross sales		1,117,000
Customer returns		25,000
Markdowns		93,000

III. Shortages and Overages

Physical inventories at current retail prices are taken at the end of the accounting period. At this same time, the "book stock" at retail is adjusted to agree with the dollar value of the physical count. Any discrepancy between the dollar value of the "book stock" and the dollar value of stock determined by the physical count of merchandise on hand is classified as a **shortage** (or shrinkage) or an **overage.** As described, shortages exist if physical inventory is lower than book inventory; overages exist if the physical count exceeds the statistical tally.

It is almost impossible to run a merchandising operation with 100% accuracy. Shortages or overages nearly always result and are actually expected to occur. The shortage or overage is commonly expressed as a percentage of the net sales. Regardless of the cause, the inventory shortage is fundamentally the buyer's or department manager's problem and responsibility. To keep discrepancies to a minimum is one of the many challenges a merchant must face. For internal control purposes, it is sometimes desirable to estimate shortages. This estimate is also expressed as a percentage of net sales. Furthermore, even though merchandise planning is devised with estimated planned shortages in mind, generally the actual shortage exceeds the expected shortage.

Figure 22, a shortage report, which is usually calculated at the end of the accounting period, shows typical shortage information. From the data in this report, a multistore operation can pinpoint prevention, causes, and shortage remedies and can attempt to improve the shortage results.

Figure 22. Shortage Report

DIV 10 STORE	---------SHORTAGES IN DOLLARS--------- CURRENT SEASON	CURRENT -1	CURRENT -2	--------SHORTAGES IN PERCENTS--------- CURRENT SEASON	CURRENT -1	CURRENT -2 DATE
00						
01	8,731	2,395	3,920	2.8	0.8	1.3
06	891-	717	1,712	0.5-	0.5	1.1
09	999-	867-	1,583	0.9-	0.9-	1.5
12	293-	668	1,518	0.3-	0.8	1.6
14	5,107	507	524	5.0	0.6	0.6
15	1,056	1,361	1,928	0.8	1.2	1.6
DIV 10	12,711	4,781	11,185	1.4	0.6	1.3

A. Causes of Shortages and Overages

Shortages may stem from inaccurate record-keeping and/or faulty physical counts. A principal cause of shortages is pilferage which, realistically, can never be prevented completely. Overages, however, can only be caused by faulty record-keeping.

The common causes of shortages and overages are:

- Clerical errors in the calculation of the book and/or physical inventory, which include:
  Failure to record markdowns properly.
  Incorrect "retailing" of invoices.
  Errors in charging invoices to departments.
  Errors in recording transfers.
  Errors in recording returns to vendor.
  Errors in recording physical inventory.
  (Please note that the computer processing of these forms has minimized these clerical errors.)
- Physical merchandise losses, which include:
  Theft by customers and/or employees.
  Unrecorded breakage and spoilage.
  Sales clerks' errors in recording sales.
  Overweighting.
  Borrowed merchandise.
  Lost or incorrect price tickets.
  Sampling.

B. Calculating Shortages and Overages

The Physical Inventory Count as a Determining Factor in the Calculation of Shortages or Overages

CONCEPT:

Shortage (or Overage) = Closing book inventory at retail − Physical inventory

PROBLEM:

Find the shortage or overage in dollars from the following figures:

Opening inventory at retail	$22,000
Purchases at retail	17,500
Net sales	18,000
Markdowns	300
Employee discounts	600
Physical inventory, end of period	19,200

SOLUTION:

Opening book inventory retail (ins)	=	$22,000
+ Purchases retail	=	+17,500
Total merchandise handled (total ins)	=	$39,500 → $39,500
Net sales	=	$18,000
+ Markdown	=	+ 300
+ Employee discounts	=	+ 600
Total deductions (outs)	=	$18,900 → = −18,900
Book inventory retail		= $20,600
− Physical inventory		= −19,200
Dollar shortage		= $ 1,400

Expressing the Amount of Shortages or Overages for a Period as a Percentage of the Net Sales for the Same Period

CONCEPT:

$$\text{Shortage \%} = \frac{\$ \text{ Shortage}}{\$ \text{ Net sales}}$$

PROBLEM:

For the period under consideration, the net sales of Dept. 23 are $100,000. The physical count revealed a $5,000 shortage. What was the shortage percentage for this period?

SOLUTION:

$$\frac{\$ \text{ Shortage}}{\$ \text{ Net sales}} = \frac{\$ \ 5,000}{\$100,000}$$

Shortage = 5%

Estimating Shortages that are Expressed as a Percentage of the Planned Net Sales Figure for Internal Control Purposes

CONCEPT:

Estimated dollar shortage = Estimated shortage percentage × Planned net sales

PROBLEM:

The seasonal plan for a department showed planned sales of $350,000 with a planned shortage of 2.5%. What was the planned dollar shortage?

SOLUTION:

$350,000 Net sales
× 2.5%   Planned shortage

Planned Dollar Shortage = $ 8,750

For assignments for the previous section, see practice problems 11–18.

PRACTICE PROBLEMS

Shortages and Overages

11. A costume jewelry department showed the following figures for a six-month period:

Net sales	$125,000
Purchases (at retail)	105,000
Opening retail inventory (Feb. 1)	64,000
Markdowns	9,000
Employee discounts	2,600
Physical count (July 31)	31,000

    (a) What was the shortage in dollars?

    (b) What was the shortage in percentage?

If the planned shortage was estimated at 2%, was the actual shortage more or less? By how much in dollars? In percentage?

12. Find the shortage or overage percentage if:

Net sales	$137,000
Opening inventory (retail)	140,000
Markdowns	7,000
Employee discounts	1,000
Retail purchases	96,000
Closing physical inventory	89,150

13. Last year, the net sales in a home fashions department were $365,000. The book inventory at year-end was $67,500, and the physical inventory was $66,000. What was the shortage percentage?

14. Find the shortage or overage percentage using the following data:

Opening inventory (retail)	$204,000
Net sales	342,000
Vendor returns	4,000
Transfers to branches	8,000
Employee discounts	1,000
Purchases (at retail)	495,000
Markdowns	46,000
Closing physical inventory	287,000

15. If the retail book inventory at the close of the year is $1,500,000 and the physical inventory totals only $1,275,000, what will be the shortage percentage, if net sales were $15,000,000?

16. The merchandise plan for Fall shows planned sales of $35,000 with an estimated shortage of .7%. What are the planned dollar shortages for Fall?

17. A new shop owner was reviewing figures with the store's accountant. Net sales for the first three months of business were $87,000 and the book inventory was $72,000. It was noted that the physical inventory was 2.5% lower than the book inventory. Find the shortage percentage for this three-month period.

18. For the six-month period ending in January, your department showed the following figures:

Opening inventory (retail)	$262,000
Customer returns	10,000
Returns to vendor	6,200
Employee discounts	3,800
Gross sales	910,000
Retail purchases	870,000
Markdowns	30,000
Transfers in	5,100
Transfers out	4,000
Physical inventory	170,000

(a) What is the percentage of employee discounts?

(b) Determine the overage or shortage in both dollars and percentage.

(c) Using a 49% markup, convert the retail opening and closing inventories to cost values.

IV. An Evaluation of the Retail Method of Inventory

A. The Advantages of the Retail Method of Inventory

The benefits of the retail method of inventory are that:

- It permits control over profit because the figures for markup obtained (i.e., the difference between the cost and the retail of the total merchandise handled) and markdowns taken (upon which the realized gross margin depends) frequently are available and immediate action can be taken to protect the desired profit margin.
- It simplifies the physical inventory process because the physical inventory is taken at retail prices, which is less difficult and less expensive. Additionally, because all entries are made rapidly and no decoding is necessary, the personnel used does not require special training or experience.
- It provides a book inventory and, therefore, discrepancies (i.e., shortages and/or overages) in stock can be determined, shortage causes may be discovered, and preventive/corrective measures can be taken.
- It provides an equitable basis for insurance and adjustment claims.

B. The Limitations of the Retail Method of Inventory

The disadvantages of the retail method of inventory are that:

- It is a system of averages and therefore does not provide a precise cost evaluation of the inventory at its present cost price. This figure (i.e., cost evaluation of inventory) is calculated by applying the markup complement percentage to the retail value of the inventory. This may result in a figure that is either greater or smaller than the invoice cost of the merchandise currently received. This is the most significant weakness of this method.
- It depends upon extensive record-keeping for system accuracy.
- It is essential that all price changes be recorded.

C. Finding the Cost of Goods Sold and the Gross Margin with the Retail Method of Inventory Valuation

The retail method of inventory was introduced in department stores because it allowed a more simplified method to constantly monitor the all-important gross margin figure. The retail method of inventory eliminated a whole system of records formerly necessary to determine the valuation of an inventory at cost. Because the calculation of profit depends on cost data, the subsequent steps shown are taken in the calculation of a book inventory, and in the determination of a continual gross margin figure. The following problem illustrates the calculation of gross margin on stock plus purchases (i.e., total merchandise handled) (see Figure 23):

PROBLEM:

A junior sportswear buyer wants to calculate the gross margin figure to ascertain whether the department is "on target" and will achieve the planned gross margin goals for the season. The available season-to-date information is:

	Cost	Retail	MU%
Opening inventory		$100,000	51%
New purchases and freight	$240,000	500,000	

Step 1: Begin with a retail opening inventory figure: $100,000. The opening inventory at retail ($100,000) was determined when the stock on hand was physically counted at the end of the previous accounting period. The cumulative markup of 51% was achieved.

Step 2: Determine a cost opening book inventory figure:
   $100,000 × (100% − 51%)
= $100,000 × 49%
= $ 49,000

Step 3: All new purchases ($240,000 cost, $500,000 retail) are added to the opening book inventory figures ($49,000 cost, $100,000 retail) to find total merchandise handled (TMH) figures ($289,000 at cost and $600,000 at retail) resulting in a 51.8% cumulative markup.

Step 4: The sum $475,000 ($425,000 total of net sales) + $45,000 (markdowns) + $5,000 (shortages) is subtracted from the retail figure of TMH ($600,000) to find the retail closing book inventory figure ($125,000).

Step 5: Determine a cost closing book inventory figure:
   $125,000 × (100% − 51.8%)
= $125,000 × 48.2%
= $ 60,250

Step 6: The closing book inventory at cost ($60,250) is subtracted from TMH at cost ($289,000) to find the cost of goods sold ($228,750).

Step 7: The cost of goods sold ($228,750) is then subtracted from the net sales ($425,000)[4] to find the merchandise margin ($196,250).

---

[4]In the calculation of a maintained markup, the margin on sales is determined before making adjustments for cash discounts earned and alteration costs.

Figure 23. Calculating Gross Margin on Stock Plus Purchases

	Cost	Retail	% of Sales	Cum. MU%
Opening Inventory	$49,000 $\big($ \$100,000 × (100% − MU%)$\big)$ $\big($ \$100,000 × 49% $\big)$	$100,000		51.0%
(Plus) New Purchases & Freight	+ 240,000	+ 500,000		
Total Mdse. Handled (Minus) Total Deductions	$289,000	$600,000 − 475,000 $\big($ Sales $\quad$ \$425,000 +Markdowns 45,000 +Shortages $\quad$ \$5,000 $\big)$		51.8%
(Minus) Closing Inventory	− 60,250 $\big($ \$125,000 × (100% − MU%)$\big)$ $\big($ \$125,000 × 48.2% $\big)$	$125,000		
Gross Cost of Mdse. Sold	$228,750	Net Sales $425,000 −Gross Cost of Mdse. Sold $\quad$ 228,750		
Merchandise Margin (Plus) Cash Discounts		$196,250 + 13,000 209,250	46.2%	
(Minus) Workroom Costs Gross Margin		− 1,000 $208,250	49%	

Step 8: The cash discounts ($13,000) are added to the merchandise margin ($196,250), which equals $209,250.

Step 9: The workroom costs ($1,000) are subtracted from $209,250 to find the gross margin ($208,250).

From an accounting viewpoint, in the calculation of gross margin, the cash discounts and workroom costs are adjusted after the margin on the merchandise itself (i.e., maintained markup) is determined. Nonetheless, because merchants frequently negotiate cash discounts or influence the workroom factor, their impact on the gross margin must be considered.

D. The Relationship of Profit to Inventory Valuation in the Retail Method of Inventory

The value placed on an inventory has a decided effect on profits. In this unit there is a detailed examination of the mathematical calculations and records adopted by departmentalized retailers who use the retail method of inventory to establish a continuing gross margin figure and to verify if a profit has been achieved. By illustrating the relationship between sales volume, cost of merchandise sold, given expenses, and the operating profit, the example that follows shows the application of the data collected through this method of inventory valuation. (For ease of comprehension of this system, the same figures are used as in the preceding calculation of gross margin to the operating profit.)

Net Sales	Cost	Retail	% of Sales
		$425,000	100%
Opening book inventory	$ 49,000		
+ Purchases	+240,000		
Total mdse. handled	= $289,000		
− Closing book inventory	− 60,250		
Gr. cost of mdse. sold	= $228,750		
− Cash discounts	− 13,000		
	$215,750		
+ Workroom	+ 1,000		
Net cost of mdse. sold	= $216,750	−216,750	− 51%
Gross margin		$208,250	49%
− Operating expenses		−191,250	− 45%
Net profit		= $ 17,000	4%

19. The shortage in the legwear department is $3,500. This is 5% of that department's net sales. What is the sales volume of the department?

20. The coat department's net sales were $225,000, markdowns taken amounted to $15,000, and employee discounts were $3,000. The retail opening inventory for this period was $75,000, the purchases made at retail were $210,000, and the buyer estimated the shortages at 2%. Determine the estimated physical count.

21. A store with net sales of $3,500,000 has estimated its shortages to be 2%. The actual dollar shortage amounted to $72,000.

    (a) Was this shortage a higher or lower percentage than anticipated? By how much?

    (b) What was the dollar difference between the estimated and the actual shortage?

22. The net sales of a lingerie department were $295,000; inventory on February 1 was $150,000; markdowns were 8% of net sales; purchases for this period were $362,000; the physical inventory taken July 31 was $188,400.

      (a) Was there a dollar shortage for this period?

      (b) What was the shortage or overage percentage for this period?

23. Describe in detail the various methods that a merchant might use to reduce excessive departmental shortage.

24. Research and Discussion: One of the major duties of any merchant is to control inventory discrepancies (e.g., excessive shortages or overages). Prepare a brief fact sheet for new assistant buyers that outlines the actions a merchant at the departmental level can take to accomplish effectively this responsibility. Briefly explain each action mentioned.

25. A men's outerwear department had an opening inventory of $340,000. The net purchases were $78,000, gross sales were $140,250, customer returns were $11,150, and markdowns—including employee discounts—were $4,800. Shortages of 1.2% were estimated. Calculate:

    (a) The closing retail book inventory.
    (b) The estimated physical inventory.

26. For the Spring Season, the hosiery department had net sales of $700,000. On July 31, the physical inventory was $174,220 and the retail book inventory was $185,220.

    (a) What was the shortage percentage for the season?
    (b) If a 2% shortage was estimated, was the actual shortage percentage higher or lower than anticipated? By how much?

27. The men's furnishings buyer received the following data:

	Cost	Retail
Total Mdse. Handled	$451,608	$940,850
Net Sales		650,000
Markdown		40,000
Employee Discounts		10,000

Calculate

    (a) The closing inventory at cost and retail.
    (b) The gross margin in dollars and percent.

RETAIL METHOD OF INVENTORY

Two years ago, Ms. Carol, the misses sportswear buyer, agreed with management that a separate petite sportswear department should be created. Because of increasing sales, she felt that petite sportswear had outgrown its status as a classification and deserved, in its own right, to become a separate department. Ms. Carol continued as the buyer for the newly created department, and with her enthusiastic and skillful attention, the impressive sales increases continued for the first year. The second year, however, the sales increases were minute. Ms. Carol now questioned if the category should remain a department or again be incorporated into the misses sportswear department. To make an appropriate judgment, she requested the following data for analysis. The department had an opening inventory of $750,000 at retail that carried a 53% markup. During this period, the gross purchases of $570,000 at retail were priced with a 56.1% markup. The freight charges were $9,600. The merchandise returned to vendors amounted to $14,000 at cost, and $30,000 at retail. Transfers from the misses sportswear department were $3,500 at cost, and $7,600 at retail. Transfers to the misses sportswear department were $8,000 at retail, with an agreed cost of $3,700. The gross sales were $720,000; customer returns and allowances were $30,000. The markdowns taken were 12%, and employee discounts were 1%.

As Ms. Carol determined the gross margin achieved by the petite sportswear department, she weighed this against the 46.1% gross margin of the misses department. Should this "new" department continue as a separate entity? Why? Justify your decision with a mathematical comparison between the performance of the petite vs. misses sportswear departments.

CONTROLLING SHORTAGES

At the end of the fall season Gary Abbott, the buyer, received the shortage report for the Gift Shop. This report revealed that the overall department shortage for this six-month period was 1.3% or .2% less than the previous season. Gary was delighted to notice this decline in shortage, small as it was. As he analyzed the results of the individual stores, he found that Store 01 had a shortage of 1.2% while Store 09 had a 5.0% shortage.

Because the store uses a bar code scanning system to take inventory, the accuracy of the amount of inventory taken is ensured. However, Gary reviews the figures for each store before trying to determine the causes of the vast shortage differences. He refers to the following data:

		Store 01			Store 09	
	Cost	Retail	MU%	Cost	Retail	MU%
Opening inventory		$450,000	52%		$300,000	52%
Purchases (including freight)	$142,500	300,000		$71,250	150,000	
Reductions		7,000			4,000	
Sales		375,000			150,000	
Shortage		1.2%			5%	

Store 01 had a physical inventory figure of $363,500, and Store 09's physical count was $288,500. Other differences between these two stores are:

1. Store 01 is one of the oldest existing branches of the chain, while Store 09 is the newest branch, having been opened one year ago.
2. Store 01 is located in a high income area, while Store 09 is in a medium-income bracket location.
3. Store 01 is one of the most profitable units of the chain, and because of its high productivity enjoys a commensurate sales force.
4. Since 09's existence is so young, it has been staffed with a minimum permanent sales organization supplemented by part-time employees.

Gary takes three steps:

1. He decided (though can the computers ever be wrong?) to first determine the closing book inventory from the above figures.
2. Having done that, he adjusted the physical count to the book inventory to determine the shortage percentage.
3. Having satisfied himself as to the accuracy of the shortage percentage, he attempted to determine the possible causes. If you were the buyer what causes would you investigate more thoroughly in order to decrease shortages and why? What effect, if any, would the large shortage % of Store 09 have on the overall department net profit?

Notes

Unit V

DOLLAR PLANNING AND CONTROL

Objectives

- Understanding and recognition of the elements of a six-month merchandise plan.
- Knowledge and ability to plan sales.
- Calculation of changes in sales as percentages.
- Facility to plan stock levels, using:
  Stock-sales ratio method.
  Week's supply method.
  Basic stock method.
- Calculation of GMROI.
- Proficiency to plan markdowns.
- Skill to plan purchases at retail and at cost.
- Calculation of open-to-buy figures.

Key Terms

average retail stock	open-to-buy (OTB)
basic stock method	planned purchases/receipts
BOM stock	six-month seasonal dollar
dollar merchandise plan	merchandise plan
EOM stock	stock-sales ratio
GMROI	turnover
on order	weeks supply method

P rofit in retailing is determined largely by maintaining a proper proportion between sales, inventories, and prices. The merchandiser is responsible for providing an inventory that reflects customer demand and also remains within the financial limits set by management. For each department, a sales goal in dollar amounts is forecast, and the size of the inventory necessary to meet these goals is planned. A budget that coordinates these sales and stocks is called a **dollar merchandise plan.** It schedules planned sales month by month, the amount of stock planned for each of these months, and the amount of projected reductions. The budget is prepared in advance of the selling period to which it applies. It typically covers a six-month period (e.g., August 1 to January 31, and February 1 to July 31).

The information in this budget permits the merchandiser to determine the amount of purchases required. In no way does the dollar merchandise plan address the issue of what merchandise should be purchased. The development of an assortment that reflects customer demands is another important aspect of the total planning process. Because of the subject of this book, this chapter focuses on the mathematics used in this process; concepts and principles are briefly defined and discussed for better comprehension.

Although the dollar merchandise plans used by different stores vary considerably in scope and detail, when properly planned and administered, the sales, stocks, markdowns. and projected cumulative markup percentage (i.e., the original retail price of the total merchandise handled minus the cost) are the indispensable figures that should result in a satisfactory net profit.

The main reason for planning purchases is to assist the buyer in making purchases at the proper time and in the correct amounts so that the stock level is in ratio to sales. Consequently, the dollar merchandise plan also provides a control figure called **open-to-buy.** This figure represents the dollar amount of merchandise the buyer may receive during the balance of a given period, without exceeding the planned stock figure at the end of the period under consideration. Because of the benefits that result from this process, most large and many small retailers are committed to comprehensive planning activities. The dollar merchandise system of planning and control discussed in this unit is designed to protect a store's major investment, that is, its inventory. As the art of this merchandising technique is broad in scope and requires an in-depth examination, this subject must be included in any study related to buying for retail.

I. Six-Month Seasonal Dollar Merchandise Plan

As a device for unifying merchandising operations, the objectives of the dollar plan are:

- To procure a net profit by providing an instrument that plans, forecasts, and controls the purchase and sales of merchandise.
- To research previous results to repeat and improve prior successes and to avoid failures.
- To integrate the various merchandising activities involved in determining the purchases necessary to achieve the estimated planned sales.

A. The Procedure of Dollar Planning by Element

Planning Sales

The planning of this figure is most significant because it is the basis for establishing the stock, markdown, and purchase figures. Thus, it should be calculated first. However, its calculation requires the greatest skill and judgment because its accuracy depends on detailed investigation and analysis.

STEP 1:
Carefully forecast future total dollar sales volume for the entire period by:

(a) Reviewing and analyzing past sales performance for the same time period.

(b) Considering factors that may cause a change in sales. These factors include:

(c) ■ Current sales trends.
   ■ Previous rate of growth patterns.
   ■ Economic conditions.
   ■ Local business conditions.
   ■ Fashion factors.
   ■ Influencing conditions within and from outside the store or department, (e.g., changes in store concepts, market direction, competition, etc.).

(d) Establishing, for the season, a percentage of estimated sales change after analyzing the sales performance and current conditions that cause sales changes. Then, calculate the total dollar sales volume for the period. The following calculations are used in this procedure.

Calculating the Percentage of Sales Increase or Decrease When Last Year's Actual Sales and This Year's Planned Sales Are Known

CONCEPT:

Percentage sales increase = TY planned sales

− LY actual sales

= Sales increase

= $\dfrac{\text{Sales increase}}{\text{LY actual sales}}$

= % Sales increase

PROBLEM:

If last year's actual sales were $1,834,900 and this year's planned sales are $2,000, what is the percentage of sales increase?

SOLUTION:

Percentage sales increase = $2,000,000 Pl. sales

−1,834,900 Actual LY sales

= $ 165,000 Sales increase

$\dfrac{\$\ \ 165,000}{\$1,834,900}$ $\dfrac{\text{Sales increase}}{\text{LY sales}}$

= .089 or 9%

Sales increase percentage = 9%

There are circumstances under which the sales volume of a department or a classification is reduced because of a decreased demand. The concept for a decrease in sales is the same as for an increase of sales.

PROBLEM:

The sales of the boot classification declined significantly because of the current fashion emphasis. Consequently, the shoe buyer planned sales for this category at $500,000 this season although last year's actual sales amounted to $650,000. What was the planned percentage of sales decrease for this classification?

SOLUTION:

% Sales decrease $=$ $\dfrac{\text{Actual LY sales} - \text{Pl. TY sales}}{\text{Actual LY sales}}$

$=$ $650,000$ LY Actual sales
      $-\$500,000$ TY Planned sales

$=$ $150,000$ Sales decrease

$=$ $\dfrac{\$150,000 \ \ \text{Sales decrease}}{\$650,000 \ \ \text{LY Actual sales}}$

Sales decrease percentage = 23.1%

Calculating a Total Planned Seasonal Sales Figure When Last Year's Sales and the Planned Percentage of Increase Are Known

CONCEPT:

Seasonal planned sales = Last year (LY) sales × Planned increase %
                           = Dollar increase
                           = LY sales + Dollar increase

PROBLEM:

If last year's seasonal sales are $1,834,900 and there was a planned 9% sales increase, what are the planned seasonal sales for this year (TY)?

SOLUTION:

Seasonal planned sales = $1,834,900   LY sales
                       ×   9%   Sales increase

            = $ 165,141   Sales increase

               $1,834,900   LY sales
             + 165,141   Sales increase

TY seasonal
planned sales   = $2,000,041[1]

STEP 2:

To set the individual monthly sales goals, use the seasonal distribution of the previous year's sales for the same period as a guideline. When adjusting the planned monthly sales increase or decrease, the three essential processes that influence a buyer's judgment are:

- Considering the department's past experience with respect to the normal percentage distribution of sales for the planning period.

---

[1]On the actual plan, the seasonal planned sales would be projected at $2,000,000.

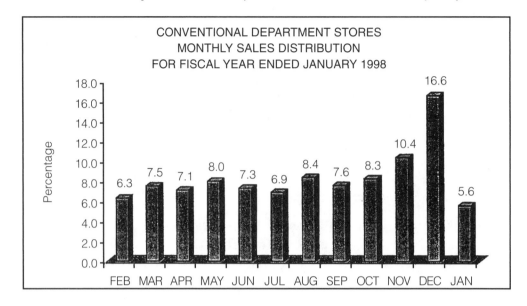

Source: U.S. Department of Commerce, Bureau of the Census: Combined Annual and Revised Monthly

- Comparing the monthly percentage distribution with industry performance. (Figure 24)
- Adjusting monthly sales figures because of shifting dates of certain holidays, planned special promotions, and other merchandising strategies. (Figure 25)

For assignments for the previous section, see practice problems 1–7.

Planning Stocks

Because the merchandising policies of retail stores differ, there is no absolute formula for developing the variety of a stock assortment. However, the planning

---

This daily report can be viewed by screen print. By department, the individual branch and the department's total sales can be obtained and any necessary action can be taken quickly. The annotated information on Figure 25 is numbered (1) to (5), and the following information corresponds to those numbers:

(1) DEPARTMENT NUMBER AND NAME (of item): Example: DEPT 220, BELTS.

(2) LOCATION: Individual store number and its location, example: 01 NY.

(3) TODAY: TY actual sales and LY sales for the current day, example: in STORE 01, NY, in DEPT 220, BELTS TY $3680, LY $2147. TOT-ALL: DEPT 220, BELTS, TOTAL TY $7837, TOTAL LY $6674, PCT 17.4% + sales increase for TY over LY.

(4) PDT ($1000): Planned to date of TY, LY, and PLAN figures. PLAN numbers represent an end-of-week cumulative total, example:

    TOT-ALL, DEPT 220, BELTS

    TY: $94

    LY: $90

    PCT: 4.5% + sales increase for TY over LY.

(5) CUMULATIVE TOT STD: STD of TY over PLAN, example:

    TOT-ALL, DEPT 220, BELTS

    TY: $675

    PLAN: $673

Figure 25. Daily Flash Sheets

Daily Flash Sales
Daily Flash Sales for Wednesday 10/14/2000   Date: per 09 wk 2 day 4

*****PLAN NUMBERS REPRESENT AN END-OF-WEEK CUMULATIVE TOTAL*****

(1) DEPT 220 — BELTS

LOC	(3) TODAY TY	LY	(4) PTD ($1000) TY	LY	PLAN	PCT	(5) STD TY	PLAN
(2) 01 NY	3680	2147	40	37	55	7.5+	277	284
02 BR	301	403	4	3	5	7.8+	32	22
03^ FM	0	0	0	0	0	0.0+	0	0
04^ ST	0	0	0	0	0	0.0+	0	0
05 BC	61	506	5	5	8	6.1-	38	36
06 SH	216	207	5	4	5	27.5+	31	28
07 CP	0	0	0	0	0	0.0+	0	0
08 NM	719	243	7	5	8	36.3+	57	46
09 GC	471	276	5	4	5	38.4+	32	27
10 PG	402	77	2	2	2	25.6+	13	8
11 CH	695	343	5	3	5	38.4+	34	31
12 WP	322	320	6	5	7	1.4+	41	42
13 WF	293	859	3	5	6	46.2-	21	27
14 TC	185	237	3	4	5	9.6-	22	23
16 KP	265	306	4	3	4	16.0+	22	21
17 WG	177	170	2	2	2	12.4+	17	14
20^ VV	0	0	0	0	0	0.0+	0	0
21* FA	0	580	0	6	7	102.9-	12	35
22* FR	0	0	0	0	0	0.0+	0	0
24 FN	0	0	0	0	0	0.0+	0	0
25* MI	50	0	3	0	6	100.0+	25	29
TOT-CMP	7787	6094	90	83	117	8.4+	638	609
TOT-ALL	7837	6674	94	90	130	4.5+	675	673
PCT	17.4+		4.5+					

*****PLAN NUMBERS REPRESENT AN END-OF-WEEK CUMULATIVE TOTAL*****

DEPT 231 — SCARVES

LOC	TODAY TY	LY	PTD ($1000) TY	LY	PLAN	PCT	STD TY	PLAN
01 NY	4822	4191	59	64	81	8.6-	316	301
02 BR	122	59-	2	2	0	35.8+	13	3
03^ FM	0	0	0	0	0	0.0+	0	0
04^ ST	0	0	0	0	0	0.0+	0	0
05 BC	661	488	8	6	10	24.8+	43	33
06 SH	478	740	6	7	9	14.8-	35	32
07 CP	0	0	0	0	0	0.0+	0	0
08 NM	368	848	7	6	11	27.0+	55	40
09 GC	407	155-	4	3	5	29.8+	24	18
10 PG	56	44	1	0	0	131.2+	4	1
11 CH	571	82	5	6	7	11.6-	35	22
12 WP	73	602	10	6	10	72.4+	53	38
13 WF	170	315	3	4	5	33.1-	19	21
14 TC	85	483	3	3	5	17.3-	18	20
16 KP	485	311	4	4	5	10.4+	22	23
17 WG	26	465	3	3	4	5.3-	19	15
20^ VV	0	0	0	0	0	0.0+	0	0
21* FA	0	57	0	1(	2	100.0-	4	7
22* FR	0	0	0	0	0	0.0+	0	0
24 FN	0	0	0	0	0	0.0+	0	0
25* MI	349	0	4	0	0	100.0+	23	0
TOT-CMP	8324	8356	113	113	152	0.2-	658	567
TOT-ALL	8673	8413	117	115	154	2.5+	685	574
PCT	3.0+		2.5+					

*****PLAN NUMBERS REPRESENT AN END-OF-WEEK CUMULATIVE TOTAL*****

MGM 105 — DRESS ACCESSORIES

LOC	TODAY TY	LY	PTD ($1000) TY	LY	PLAN	PCT	STD TY	PLAN
01 NY	13709	12232	162	163	223	0.6-	1038	1008
02 BR	1001	1376	16	15	20	3.9+	122	97
03^ FM	0	0	0	0	0	0.0+	0	0
04^ ST	0	0	0	0	0	0.0+	0	0
05 BC	1324	2362	20	20	30	2.3+	151	129
06 SH	1284	1786	23	21	27	12.9+	152	136
07 CP	0	0	0	0	0	0.0+	0	0
08 NM	2636	2871	29	29	44	0.7-	231	215
09 GC	1163	687	14	13	17	13.8+	96	80
10 PG	874	519	7	5	8	24.1+	44	38
11 CH	2751	821	19	17	22	8.0+	139	110
12 WP	968	1248	27	21	30	32.0+	176	151
13 WF	1043	2045	11	17	21	33.4-	83	100
14 TC	921	1389	12	13	17	10.3-	88	80
16 KP	1504	1352	13	11	15	22.1+	86	80
17 WG	616	1008	9	11	12	11.5+	63	58
20^ VV	0	0	0	0	0	0.0+	0	0
21* FA	0	1847	0	17	23	101.1-	41	114
22* FR	0	0	0	0	0	0.0+	0	0
24 FN	0	0	0	0	0	0.0+	0	0
25* MI	634	0	13	0	16	100.0+	102	85
TOT-CMP	29794	29696	363	355	486	2.2+	2470	2282
TOT-ALL	30428	31543	376	372	525	0.9+	2613	2481
PCT	3.5-		0.9+					

*****PLAN NUMBERS REPRESENT AN END-OF-WEEK CUMULATIVE TOTAL*****

DEPT 252 — SOCKS

LOC	TODAY TY	LY	PTD ($1000) TY	LY	PLAN	PCT	STD TY	PLAN
01 NY	6382	6578	76	82	81	7.6-	334	386
02 BR	368	313	3	3	0	0.3-	22	7
03^ FM	0	0	0	0	0	0.0+	0	0
04^ ST	0	0	0	0	0	0.0+	0	0
05 BC	1017	1673	12	13	10	2.0-	52	54
06 SH	754	1002	13	11	9	18.5+	56	52
07 CP	0	0	0	0	0	0.0+	0	0
08 NM	1348	1133	16	15	11	6.2+	77	85
09 GC	839	1000	12	11	5	7.1+	51	44
10 PG	38	27	1	1	0	16.0-	6	7
11 CH	802	516	8	7	7	21.8+	35	33
12 WP	1129	775	13	13	10	0.4-	59	62
13 WF	399	958	6	9	5	35.7-	25	42
14 TC	469	429	6	6	5	4.2+	22	24
16 KP	335	772	4	6	5	26.2-	19	31
17 WG	307	515	4	5	4	15.3-	17	21
20^ VV	0	0	0	0	0	0.0+	0	0
21* FA	0	296	0	3	2	100.0-	5	21
22* FR	0	0	0	0	0	0.0+	0	0
24 FN	0	0	0	0	0	0.0+	0	0
25* MI	534	0	4	0	0	100.0+	23	45
TOT-CMP	14187	15691	175	181	152	3.7-	776	848
TOT-ALL	14721	15987	179	184	154	3.2-	805	914
PCT	7.9-		3.1-					

phase of stock investment is accomplished through the dollar plan. In the planning and control of dollar stocks, every merchandiser's objective is to:

- Maintain adequate assortments (i.e., reasonably complete from a customer's viewpoint).
- Regulate the dollar investment of stocks in relation to sales to obtain a satisfactory balance between these two factors.

Daily computerized sales reports provide the buyer with information on the actual performance and any variance from the planned performance. This information requires analysis for appropriate action and decisions. These computerized reports provide the basis for dollar control of inventories. This report helps alert the merchandiser to the most current sales position to make any revisions deemed necessary.

After planned monthly sales are established, the amount of dollar stock that is required on hand at the beginning of each month (**BOM stocks**) and/or the end of each month (**EOM stocks**) must be determined. The EOM stock for a particular month is the same as the BOM stock for the following month; for example, if $230,00 is the EOM stock for February, this same figure is the BOM stock for March.

There are variations in the methods of calculating individual monthly stock figures. Before discussing these possible techniques, it is essential to examine **turnover** because it represents the degree of balance between sales and stocks. The rate of stock turnover measures the velocity with which merchandise moves into and out of a department or store. Turnover, or rate of stock turnover, is a merchandising figure. It indicates the number of times that an average stock has been sold and replaced during a given period, the number of times goods have been turned into money, and subsequently, money turned back into goods. Although turnover is a resultant figure, it can be planned, controlled, and, for convenience of comparison, is usually expressed as an annual or semiannual figure.

Determining the Turnover Figure

Every retailer should understand the importance of turnover to make better use of capital investment, to control inventories, and ultimately, to realize optimum profits. It acts as an index to efficient merchandising. Successful stock planning does not begin with turnover, but results in achieving the desired rate of stock turnover. This term indicates the number of times that an average stock is sold for a given period of time, which, unless otherwise stated, refers to a period of one year. However, turnover may be computed on a weekly, monthly, or seasonal basis. The actual number of stock turns varies with the type of merchandise and price. Generally speaking, lower price ranges turn more rapidly than higher ranges; apparel and accessories turn more rapidly than home furnishings. Typical average turnover figures for a particular type of goods are most important as a method of comparison. The following average rate of turnover figures[2] show the range that may occur:

Misses Dresses:	2.8
Men's Furnishings:	2.1
Loungewear and Robes:	2.1
Children's Footwear:	1.9
Linen & Domestics:	1.9
Handbags:	2.8

Turnover is important to a merchandising operation because it:

■ Stimulates sales by presenting fresh merchandise to the customer.

■ Reduces markdowns by keeping the flow of new goods constant, thereby curbing the accumulation of large amounts of older stock.

■ Lowers cost of goods sold because the "open-to-buy" position permits the buyer to take advantage of special prices and offerings.

■ Decreases interest, merchandise taxes, and other operating expenses as a percentage of net sales.

The stock turnover rate can be calculated on either a unit or dollar basis, but for the purposes of this text, the dollar basis will be examined.

Calculating Turnover When Average Retail Stock and Sales for the Period Are Known[3]

The dollar figures of stock turn can be determined on either a cost or retail basis. Generally, in stores that use the retail method of inventory, the rate of stock turn is determined on a retail basis. Essential for accuracy, however, is that both sales and inventory be calculated on the same foundation.

CONCEPT:

$$\text{Turnover} = \frac{\text{Net sales for period}}{\text{Average retail stock for same period}}$$

PROBLEM:

For the year, the infants' department had net sales of $2,000,000. The average retail stock during this period was $500,000. What was the rate of stock turn?

---

[2]Most current figures from FOR/MOR, The Combined Financial, Merchandising & Operating Result of Retail Stores, NATIONAL RETAIL FEDERATION. These figures represent performance at the time of publication and should not be construed to be ideal.

[3]The same method can be used to calculate either a monthly or yearly turnover figure.

SOLUTION:

Turnover for the period = $\dfrac{\$2,000,000 \ \text{Net sales}}{\$\ 500,000 \ \text{Average retail stock}}$

Turnover = 4

Calculating Average Retail Stock When Planned Sales and Turnover Are Known

CONCEPT:

Average retail stock = $\dfrac{\text{Planned sales for period}}{\text{Turnover rate}}$

PROBLEM:

The hosiery department planned sales of $2,000,000 with a stock turn of 4 as the goal. What should be the average stock carried for the period under consideration?

SOLUTION:

Average stock for period = $\dfrac{\$2,000,000 \ \text{planned sales}}{4 \ \text{Turnover rate}}$

Average retail stock = $\ 500,000

By understanding the relationship of the average stock, planned sales, and turnover, and by substituting the known factors of the basic formula, the unknown can be calculated (e.g., net sales = stock turnover × average stock at retail).

Calculating Average Retail Stock When Monthly Inventories Are Known

Because the determination of the average inventory directly affects the rate of stock turn, there is a need for a common method among stores and retail establishments to determine the average stock amounts so that the comparison of stock turns can be meaningful. Under the retail method of inventory, an **average retail stock** is the sum of the retail inventories at the beginning of each year, season, month, or week. This is added to the ending inventory and then divided by the number of inventories used. This is the most accurate and commonly used method because a monthly book inventory figure is available through the Retail Method of Inventory. For example, to obtain an average retail stock figure for a year, the 12 stock inventories at the beginning of each month are added to the ending inventory and the total sum is divided by 13. If the stock turnover rate is computed for a shorter period than one year, the same principle is applied (e.g., for determining a six-month turnover rate, add the seven stock-on-hand figures and divide by 7). This turnover rate, which has been computed for a period of less than a year, can then be converted to an equivalent annual rate.

In addition, an average stock figure can be calculated in cost as well as retail dollars. The method of finding an average monthly inventory at cost is exactly the same as determining the average stock at retail. For reasons that should be apparent, it is incorrect to mix cost figures with those at retail in the same turnover calculation, so when this type of figure is desired, only the cost inventory figures are used.

CONCEPT:

Average retail stock = $\dfrac{\text{Sum of beginning inventories} + \text{Ending inventory for given period}}{\text{Number of inventories}}$

PROBLEM:

Find the average retail stock and the turnover for this period.

	Sales		BOM stocks
January	$10,000	Jan. 1	$13,000
February	8,000	Feb. 1	12,000
March	14,000	Mar. 1	17,000
April	16,000	Apr. 1	19,000
May	12,000	May 1	15,000
June	14,000	June 1	18,000
July	10,000	July 1	14,000
August	6,000	Aug. 1	10,000
September	12,000	Sept. 1	16,000
October	11,000	Oct. 1	15,000
November	12,000	Nov. 1	15,000
December	15,000	Dec. 1	18,000
		Dec. 31 ($13,000 is ending inventory)	

SOLUTION:

Sum of 12 BOM stocks	=	$182,000
+ EOM stock	=	+ 13,000
	=	195,000

Average retail stock = $\dfrac{\$195,000 \;\;\text{(Sum of 13 figures)}}{13 \;\;\text{(Number of inventories)}}$

Average retail stock for one year = $ 15,000

After calculating an average stock figure, the formula of net sales for the period under consideration divided by the average stock is applied to determine the turnover rate. For example:

Turnover = $\dfrac{\$140{,}000 \;\text{(Sum of 12 monthly sales figures)}}{\$15{,}000 \;\text{(Average retail stock for the period)}}$

Turnover = 9.3

This same method is used to calculate an average retail stock for a shorter period. The next problem applies the formulas for average inventory and turnover. It illustrates how to determine the average retail stock for a period shorter than one year and how to convert the turnover to an annual rate.

EXAMPLE:

	Sales	Stock-on-hand (Book inventory)	
Feb. 1	$ 20,000	$ 50,000	
Mar. 1	27,500	60,000	
Apr. 1	35,000	75,000	
May 1	32,500	70,000	
May 31		60,000	
Total sales	$115,000	$315,000	Sum of inventories

Average stock = $\dfrac{\$315{,}000 \;\text{Sum of inventories}}{5 \;\text{Number of inventories}}$

Average stock = $ 63,000

Stock turn rate = $\dfrac{\$115{,}000 \;\text{Net sales}}{\$63{,}000 \;\text{Average stock}}$

= 1.83 for 4 months or 1/3 year

Annual Rate = 1.83 × 3

Annual turnover rate = 5.49

In planning stocks for a season, from the standpoint of stock turnover, merchandise is apportioned so that the average stock is related to the sales for the entire period. This approach does not offer a basis for planning a specific amount of stock to be on hand to achieve a planned sales figure.

Determining Gross Margin Return by Dollar Inventory

While retailers have stock turn goals to judge the efficiency of the balance between sales and stocks, when money is tight greater emphasis is placed on the relationship between the inventory investment, or working capital, and its ability to produce gross margin dollars. The objective to produce a maximum gross margin from a minimum dollar amount investment.

The ratio of productivity of each dollar invested in inventory is similar to a share of stock, and the productivity of this dollar is equivalent, to some degree, to earnings per share. Stock turnover influences and affects the utilization of money invested in inventory. The more times money is converted into sales and gross margin, the greater the return per dollar of inventory. Today, the frequency of this "reinvestment" is an increasingly significant factor. The measurement of the efficiency of investment in inventory is referred to as **gross margin return per dollar of inventory,** which is commonly known as **GMROI** (pronounced jim-roy). This element is used by financial analysts to measure capital turnover.

Merchandisers in retailing are responsible for a successful stock turnover and consequently are focused on it. Both stock turn and GMROI are involved with inventory productivity and the relationship between these two elements is that the calculation of stock turn utilizes an average inventory at retail, and GMROI uses an average inventory at cost.

The following example illustrates this concept:

Given:

Net sales	=	$1,200,000
Gross margin	=	480,000
Average inventory (retail)	=	480,000
Average inventory (cost)	=	240,000

Find:

(a) Stock turnover $= \dfrac{\$1,200,000 \text{ Net sales}}{\$\,480,000 \text{ Average inventory at retail}}$

$= 2.5$

(b) GMROI $= \dfrac{\$\,480,000 \text{ Gross margin}}{\$\,240,000 \text{ Average inventory at cost}}$

$= 2.0$

This is the simplest level of calculating GMROI. It is apparent that as more sales and gross margin dollars are generated, without increasing inventory, GMROI will increase.

It is more practical to think of GMROI in terms commonly used in merchandising. These factors, which can be managed and influenced, are:

- Markup percentage.
- Gross margin percentage.
- Turnover.

Another way to think of the calculation is:

$$\frac{\text{How much is made on a sale} \times \text{How long it takes to sell it}}{\text{How much was paid for it}}$$

This results in the following calculation:

CONCEPT:

$$\frac{\text{Gross margin \%} \times \text{Turnover}}{100\% - \text{Markup \%}}$$

PROBLEM:

The year-to-date results of the intimate apparent department are:

Gross margin: 40%
Turnover: 2.5
Markup: 50%

What is the GMROI achieved by this department?

SOLUTION:

$$\text{GMROI} = \frac{\text{G.M. \%} \times \text{T.O.}}{100\% - \text{MU \%}}$$

$$= \frac{40\% \text{ G.M.} \times 2.5 \text{ T.O.}}{100\% - 50\% \text{ MU}}$$

$$= \frac{.40 \times 2.5}{100\% - .50}$$

$$= \frac{1}{.50}$$

$$= 2$$

The GMROI result is identical for either calculation but the second example shows the relationship of the components and demonstrates how future results can be improved.

The key to successful retailing is achieving more dollar sales without a corresponding increase in inventory. Through the determination of turnover, the stock level that produce an optional sales level can be measured. The calculation of GMROI shows the profitability or cash flow that these sales produce.

Figure 26 charts the inventory productivity or stock turn and the profitability or GMROI for a 5-year period.

Figure 26. Inventory Productivity and Profitability

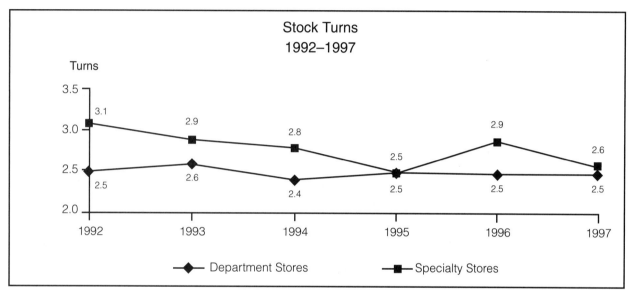

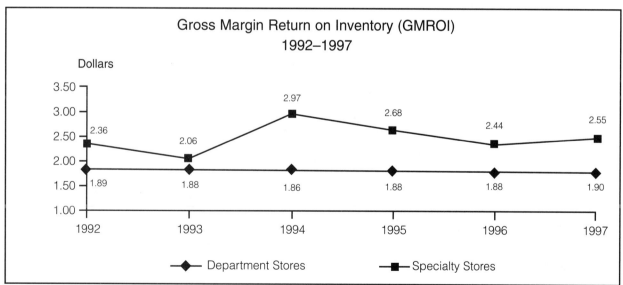

Note: Department and Specialty store figures are weighted by the aggregate net sales of the companies reporting. For further detail, please refer to the FOR Reference Calculation, Classification and Organization of Data.

For assignments for the previous section, see practice problems 8–22.

Figure 27. Stock Sales Ratio for Fiscal Year 1997

Feb	Mar	Apr	May	June	July	Aug	Sept	Oct	Nov	Dec	Jan
5.43	4.17	5.19	4.95	4.03	4.83	4.75	4.34	5.13	4.18	2.10	6.17

Methods of Stock Planning

It is common to plan monthly stock figures for the beginning of the period by a **stock-sales ratio** method. This technique, illustrated in the following examples, indicates the relationship between stock-on-hand at the beginning of the month and the retail sales for the same month.

Setting Individual First of Month Stock Figures by Stock-Sales Ratio Method

After planned monthly sales figures are established, the amount of dollar stock that is required on hand at the beginning of each month (BOM stocks) and the end of each month (EOM stocks) must be determined. This relationship is referred to as a stock-sales ratio. Generally, the BOM stock-sales ratio is used to balance planned monthly stocks with the planned monthly sales. Standard stock-sales ratios in departments can be established by evaluating the actual past stock-sales ratio performance of the department that has proven to provide the proper relationship. Additionally, researched guidelines of data showing typical monthly stock-sales ratios are available in the FOR/MOR, published by the National Retail Federation, and this can be used as a source of information in planning monthly stock proportions. Because monthly stock-sales proportions vary, it is necessary to establish the proper ratio for an individual month. Figure 27 illustrates typical department store stock-sales ratios for each month.

Calculating Stock-Sales Ratio When Retail Stock and Sales for a Given Period Are Known

CONCEPT:

$$\text{Stock-sales ratio} = \frac{\text{Retail stock at given time in the period}}{\text{Sales for the period}}$$

PROBLEM:

On February 1, the boys' wear department had a retail stock of $120,000. The planned sales for this month were $20,000. Find the stock-sales ratio for the month of February.

SOLUTION:

$$\text{Stock-sales ratio} = \frac{\$120,000 \ \text{BOM Stock}}{\$ \ 20,000 \ \text{February sales}}$$

Stock-sales ratio = 6

Calculating BOM Stock When Planned Sales and Stock-Sales Ratio Are Known

CONCEPT:

BOM stock = Planned monthly sales × stock-sales ratio

PROBLEM:

The fabric department planned sales of $40,000 for the month of July. Experience in the department showed an 8.2 stock-sales ratio was successful. What should be the planned BOM stock for July?

SOLUTION:

BOM July stock = $ 40,000 Planned July sales

× 8.2 Stock-sales ratio

BOM stock = $328,000

For assignments for the previous section, see practice problems 23–26.

Setting Stock Figures by the Weeks Supply Method

The **weeks supply method** plans inventory size on a weekly basis. The set amount of stock equals a calculated number of weeks supply. The number of weeks supply that is to be "on hand" depends on the planned turnover figure to be achieved and is used as a guide to set the number of weeks inventory supply. This technique of stock planning is best used in a department that primarily carries staple merchandise and/or has a relatively stable sales volume. Note that because the stock size is in direct relation to the planned weekly sales, it can result in an excessive stock condition at the peak selling periods or in dangerously low stocks during the slower months.

Calculating the Number of Weeks Supply

CONCEPT:

Number of weeks supply = Weeks ÷ Desired turnover

PROBLEM:

Department #32 has a planned stock turnover of 4.0 for the six-month period. Determine the number of weeks supply needed to achieve the desired turnover.

SOLUTION:

Number of weeks supply = $\dfrac{26 \text{ weeks (6 months)}}{4.0 \text{ turnover}}$

Number of weeks supply = 6.5

Finding Planned Stock, Given Turnover, and Weekly Rate of Sales

CONCEPT:

Planned stock = Average weekly sales × Number of weeks supply

PROBLEM:

A department has an average weekly sales rate of $9,800 and a planned turnover of 4.0 for the six-month period. Calculate the amount of stock to be carried.

SOLUTION:

Step 1: Find the number of weeks supply given the turnover and the supply period.

$$\text{Number of weeks supply} = \frac{26 \text{ weeks (6 months)}}{4.0 \text{ turnover}}$$

Number of weeks supply = 6.5

Step 2: Find planned stock given the average weekly sales and the number of weeks supply.

Planned stock = $ 9,800 Average weekly sales × 6.5 No. of weeks supply

Planned stock = $63,700

For assignments for the previous section, see practice problems 27–30.

Setting Beginning of the Month Stock Figures by Basic Stock Method

Another approach to balancing stocks and sales is the **basic stock method,** which is the average inventory for the period. This average inventory is derived simply from the planned sales and turnover. For example, if the anticipated six-month sales total $960,000 and a turnover of 2 is desired for the season, average inventory can be calculated by applying the formula:

$$\frac{\text{Sales}}{\text{Turnover}} = \frac{\$960,000}{2} = \$480,000 \text{ Average inventory}$$

This technique presumes that the retailer will begin each month with a minimum amount of basic stock that remains constant regardless of the monthly sales to be achieved. Generally, it is best to apply this basic stock (i.e., fixed quantity of stock maintained throughout the season) when the annual turnover rate is 6 or less because using it with higher stock-turn merchandise would result in unrealistic basic stocks.

Calculating the Average Monthly Sales

Planned sales

February	$110,000
March	150,000
April	160,000
May	180,000
June	210,000
July	+150,000
Total Sales	$960,000 ÷ 6 = $160,000 Average monthly sales

Finding a Basic Stock Given the Average Monthly Sales and the Average Inventory

The average inventory minus the average monthly sales produces a basic stock at retail. For example:

Average inventory	=	$480,000
− Average monthly sales	=	−160,000
Basic stock	=	$320,000

Finding a BOM Stock When a Basic Stock and Planned Sales for the Month Are Known

The calculated basic stock figure is added to each month's planned sales to determine the BOM amount for the month.

CONCEPT:

BOM stock = Basic stock + Planned sales for the month.

PROBLEM:

In an accessories department that has planned a turnover of 4 for the Fall season, the estimated sales are as follows:

August	$28,000	November	$36,000
September	30,000	December	40,000
October	32,000	January	26,000

Calculate the BOM stocks using the basic stock method.

SOLUTION:

Step 1: Determine average monthly sales.

August	$ 28,000
September	30,000
October	32,000
November	36,000
December	40,000
January	+ 26,000
Total for the season	$192,000 ÷ 6 = $32,000

Average monthly sales = $32,000

Step 2: Calculate average inventory.

Average inventory = $192,000 Sales ÷ 4 Turnover = $48,000

Step 3: Find basic stock.

Basic stock at retail =	Average inventory	$48,000
	− Average monthly sales	−32,000
	Basic stock =	$16,000

Step 4: Calculate BOM stock by adding basic stock to monthly planned sales.

BOM STOCK =	*Monthly sales*		*Basic stock*		*BOM stock*
August	$28,000	+	$16,000	=	$44,000
September	30,000	+	16,000	=	46,000
October	32,000	+	16,000	=	48,000
November	36,000	+	16,000	=	52,000
December	40,000	+	16,000	=	56,000
January	26,000	+	16,000	=	42,000

For assignments for the previous section, see practice problems 31–33.

Planning Markdowns

In dollar planning, markdowns are important because they reduce the total value of the stock available for sale. Careful planning of markdowns helps reduce the amount of markdowns taken, which helps increase net profit figures. The amount of planned markdowns to be taken is expressed both in dollars and as a percentage of planned sales. Because the dollar markdowns vary greatly, the percentage data is more significant for comparison between past and present performance. The percentage of markdowns also varies with different lines of merchandise, different months, and different seasons. The planned markdown figure is usually based on a normal amount determined from experience. Typical markdown percentages by department are available for industry comparison, as illustrated in Figure 28.[4]

Figure 28. Typical Markdown Percentages (Including Employee Discounts)

Women's Footwear—	19.4%	Boys' Clothing—	21.8%
Fine Jewelry & Watches—	5.6%	Small Appliances—	15.7%
Infants & Toddlers—	22.9%	Cosmetics & Toiletries—	1.9%

[4]Current figures from FOR/MOR 1998 Edition, National Retail Federation. These figures represent performance at the time of publication and should not be construed to be ideal.

Figure 29. Monthly Markdowns (% of Monthly Total Company Net Owned Sales) for Fiscal Year 1997

Feb	Mar	Apr	May	June	July	Aug	Sept	Oct	Nov	Dec	Jan
13.88	10.74	10.93	7.87	12.57	17.88	15.73	8.60	10.43	10.16	15.95	17.54

It is common when planning markdowns for a season to:

Step 1: Set the total markdown amount (stated as a percentage of total season's sales) for the entire period by:

(a) Reviewing and analyzing past markdown performance for the same period and for the entire period under consideration.

(b) Considering factors that may effect a change in markdowns.

Step 2: Convert the planned markdown percentage of sales to a total dollar figure for the season.

Step 3: Apportion total dollar planned markdowns by month. (Note that the distribution of monthly markdown goals does not mean necessarily that markdowns and sales will be in the same proportion during each of the months of the season.) Figure 29 illustrates store-wide monthly markdown percentages.

EXAMPLE:

Last year, net sales for the season in the swimwear department were $100,000. The total amount of markdowns taken during the entire period totaled $5,000. The buyer, upon reviewing the performance of the department and in preparation for planning markdowns for the same period this year, decided the $5,000 markdown figure taken previously was normal and compared favorably with standard markdown percentages established for this type of merchandise. Consequently, last year's dollar markdown amount was converted to a percentage:

$$\frac{\text{Last year's markdown}}{\text{Last year's net sales}} = \frac{\$ 5,000}{\$100,000} = 5\% \text{ Markdowns}$$

The total planned sales figure established by the buyer for the season under consideration was set at $110,000. Because a repetition of the percentage of markdowns was desired for the forthcoming season, the dollar amount of markdowns to be taken was determined by:

$110,000 Planned sales × 5% Planned markdowns = $5,500 Planned total markdown for the season

The amount of $5,500 would then be apportioned by dollars to the individual months of the period.

Planning Markups

Although markup planning and calculations are discussed in Unit III, it is necessary to understand that after the initial markup has been carefully planned, the buyer will have to constantly manipulate the actual markup to date in relation to the markup on additional purchases for the season to obtain the planned seasonal markup percentage. To "protect" profitability, the gross profit figure, including an estimated shortage amount, can be calculated easily as in the following example, which shows the facts that should be considered:

(1) For the Spring season, a department has planned:
- Sales @ $2,000,000
- Markdowns @ $ 200,000 (10%)
- Shortages @ $ 40,000 (2%).

(2) The department came into the period under consideration with an opening inventory at retail of $500,000, and a cumulative markup for the period of 52%.

(3) A closing inventory of $500,000 at retail is projected for the end of the Spring period.

(4) Management projects a desired gross margin of 48.5% for the Spring period.

(5) Based on a 48.5% gross margin, the cumulative markup (stock + purchases) is calculated:

$$\text{Cumulative MU\%} = \frac{48.5\% \text{ GM} + 12\% \text{ Red (10\% MDs} + 2\% \text{ SH)}}{100\% \text{ Sales} + 12\% \text{ Reductions}}$$

$$= \frac{60.5}{112}$$

$$= 54\%$$

(6) The markup percentage required on new purchases to meet desired goals is determined by the following method:

	Retail	Cost	Markup %
$2,000,000 Net Sales	$2,740,000	($1,260,400)	54
+ 200,000 Markdowns		($2,740,000	
+ 40,000 Shortages		× 46%)	
+ 500,000 Closing Retail Inventory			
= 2,740,000 TOTAL MDSE Requirements			
− Opening inventory	− 500,000	− 240,000	52
		↓	
		(500,000 × 48%)	
New purchases	= $2,240,000	$1,020,400	54.4

Markup % on new purchases is

$$= \begin{array}{l} \$2,240,000 \text{ Retail} \\ -1,020,400 \text{ Cost} \\ \hline 1,219,600 \text{ Markup} \end{array}$$

$$= \frac{\$1,219,600 \text{ Markup}}{2,240,000 \text{ Retail}}$$

$$= 54.446 \text{ or } 54.4\%$$

Given:

Dollar sales (from plan)	=	$2,000,000
Dollar markdown (from plan) (10%)	=	200,000
Anticipated dollar shortage	=	40,000

Shortage % × Total planned dollar sales	=	$ 40,000 (2% × 2,000,000)
Planned Markup % on stock + Purchases		= 54.0%
Cost or complement % on planned stock + Purchases = 46.0%		

Cost of planned sales:

Planned markdown = $200,000 × .46%	= $	92,00
Planned shortage = 40,000 × .46%	=	18,400
Planned sales = $2,000,000 × .46%	= +	920,000
Total	=	$1,030,400
Planned $ sales	=	$2,000,000
Cost of planned sales	=	−1,030,400
Planned $ gross profit	=	$ 969,600
Planned gross profit %	=	$ 969,600
		2,000,000
	=	48.5%

For an assignment for the previous section, see practice problem 34.

Planned Purchases—Planned Receipts

One objective of planning is to assist the buyer in proper timing and in purchasing the correct amounts of goods. Therefore, when the planned sales, stocks, and markdowns have been determined, the amount of monthly purchases is automatically calculated by a formula. **Planned purchases,** which is more accurately termed **planned receipts,** refers to the dollar amount of merchandise that can be brought into stock during a given period. Store reports frequently identify these figures as receipts. (See Figures 30 and 31.) Generally, purchases are preplanned at retail value for each month and then converted, by formula, to a cost figure by applying the planned markup.

Calculating Planned Monthly Purchases at Retail

CONCEPT:

Planned monthly purchases   = Planned EOM stock
at retail
                        + Planned sales for month

                        + Planned markdowns for month

                        = Total merchandise requirements

                        − Planned BOM stock

                        = Planned purchase amount

PROBLEM:

From the following planned figures for the lingerie department, calculate the planned purchase amount for June:

Planned stock June 1	$ 38,000
Planned sales for June	100,000
Planned markdowns for June	5,000
Planned stock for July 1	40,000

SOLUTION:

Planned June sales		$100,000
+ Planned EOM stock (July 1)		40,000
+ Planned June markdowns		+ 5,000
Total merchandise requirements	=	$145,000
− Planned BOM stock (June 1)		− 38,000
Planned monthly retail purchases		$107,000

Converting Retail Planned Purchases to Cost

The planned purchase figure at retail must be established first before the planned purchase figure at cost is determined by conversion.

CONCEPT:

Planned purchase at cost = Planned retail purchases (R) × (100% − Planned markup MU%)

PROBLEM:

The planned retail purchases for June were $107,000, and the planned MU% was 41.5%. Calculate the planned purchase amount at cost.

SOLUTION:

$$\text{Planned purchases} = \$107,000 \text{ Pl. re. pur.} \times (100\% - 41.5\% \text{ Pl. MU\%})$$
$$= \$107,000 \times 58.5\%$$
$$= \$ 62,595$$

Planned Purchases at Cost = $62,595

Based on the above examination of the procedures, elements, and computations that relate to the creation of a dollar plan, analyze Figures 30–34, which are examples of typical six-month seasonal dollar merchandise plans. The formats differ, yet there are certain common features. These forms are included for familiarization with their differences and similarities. In large stores, the statistical departments furnish this kind of historical data to assist the buyers and the divisional merchandise managers in making decisions on which the required purchases—currently referred to as planned receipts—are calculated. It is common for a general merchandise manager and/or controller to contribute to the planning function.

Figure 30. Worksheet for Annual Merchandise Plan

$(000)														
SALES ($)	FEB.	MARCH	APRIL	MAY	JUNE	JULY	SPRING	AUG.	SEPT.	OCT.	NOV.	DEC.	JAN.	FALL	ANNUAL
00 PLAN							20500								
99 ACT.	1817	3396	3476	3066	3041	2070	16865	2303						2303	19168
99 PLAN	1643	3265	3207	3238	3034	1608	15996	2231	4095	3071	3161	4233	1681	18471	34467
98 ACT.	1427	2619	2550	2701	2742	1438	13478	1766	3157	2322	2112	3077	1457	13891	27368
97 ACT.	1224	2250	2065	2366	2447	1379	11730	1725	2536	1842	1847	2620	959	11530	23260
96 ACT.	1115	2018	1947	1977	1951	1170	10177	1451	2159	1412	1377	1988	833	9221	19399

SALES % CHG.	FEB.	MARCH	APRIL	MAY	JUNE	JULY	SPRING	AUG.	SEPT.	OCT.	NOV.	DEC.	JAN.	FALL	ANNUAL
96P/92A															
95A/91A	27.3	29.6	36.3	13.5	10.9	43.9	25.1	30.4	−100.0	−100.0	−100.0	−100.0	−100.0	−83.4	−30.0
94P/91A	15.1	24.7	25.8	19.9	10.6	11.9	18.7	26.3	29.7	32.3	49.7	37.6	15.3	33.0	25.9
93A/90A	16.6	16.4	23.5	14.2	12.1	4.3	14.9	2.4	24.5	26.0	14.3	17.4	52.0	20.5	17.7
92A/89A	9.8	11.5	6.1	19.7	25.4	17.9	15.3	18.9	17.5	30.4	34.1	31.8	15.1	25.0	19.9

EOM STOCK	FEB.	MARCH	APRIL	MAY	JUNE	JULY	AVG. SPRING	AUG.	SEPT.	OCT.	NOV.	DEC.	JAN.	AVG. FALL	AVG. ANNUAL
00 PLAN							10513								
99 ACT.	7449	9578	9714	8979	8518	7581	8337	10555							
99 PLAN	8971	9703	9586	8712	7410	6950	8241	11613	12270	11810	11256	9000	8431	10190	9390
98 ACT.	7204	8802	9009	8225	6474	6105	7339	7577	8098	8536	8138	5959	6538	7279	7401
97 ACT.	5389	5986	6182	6056	5261	5140	5477	6122	6120	6460	6692	5368	5551	5922	5742
96 ACT.	5349	6188	5614	4691	4069	4481	4916	4578	5285	5031	4998	4057	4323	4679	4822

EOM – WKS OF SUPPLY	FEB.	MARCH	APRIL	MAY	JUNE	JULY	TURNOVER SPRING	AUG.	SEPT.	OCT.	NOV.	DEC.	JAN.	T.O. FALL	T.O. ANNUAL
00 PLAN							1.95								
99 ACT.	9.8	13.0	15.7	14.9	13.1	10.5	2.02	13.3							
99 PLAN	12.1	13.6	16.1	15.2	12.4	9.8	1.94	14.5	17.3	18.1	17.7	14.9	12.1	1.81	3.67
98 ACT.	12.0	15.2	17.6	16.6	13.2	11.0	1.84	13.0	15.0	18.1	16.6	13.0	10.5	1.91	3.70
97 ACT.	10.8	11.2	13.0	14.0	12.3	10.9	2.14	12.8	12.6	15.9	16.2	13.6	11.4	1.95	4.05
96 ACT.	11.8	14.1	14.4	13.3	11.4	11.5	2.07	11.9	15.4	15.7	15.1	12.4	10.6	1.97	4.02

NET RECEIPTS	FEB.	MARCH	APRIL	MAY	JUNE	JULY	SPRING	AUG.	SEPT.	OCT.	NOV.	DEC.	JAN.	FALL	ANNUAL
00 PLAN															
99 ACT.	2728	5525	3611	2331	2580	1133	17909	5276						5276	23185
99 PLAN															
98 ACT.	3080	4217	2756	1918	992	1069	14032	3238	3677	2760	1714	898	2036	14323	28355
97 ACT.	2290	2846	2261	2240	1652	1258	12547	2707	2534	2183	2079	1296	1142	11942	24489
96 ACT.	2442	2857	1373	1054	1330	1581	10637	1549	2866	1158	1345	1047	1099	9064	19700

MARKDOWN ($)	FEB.	MARCH	APRIL	MAY	JUNE	JULY	SPRING	AUG.	SEPT.	OCT.	NOV.	DEC.	JAN.	FALL	ANNUAL
00 PLAN															
99 ACT.	395	380	456	773	797	448	3249	452						452	3700
99 PLAN															
98 ACT.	165	533	342	628	743	122	2533	314	488	479	578	996	31	2885	5418
97 ACT.	250	233	294	228	649	162	1816	253	365	489	362	1002	90	2560	4376
96 ACT.	216	216	350	252	504	292	1830	168	223	315	366	450	204	1725	3555

MARKDOWN %	FEB.	MARCH	APRIL	MAY	JUNE	JULY	SPRING	AUG.	SEPT.	OCT.	NOV.	DEC.	JAN.	FALL	ANNUAL
00 PLAN															
99 ACT.	21.7	11.2	13.1	25.2	26.2	21.6	19.3	19.6						19.6	19.3
99 PLAN															
98 ACT.	11.6	20.3	13.4	23.2	27.1	8.5	18.8	17.8	15.5	20.6	27.4	32.4	2.1	20.8	19.8
97 ACT.	20.4	10.3	14.3	9.6	26.5	11.7	15.5	14.7	14.4	26.6	19.6	38.2	9.4	22.2	19.8
96 ACT.	19.4	10.7	18.0	12.8	25.8	25.0	18.0	11.5	10.3	22.3	26.6	22.6	24.5	18.7	18.3

| A13 – RTW C DRESSES |
| A13 – RTW C DRESSES |

Figure 31. Six-Month Merchandise Plan (By Store)

SALES

STORE	FEBRUARY PLAN	FEBRUARY L Y	MARCH PLAN	MARCH L Y	APRIL PLAN	APRIL L Y	MAY PLAN	MAY L Y	JUNE PLAN	JUNE L Y	JULY PLAN	JULY L Y	TOTAL SEASON PLAN	TOTAL SEASON L Y	STORE
01	27.8	26.5	43.9	40.4	57.6	55.0	79.0	75.5	46.1	43.5	26.8	25.4	281.2	266.3	01
02	43.8	42.3	59.5	55.8	84.1	81.3	120.1	116.0	61.2	58.4	39.2	37.9	407.9	391.7	02
03	44.3	42.8	56.7	53.6	84.7	81.8	123.2	118.9	69.3	65.7	43.8	42.4	422.0	405.3	03
05	14.9	14.1	23.8	22.2	33.2	31.7	48.8	46.6	27.5	26.3	15.6	15.0	163.8	155.9	05
07	10.8	10.5	15.0	14.3	18.6	18.1	29.3	28.3	17.7	17.1	9.8	9.4	101.2	97.7	07
08	18.8	18.1	32.1	30.3	39.1	37.7	59.4	57.2	33.9	32.6	20.3	19.4	203.6	195.3	08
09	10.8	10.3	13.9	12.9	19.0	18.2	31.9	30.5	20.3	19.3	11.0	10.5	106.9	101.7	09
12	23.3	22.2	27.3	25.5	47.4	43.8	77.5	72.0	44.5	41.3	31.1	28.9	251.1	233.7	12
13	28.0	26.2	34.1	31.6	60.1	56.1	96.3	89.7	52.8	49.4	31.2	29.1	302.5	282.1	13
14	7.3	6.6	8.4	7.5	10.5	9.5	21.8	19.5	13.3	12.0	6.5	5.9	67.8	61.0	14
15	10.1	8.7	12.5	10.4	20.2	16.9	35.6	30.7	24.9	22.2	16.1	14.6	119.4	103.5	15
16	17.2	15.8	21.5	19.5	32.1	29.5	52.8	48.2	30.2	27.9	17.3	15.9	171.1	156.8	16
17	1.4	1.4	2.2	2.2	3.7	3.6	5.8	5.7	4.3	4.2	4.1	4.0	21.5	21.1	17
18	12.0	11.2	15.1	13.7	24.9	23.3	43.9	40.1	18.4	17.0	15.2	14.0	129.5	119.3	18
19	14.3	13.6	16.9	15.6	23.0	21.7	40.3	38.0	25.5	24.0	14.7	13.8	134.7	126.7	19
20	10.8	9.7	14.6	12.9	14.4	13.4	34.5	31.4	23.7	21.6	10.9	10.0	108.9	99.0	20
21	6.1	5.5	11.6	10.2	8.9	8.3	17.9	16.3	17.0	15.5	9.9	9.0	71.4	64.8	21
TOT	301.7	285.5	409.1	378.6	581.5	549.9	918.1	864.6	530.6	498.0	323.5	305.2	3064.5	2881.8	TOT

STOCK

STORE	FEBRUARY PLAN	FEBRUARY L Y	MARCH PLAN	MARCH L Y	APRIL PLAN	APRIL L Y	MAY PLAN	MAY L Y	JUNE PLAN	JUNE L Y	JULY PLAN	JULY L Y	TOTAL SEASON PLAN	TOTAL SEASON L Y	STORE
01	58.0	42.8	72.0	50.1	88.0	73.4	116.0	99.2	80.0	77.7	72.0	59.8	69.0	51.6	01
02	94.0	95.5	99.0	70.6	121.0	94.8	159.0	152.3	110.0	106.6	99.0	87.3	95.0	63.1	02
03	79.0	73.3	108.0	63.5	132.0	110.0	174.0	169.6	120.0	146.9	108.0	105.9	102.2	73.1	03
05	36.0	24.3	54.0	37.6	66.0	49.6	87.0	41.8	60.0	46.0	54.0	30.3	51.0	25.0	05
07	29.0	19.5	36.0	29.4	44.0	42.0	58.0	39.4	40.0	38.5	36.0	31.4	27.0	20.9	07
08	44.0	31.3	63.0	33.8	77.0	49.7	102.0	56.7	70.0	47.7	63.0	48.9	58.0	35.5	08
09	29.0	23.0	45.0	30.5	55.0	48.6	73.0	44.5	50.0	53.8	45.0	36.2	43.0	20.3	09
12	65.0	49.3	76.0	42.6	94.0	70.5	123.0	115.0	85.0	87.5	77.0	47.9	74.0	40.0	12
13	72.0	53.0	81.0	50.0	99.0	67.1	130.0	107.7	90.0	72.7	81.0	60.0	77.0	54.7	13
14	15.0	12.2	27.0	21.6	33.0	21.2	44.0	24.3	30.0	25.5	27.0	26.2	26.0	16.9	14
15	33.0	18.1	41.0	25.8	49.0	38.1	65.0	40.9	45.0	49.7	40.0	37.1	38.0	29.2	15
16	44.0	34.3	54.0	35.5	66.0	53.1	87.0	73.9	60.0	63.7	54.0	49.0	52.0	43.2	16
17	7.0	8.6	9.0	11.0	11.0	13.8	15.0	21.5	10.0	16.8	9.0	13.7	9.0	5.7	17
18	33.0	25.3	41.0	39.7	50.0	50.4	65.0	63.9	45.0	59.8	41.0	42.5	39.0	31.7	18
19	40.0	26.0	40.0	33.5	49.0	46.1	65.0	69.7	45.0	71.9	40.0	38.4	39.0	33.8	19
20	29.0	24.0	32.0	31.4	39.0	43.6	51.0	51.5	35.0	50.3	32.0	35.9	30.0	31.8	20
21	18.0	12.8	22.0	37.1	27.0	35.8	36.0	28.2	25.0	38.6	22.0	26.8	21.0	15.8	21
TOT	725.0	573.3	900.0	643.7	1100.0	907.8	1450.0	1200.1	1000.0	1053.7	900.0	777.3	850.0	592.3	TOT

	FEBRUARY		MARCH		APRIL		MAY		JUNE		JULY		TOTAL SEASON		
PL. RCPTS.	476.7		609.1		931.5		468.1		430.6		273.5		3189.5		PL. RCPTS.
*MD	125.0	126.3	70.0	52.0	113.0	117.2	285.0	264.6	172.0	195.6	45.0	32.3	810.0	788.0	*MD

TOTAL SEASON	PLAN	L Y		PLAN	L Y	DEPT. NUMBER:_____
MARKUP %	58.0	57.4	GM & DISC %	50.6	49.9	DEPT. NAME: MS. BUDGET COORDINATES
MD & ED %	26.9	27.8	TURNOVER	3.1	3.5	BUYER:_____

*(EXCLUDING ED)

Figure 32. Six-Month Merchandise Plan

		AUGUST SALES	BOM STOCK	SEPTEMBER SALES	BOM STOCK	OCTOBER SALES	BOM STOCK	NOVEMBER SALES	BOM STOCK	DECEMBER SALES	BOM STOCK	JANUARY SALES	BOM STOCK	SEASON SALES	AVER STOCK	FEBRUARY SEASON T.O.	BOM STOCK
CHAIN	LY	365.8	576	348.8	790	306.4	704	376.5	612	310.0	607	130.9	278	1836.4	595	3.09	321
	PLAN																
T.O.	LY	.63		1.04		1.48		2.08		2.59		3.09		3.09			
	PLAN																
O.T.B.	LY																
	PLAN																
M.D.$	LY	64.8		46.3		37.8		70.8		59.2		75.1		354.0			
	PLAN																
M.D.%	LY	17.72		13.36		12.33		18.80		19.10		57.40		19.28			
	PLAN																
MU: PUR	LY	50.40		49.73		48.80		50.07		44.64		48.61		49.64			
	PLAN																
MU% S&P	LY	50.12		49.69		49.20		49.49		49.26		49.07		49.07			
	PLAN																
SHORT%	LY	2.07		2.04		2.08		2.18		2.15		2.18		2.11			
	PLAN																
G.P.$	LY	147.2		143.6		124.3		149.9		115.5		20.6		701.0			
	PLAN																
G.P.%	LY	40.24		41.40		40.55		39.80		37.25		15.76		38.17			
	PLAN																
BEG SEAS MU% STK	LY	49.80															
	PLAN																

As a guide to merchandising, the real value of dollar planning is that the figures projected for each element reflect goals that are reasonably attainable. Because the buyer is responsible for interpreting and achieving the projected figures, it is essential that the buyer be involved in the preparation of the figures. Also, a buyer who has helped to set these guidelines will be more inclined to use them. Once completed, a dollar plan must be adjusted to actual conditions and results during the season under consideration.

Adjusting the Planned Purchases

During the season, as the merchandising activities are performed, the actual re-sults are checked against the planned figures. Sometimes this reveals the need to adjust the original planned figures for either a month or for the balance of the season, because of a deviation from the planned sales thus far or because of a change in circumstances. For example, if sales and/or markdowns are actually larger than planned, purchases must be greater than planned to achieve the level of stock planned. Conversely, if these factors are actually less than planned, a downward revision of purchases is required. Figure 34 illustrates the variation between planned figures and actual results.

For assignments for the previous section, see practice problems 35–42.

Figure 33. Total Corporate Six-Month Plan

SPRING 2000	**Total Corporate Six-Month C-1 Plan**																									AUG	TOTAL	AVE.		RECEIPTS	
CLASS		FEB				MAR				APR				MAY				JUN				JUL									
		BOM	SALE	MD	REC	BOM	SALE	MD	REC	BOM	SALE	MD	REC	BOM	SALE	MD	REC	BOM	SALE	MD	REC	BOM	SALE	MD	REC	BOM	SALE	STOCK	TURN	RETAIL	LCC
EARS R.PLAN						548			120				120				126				127				212						
ACT.		533	58	42	115																										
P.PLAN		533	58	42	115	548	100	25	120	543	105	25	120	539	135	35	126	504	125	35	135	559	180	50	130	459	703	526	1.34	841	210
LY		371	60	4	66	365	90	4	140	398	85	8	140	406	113	5	207	564	99	20	232	534	145	9	106	323	592	423	1.40	867	217
STRAN R.PLAN						296			37								55				84				73						
ACT.		268	31	2	61																										
P.PLAN		268	31	2	61	296	50	10	40	276	55	10	40	268	70	15	57	268	60	10	85	296	90	20	64	250	356	275	1.30	405	101
LY		301	34	0	0	256	48	2	47	245	50	2	47	259	69	0	83	282	61	2	114	308	89	0	68	241	351	270	1.30	418	105
FASHI BASIC R.PLAN						239			24				40				53				80	202	90	20	183	275					
ACT.		170	21	3	93																										
P.PLAN		170	21	3	93	239	45	10	24	208	45	10	40	193	55	10	54	182	50	10	85	207	75	15	66	183	291	197	1.47	362	91
LY		119	18	3	9	103	36	3	59	118	31	3	91	165	46	4	130	229	38	6	32	206	50	3	34	119	219	151	1.45	355	89
COLO R.PLAN						93			117				117				23				0				0						
ACT.		114	17	4	0																										
P.PLAN		114	17	4	0	93	15	5	117	190	20	10	23	188	30	10	23	148	30	10	0	124	35	10	16	99	147	137	1.08	176	44
LY		114	24	10	59	143	34	3	135	240	39	16	55	248	49	16	55	230	39	8	40	266	52	6	79	266	237	215	1.10	415	104
GOLD R.PLAN						160			79				43				0				0				16						
ACT.		170	8	2	0																										
P.PLAN		170	8	2	0	160	25	10	79	204	25	10	44	218	20	10	0	188	25	10	0	168	40	15	15	143	143	179	0.80	168	42
LY		26	5	0	42	58	16	1	41	81	20	1	107	160	11	14	22	145	19	3	22	223	43	2	106	116	114	116	0.99	361	90
FASHI R.PLAN						261			102				214				60				60				64						
ACT.		172	26	3	118																										
P.PLAN		172	26	3	118	261	60	15	98	284	50	20	210	424	60	20	68	412	55	20	60	397	75	30	40	322	326	325	1.00	594	149
LY		301	33	6	38	291	59	8	122	301	52	10	86	304	61	11	112	315	42	12	44	283	42	11	16	224	289	288	1.00	418	105

FIGURE 34. Purchase Planning

	Planned	
Planned retail purchases for October based on *planned* figures	$20,000	Planned Sales
	+42,000	Planned E O M Stock
	+ 500	Planned Markdowns
	$62,500	Total Merchandise Requirements
	–40,000	Planned B O M Stock
PLANNED RETAIL PURCHASES—	$22,500	
	Revised	
	$22,000	Revised Sales Plan
Planned retail purchases for October based on *revised* figures	+42,000	Planned E O M Stock
	+ 500	Revised Markdowns
	$64,500	Total Merchandise Requirements
	–40,000	Revised B O M Stock
ADJUSTED RETAIL PLANNED PURCHASES—	$24,500	

Explanation of Merchandise Statistics Report (Figure 35)

The elements that affect profit are included in this report as well as the status of the size of the stock, and sales trends. It is a guide to the six-month projections, shows the current performance, and enables the buyer to make necessary adjustments. The annotated information on Figure 35 is numbered (1) to (8), and the following information corresponds to those numbers:

(1) WEEK ENDING and WEEK NO.: Example: FEB 05 is WEEK NO. 01.

(2) NET SALES (in 100's): This category is divided into the following two sections:

    (a) WEEKLY: Figures that show the sales of TY, PLAN, and LY, example:

        WEEK ENDING FEBRUARY 05

TY	$62.5
PLAN	68.8
LY	62.7

    (b) CUMULATIVE: Cumulative sales for the period for TY, PLAN, LY, and % CHG, for existing stores, but also excluding any new store(s), example:

        WEEK ENDING FEBRUARY 12

TY	$122.7
PLAN	123.8
LY	123.5
% CHG	– .7%
EXCLUDE NEW STORE:	– 4.6%

(3) MARK ON % CUMULATIVE SALES: Mark on of all merchandise handled, season to date before the adjustments of cash discounts for TY and LY, example:

        WEEK ENDING FEBRUARY 05

Opening: TY	38.2%
LY	37.8%

Figure 35. Merchandise Statistics Report

MERCHANDISE STATISTICS REPORT

CURRENT WEEK — SALES, MARKDOWNS, STOCK, GROSS MARGIN DATA ESTIMATED

DEPT _____ SPRING 19___

WEEK ENDING	WK NO	(2a) WEEKLY TY	PLAN	LY	%CHG	(2b) CUM PLAN	CUM LY	%CHG	EXCL NEW STORE %CHG	CUM TY	(3) MARK ON CUM % TY	LY	(4) MD $ TY	MD $ LY	MD % TY	MD % LY	(5) STOCK PLAN	STOCK TY	STOCK LY	(6) PLATFORM TY	LY	(7) OUTSTD ORD TY	LY
OPENING											38.2	37.8					1400.0	1748.3	1455.1				
FEB 05	01	62.5	68.8	62.7	-.4	68.8	62.7	-.4	-3.6	62.5	33.2	37.3	3.6	6.6	5.7	10.5	1450.0	1954.2	1498.8	74.7	118.0	394.5	126.9
FEB 12	02	60.2	55.0	60.6	-.7	123.8	123.5	-.7	-4.6	122.7	36.3	37.1	27.6	10.2	27.5	8.3	1450.0	1865.6	1544.7	197.9	101.9	360.2	131.6
FEB 19	03	86.4	55.0	48.3	23.1	178.8	189.8	23.1	18.6	209.1	36.2	37.0	54.8	-47.1	26.2	27.7	1450.0	1853.7	1601.3	105.5	48.5	175.3	127.3
FEB 26	04	69.5	66.2	63.2	19.6	245.0	233.0	19.6	16.0	278.0	37.6	37.0	76.3	-29.5	27.4	12.6	1450.0	1888.1	1598.4	125.9	77.7	106.7	153.2
PLAN 4					5.2			5.2	-.3		37.8	37.8	16.0		7.8								
MAR 05	05	63.1	55.0	41.5	24.5	360.8	274.5	24.5	18.1	341.7	37.8	36.9	55.7	-1.2	16.3	-2.6	1500.0	1901.9	1816.5	62.1	82.0	159.3	121.3
MAR 12	06	52.1	55.0	43.9	26.7	355.0	316.5	26.7	17.0	393.6	37.7	37.0	82.8	54.0	16.0	10.7	1500.0	1853.5	1809.2	13.9	81.3	204.9	127.0
MAR 19	07	55.2	55.0	47.6	22.7	410.0	369.9	22.7	16.1	449.0	37.8	37.0	122.8	73.7	27.4	20.1	1500.0	1888.7	1554.5	122.3	29.5	156.4	330.9
MAR 26	08	62.4	75.0	76.9	15.6	485.8	442.8	15.6	6.9	511.5	37.1	37.1	38.8	78.0	60.1	17.6	1500.0	1913.1	1524.7	7.3	52.2	164.9	340.2
APR 02	09	48.1	63.5	68.8	9.0	546.5	511.6	9.0	2.8	557.5	37.8	37.2	33.4	91.2	8.2	17.8	1500.0	1870.2	1593.2	4.4	150.5	259.8	352.2
PLAN 9					7.2			7.2	-.1		37.6	37.6	34.6		6.2								
APR 09	10		60.0	51.5		688.5	583.5				37.0	37.0	169.6	188.9	19.4	18.8	1600.0		1461.2	CUR ORD	-58.5	215.1	422.2
APR 16	11		48.0	40.5		656.5	610.5				37.1	37.1	114.8	153.7	18.8	15.6	1600.0		1515.5	NXT ORD	105.4	10.0	416.2
APR 23	12		85.0	44.8		721.5	654.5				36.9	36.9	144.2	151.0	22.8	14.5	1600.0		1458.0	FUT ORD	18.9	54.5	459.9
APR 30	13		85.2	92.2	7.8	604.7	746.7	2.0			38.1	36.9	173.7	168.3	23.3	14.9	1600.0		1401.0		64.5		193.2
PLAN 13													49.0		6.1								
MAY 07	14		145.1	151.4		944.8	898.1					37.1		188.9		18.8	1550.0		1281.2		26.7		234.0
MAY 14	15		75.0	71.0		1824.6	989.7					36.9		153.7		15.6	1550.0		1383.7		160.8		517.1
MAY 21	16		95.0	71.2		1119.8	1040.9					36.7		151.0		14.5	1550.0		1483.4		169.5		497.3
MAY 28	17		100.0	90.5	7.8	1219.8	1131.4	2.0			36.2	36.9	63.6	168.3	5.2	14.9	1550.0		1561.7		172.5		603.4
PLAN 17																							
JUN 04	18		80.0	76.1		1299.8	1204.6					36.9		182.9		15.2	1500.0		1615.5		142.0		530.6
JUN 11	19		105.8	181.5		1465.6	1306.1					37.6		181.8		13.9	1500.0		1699.1		162.8		405.1
JUN 18	20		84.0	75.0		1489.6	1361.0					36.9		188.7		13.7	1500.0		1700.4		76.2		494.0
JUN 25	21		85.0	76.6		1572.6	1457.6					36.9		172.7		11.8	1500.0		1799.2		148.7		200.6
JLY 02	22		75.0	73.5	7.6	1647.6	1531.0	1.8			36.4	36.8	75.0	167.9	4.6	11.0	1500.0		1777.9		45.0		251.0
PLAN 22																							
JLY 09	23		60.0	88.8		1707.6	1599.4					36.8		140.1		8.8	1500.0		1722.8		-16.1		266.9
JLY 16	24		55.0	47.7		1762.6	1647.0					36.4		141.3		8.6	1500.0		1622.4		-38.1		289.9
JLY 23	25		60.0	52.6		1822.6	1699.8					36.7		128.8		7.8	1500.0		1608.5		15.6		368.5
JLY 30	26		54.0	43.8	7.6	1876.6	1743.5	1.8						112.7		6.5	1500.0		1582.5		32.8		402.1
PLAN 26																							

STATISTICS BELOW ON FISCAL MONTH BASIS

	4 WEEKS TY	PLAN	LY	9 WEEKS TY	PLAN	LY	13 WEEKS TY	PLAN	LY	17 WEEKS PLAN	LY	22 WEEKS PLAN	LY	28 WEEKS PLAN	LY
WEEKS SUPPLY				22.0	18.0	20.7							20.7		
GROSS MARKDOWN MMO AFTER SHTG %	17.5	29.7	41.6	30.5	30.6	22.6		30.9	18.8	31.6	24.1	32.2	26.5	32.4	28.7
Disc Earned %	6.6	6.0	4.7	5.6	6.0	6.2		5.6	6.1	5.8	8.1	5.7	5.9	5.7	5.7
Alteration %	.1	.1	.4	.1	.1	.1		.1	.1	.1	.1	.1	.1	.1	.1
Gross Margin %	24.0	35.6	46.2	36.3	36.5	28.7		36.6	25.2	37.3	30.1	37.8	32.3	38.0	34.3
Gross Margin $	67.0	87.3	107.5	200.2	200.2	146.7		294.6	136.2	355.0	340.7	622.8	394.8	713.3	597.8
SELECTIVE DATA															
Cash Disc to BOM V P %	.8	.2	.2			.4		.8	.8	.8	.5	.8	.6		.3
Stock Turn	.2	.2	.2			.3		.2	.5		.7		1.0		1.1
Transactions	123.3		13.3	22.0		22.0			25.6		62.0		84.9		98.6
% Chg	-6.2		-22.3	-22.3		13.3									
Avg Sales Chk	24.70	19.36	19.57	27.49	19.57	19.67		19.67	.6						19.16
Ret % to Gr Sales	8.2	8.1	7.9	7.9	7.8	7.8		7.3					7.3		7.7
Setting Salary		6.8	6.8	4.3	9.0	4.3		9.1	9.0		9.1		9.1		9.6
Direct Pub															
Gr Lineage $	18.2	9.9	16.2	16.2	39.6			58.8		101.7			137.0	140.3	
Rebates $	2.5	2.5	2.5		30.6			67.7		91.5			110.2	119.2	
Net Lineage %	2.7	4.3	1.4	1.4	1.7			1.5		.9			1.2	1.2	
Direct Mail $		4.6	-3.4	-3.4	-5.1			-5.1		-5.3			-2.8	.4	

COST PURCH & DISC EARNED INCL LOAD TO 8.6%

Totals (bottom summary): 7.6 | 1.8 | 36.5 | 84.4 | 4.5 | 20.7

(8)

(4) MARKDOWNS-CUMULATIVE INCLUDING EMPLOYEE ALLOWANCE: Markdowns both in DOLLARS and the % (of change), TY and LY, example:

WEEK ENDING FEBRUARY 05

	DOLLARS	%
TY	$3.6	5.7%
LY	6.6	10.5%

(5) STOCK ON HAND: Merchandise in stock for TY, PLAN, and LY, example:

WEEK ENDING FEBRUARY 05

TY	$ 1954.2
PLAN	1450
LY	1498

(6) PLATFORM RECEIPTS: Merchandise received TY and LY for the reported end of week, example:

WEEK ENDING FEBRUARY 05

TY	$ 74.7
LY	118.0

(7) OUTSTANDING ORDERS: Amount of open orders, example:

WEEK ENDING FEBRUARY 05

TY	$394.5
LY	126.9

(8) STATISTICS BELOW ON FISCAL MONTH BASIS: Comparison of such operational factors that affect ultimate profit as GROSS MARGIN, STOCK TURN, DISC. EARNED, etc., TY over LY, example:

9 WEEKS—GROSS MARGIN MMO After Shortage %

TY	30.5%
PLAN	30.6%
LY	22.6%

Applying the Concepts to Figure 35

CONCEPT:

Buyers use reports to plan future sales and stock levels. Use Figure 35 from "WEEK ENDING DATE FEB 05 TO APR 30," columns "NET SALES-WEEKLY-TY/ PLAN/LY" (2a), and columns "STOCK-ON-HAND TY/PLAN/LY" (5) to answer the following six questions.

1. Calculate the percentage by which current sales in March were above or below planned sales.
2. Calculate the percentage by which current sales in March were above or below last year's sales.
3. Based on this information, how would you evaluate the planned sales for April?
4. What was the opening cumulative mark on % for this department? What percentage change was this over LY?

5. Season to date, which week ending had the largest dollar sales TY? What was the dollar amount of those sales? Which week ending had the best sales increase percentage for the season TY over LY?
6. For both the months of February and March, were the sales TY larger or smaller than PLAN? State the percentage of change for each month.

PRACTICE PROBLEMS

Planning Sales

1. In the children's department, the August sales were planned at $247,500 because of additional promotional events. The actual sales for this month last year were $225,000. What is the percentage increase in planned sales for August of this year?

2. For the Spring period, the handbag department's total seasonal sales volume for last year was $750,000. If there is an 8% increase this year, what is the dollar amount of sales planned?

3. During the month of August, sales for a sporting goods store are planned at $900,000, which is 15% of the planned season's total sales. Calculate the monthly sales for the balance of the season, if sales are planned as follows:

August :	15%	November:	18%
September:	14%	December:	25%
October:	16%	January:	12%

4. A small retailer is planning a 10% reduction in sales due to competition from a major new department store. If last year's sales were $500,000, what sales figure should be planned for this year?

5. After a detailed analysis of sales by classification, the hosiery buyer determined a decline in the knee-hi category. Last year's sales for this category were $75,000. This year the sales for this classification are planned at $60,000. What is the percentage of sales decline?

6. Seasonal sales for last year were $855,000 and this year the merchandise manager planned for a sales increase of 8%. What is the estimated planned dollar sales figure for this year?

7. If actual sales for last year were $855,000 and this year's planned sales are $923,400, calculate the percentage of sales increase for this year.

Calculating Average Retail Stock Turnover and GMROI

8. The net sales in the neckwear department were $240,000, with a stock turnover of 3. Find this department's average stock at retail.

9. What amount of average stock should be carried by a costume jewelry department with net sales of $920,000 for the year and a stock turn of 4?

10. What is the average stock of a department with annual sales of $1,350,000 and an annual stock turn of 4.5?

11. Find the average stock from an activewear department's inventory figures:

BOM January	$ 62,000	BOM July	$120,000
BOM February	64,000	BOM August	78,000
BOM March	70,000	BOM September	78,000
BOM April	74,000	BOM October	68,000
BOM May	88,000	BOM November	64,000
BOM June	100,000	BOM December	60,000
		BOM January	62,000

12. Determine the seasonal stock turnover on the basis of the following information:

	Retail inventory	Sales
Aug. 1	$36,000	$20,000
Sept. 1	68,000	28,000
Oct. 1	60,000	44,000
Nov. 1	40,000	28,000
Dec. 1	28,000	24,000
Jan. 1	28,000	10,000
Jan. 31	18,000	

13. A housewares department has an average inventory of $112,000 at retail, with a stock turnover of 2. What are the department sales for the period?

14. Calculate the yearly turnover using the following figures from an outerwear department:

Gross sales	$497,500
Customer returns	47,500
Inventory 8/1	85,000
Inventory 10/1	105,000
Inventory 12/1	250,000
Inventory 2/1	53,000
Inventory 4/1	90,000
Inventory 6/1	80,000
Inventory 8/1	85,000

15. For the year, a shoe department has net sales of $2,500,000. The average stock carried during this period was $1,000,000. What was the annual rate of stock turn?

16. Departmental gross sales for the year were $220,000 with customer returns of 10%. During the year these inventories were taken:

Date	Inventory value (retail)
January 1	$37,000
April 1	36,500
July 1	41,500
October 1	46,500
Jan. 1 of following year	38,500

Find:

    (a) The average stock for the year.
    (b) The annual rate of turn.

17. The sales for October were $8,000; the stock on October 1 at retail value was $24,000; the stock on October 31 was $28,000. What was the stock turn for the month?

18. The sales in the children's department for the year amounted to $416,000. The stock at the beginning of the year was $120,000 at retail, and for the end of the year, the retail stock figure was $140,000. What was the stock turn for the year?

19. The men's furnishings department had the following performance for the period under consideration:

- 26.1% Gross margin.
- 2.8 Turnover.
- 30.7% Markup.

What GMROI was achieved?

20. The same men's furnishings buyer (in problem 19) made some spectacular purchases for an annual store event that increased the markup to 33.8%, with the other factors being constant. What GMROI resulted from this strategy?

21. Last Fall, the active sportswear department achieved a 45.9% gross margin with a stock turn of 2.1. The markup was 60.3%. During this Fall season, the gross margin was increased to 50.5%. Compare the GMROI performance from last year with this year.

22. The budget sportswear department achieved a 26.1% gross margin and had the same 30.7% markup as the men's furnishings department, with a stock turn of 8. What was the resultant GMROI for this department?

Calculating Stock-Sales Ratios

23. What is the planned stock-sales ratio in the handbag department when beginning of the month stock is planned at $19,000 and planned sales are $9,100?

24. Planned sales in the costume jewelry department for April are $130,000 and the planned stock-sales ratio is 2.4. What should be the stock figure on April 1?

25. The outerwear department buyer decided that a stock-sales ratio of 2.5 for the month of February would be appropriate. If the sales for February were planned at $12,000, how much stock should be carried on February 1?

26. The glove department's stock at the beginning of March was $67,500, with sales for the month at $15,900. What was the stock-sales ratio for March?

Finding Weekly Rate of Sales

27. The hosiery department sells control top pantyhose at the rate of 48 dozen per week at a retail price of $4.50 per pair. Calculate the amount of stock that should be carried to achieve a turnover of 6 for the six-month season in this category.

28. A stationery store has sales of $18,000 per week and a planned turnover of 4 for a six-month period. Calculate the amount of stock that should be carried in this store.

29. A handbag department plans a stock turn at 6.0 for a twelve-month period. What figure represents the number of weeks supply needed to achieve the desired turnover?

30. A knit accessories department has an average weekly sales figure of $14,500 and a planned turnover rate of 3.0 for the six-month period. Calculate the amount of stock to be carried.

Using Basic Stock Method

31. Calculate the basic stock figure of a men's suit department that has annual sales of $1,650,000 and an annual stock turn of 4.0.

32. For May, the gift department had planned sales of $180,000. For the Spring season, the department's planned sales were $900,000, with a planned stock turnover of 3. Determine the BOM figure for May, using the basic stock method.

33. The small leather goods department had planned the following figures for the Fall season:

Planned total sales for season: $102,000
Planned turnover for season: 2
Planned sales for November: $ 26,000

Calculate the November BOM for this department, using the basic stock method.

Planning Markup

34. Calculate the planned gross profit, in dollars, given the following data:

Planned dollar sales (given)	$900,000
Planned dollar markdowns (given)	135,000
Estimated planned dollar shortage	18,000
Percentage planned markup on stock & purchases	48.5%
Reciprocal percentage planned markup	51.5%

Planned Purchases

35. Find the planned purchases for June, if:

Planned June sales	$ 72,000
Planned June markdowns	3,000
Planned stock June 1	150,000
Planned stock July 1	155,600

36. Calculate the planned July purchases at cost using the following figures:

Planned July sales	$175,000
Planned July markdowns	20,000
Planned stock July 1	250,000
Planned stock July 31	125,000
Planned markup	52%

37. Note the following figures:

Planned September sales	$18,000
Planned September markdowns	800
Planned stock September 1	49,200
Planned stock October 1	50,400
Planned markup	51.5%

Determine:

(a) The planned September purchases at retail.

(b) The planned September purchases at cost.

(c) The turnover for September.

38. The hosiery department has an initial markup of 54%. The planned sales for April are $10,000 and $12,000 for May. The desired BOM stock-sales ratio for April is 2 and 1.5 for May. The planned markdowns are $600.

Calculate:

(a) The planned April purchases at retail.

(b) The planned April purchases at cost.

39. The following figures are from a shoe department:

Planned stock November 1	$147,000
Planned stock December 1	110,000
Planned November markdowns	2,000
Planned November sales	63,000
Actual stock November 1	140,000
Actual November sales	61,000

Find:

(a) The original planned purchases.
(b) The adjusted planned purchases.

40. The petite sportswear department had the following seasonal planned figures for October:

	Dollars	Percentages
Sales	$150,000	
Markdowns		11%
BOM Stock	136,000	
EOM Stock	108,000	
Markup		51.5%

Determine:

(a) The planned purchases at retail.
(b) The planned purchases at cost.

41. The children's clothing department had projected the following figures for January:

- Sales of $46,000.
- Stock-sales ratio of 3.0.
- Reductions of $13,800.
- EOM inventory of $140,000.

What are the planned retail purchases for January?

42. A men's furnishings department had the following figures planned for December:

Planned sales	$450,000
Planned markdowns	45,000
Planned stock (December)	900,000
Planned stock (January)	600,000

However, the following figures reflect the actual performance:

Actual sales	$430,000
Actual stock (January 1)	$620,000

Find:

(a) The original planned purchases.
(b) The adjusted planned purchases.

Notes

II. Open-to-Buy Control

Merchandise control results from effective use of data that is available through the dollar planning procedure. In purchasing merchandise, a buyer is guided by the timing and quantity goals established in the six-month seasonal dollar plan. To provide an even tighter control on the amount of merchandise received in a specific period and to achieve as precisely as possible the sales and stock plans, the buyer refers to a merchandising figure called OPEN-TO-BUY. This term, abbreviated OTB, denotes the amount of unspent (i.e., order limit) money that is available for purchasing merchandise that will be delivered during a given period. Usually, it is calculated on a monthly basis and indicates that the buyer has not yet spent all of the planned purchases or receipts for the period in question. It represents the difference between the planned purchases for a period and the merchandise orders already placed for that period. Unfilled orders, generally known as open orders, or "**on order,**" should be charged to those months during which delivery is expected so that the buyer is able to control and time buying activities to correlate with selling activities. The purpose of this control is to identify the deviations between actual results and planned goals and so the buyer can take corrective measures when needed.

The planned purchase figure for a particular month indicates the sum available to purchase goods during the month, but this figure does not indicate the distribution of the money throughout the month. Experienced buyers attempt to distribute purchases over the entire month to:

- Reorder or replace fast-selling goods.
- Fill in stocks so that complete stocks are offered.
- Compete advantageously when buying special purchases and/or new and interesting items as they become available.
- Test offerings of new resources.

Information that shows current developments helps assure that all the planned factors will proceed according to plan. Consequently, it is common in large stores that the controller's office periodically issues a report. The typical report (see Figure 36) contains information that covers:

- **Sales, including:**
  Plans for the month.
  This month to date.
  Adjusted plan for month.
- **Stocks, including:**
  First of month.
  Receipts to date (additions).
  On hand today.

- **Outstanding Orders, including:**
  For delivery by month.
- **Markdowns, including:**
  Season to date at BOM in dollars.
  Season to date at BOM in % to sales.
  Month to date.
- **Open-to-Buy, including:**
  Balance for current month.

Figure 36. Open-to-Buy Monthly Report

CO P1, MD A, RD 4, DG 026 SUITS					Open-to-Buy Report						(CGMRTO)	PAGE: 58 09:50 AM
THIS WEEK (JUN:3/5) #24	Last Month (MAY)	Current Month (JUN)	JUN :1/5 #22	JUN :2/5 #23	JUN :3/5 #24	JUN :4/5 #25	JUN :5/5 #26	JUL :1/4 #27	CURR. MO. (MTD)	Next Month (JUL)	2 Nxt Month (AUG)	3 Nxt Month (SEP)
$ NET SALES LAST YEAR	0	0	0	0	0	0	0	0	0	0	0	0
PLAN	10,000	5,000	950	1,000	1,000	1,050	1,000	0	1,950	0	8,000	20,000
ACTUAL	3,801	0	558	0					558			
% PLAN: LY												
% ACT.: LY	(62)		(41)	(100)					(71)			
% ACT.: PLAN												
$ STOCK/SALES LAST YEAR			0.0	0.0	0.0	0.0	0.0	0.0				
ACTUAL			9.4	0.0	0.0	0.0	0.0	0.0				
$ MARK-DOWNS LAST YEAR	0	0	0	0	0	0	0	0	0	0	0	0
PLAN	2,000	5,000	950	1,000	1,000	1,050	1,000	0	1,950	0	0	1,000
HOME OFF.			0	0					0			
P.O.S.			0	0					0			
TOTAL			0	0					0			
MARK-DOWNS/ SALES % LAST YEAR	0	0	0	0	0	0	0	0	0	0	0	0
% PLAN	20	100	100	100	100	100	100	0	100	0	0	5
% ACTUAL	0	0	0	0					0			
# NET SALES LAST YEAR	0	0	0	0	0	0	0	0	0	0	0	0
PLAN	68		10	0					10			
ACTUAL			0.0	0.0	0.00	0.0	0.0	0.0				
# STOCK/SALES LAST YEAR	0.00	0.00	0.0	0.0	0.00	0.0	0.0	0.0				
ACTUAL			9.2	0.0								
# AVERAGE SALE LAST YEAR	0.00	0.00	0.00	0.00	0.00	0.00	0.00	0.00	0.00	0.00	0.00	0.00
PLAN												
ACTUAL												
# AVERAGE STOCK LAST YEAR	55.90	55.80	55.80	0.00	0.00	0.00	0.00	0.00	55.80	0.00	0.00	0.00
PLAN	0.00	0.00	0.00	0.00					0.00			
ACTUAL												
LAST YEAR	58.55	57.05	57.05	57.07	0.00	0.00	0.00	0.00	0.00	0.00	0.00	0.00
PLAN	0	0	0	0	0	0	0	0	0	0	0	0
ACTUAL	22,000	10,000									15,000	30,000
$ RECEIVED NOT SHIPPED	6,558	5,249	5,249	4,680	0	0	0	0	0	0		
$ SHIPMENTS	2,568				0				0			
MARK UP % LAST YEAR	0	0	0	0	0	0	0	0	0	0	0	0
% PLAN	32	32							32		35	35
% ACTUAL	35											
# RECEIVED NOT SHIPPED			0	0					0			
# SHIPMENTS	48		0	0					0			

	CURR. MO. (MTD)	Next Month (JUL)	2 Nxt Month (AUG)	3 Nxt Month (SEP)
# OPEN-TO-RECEIVE	0	0	0	0
# ON ORDER	0	0	0	0
# OPEN TO BUY	0	0	0	0
$ OPEN-TO-RECEIVE	0	15,000	23,160	16,400
$ ON ORDER	0	0	0	0
% MARK UP	0	0	0	0
$ OPEN TO BUY	0	15,000	23,160	16,400
$ CUM. OPEN-TO-BUY	0	15,000	38,160	54,560

Planned EOM stock.

Adjusted EOM stock.

■ **Purchases, including:**

Plans for month.

Adjusted plan for month.

Plan for next month.

■ **Cumulative Markup, including:**

Plan for month.

Actual to date.

Because it is critical to determine at any time the dollar amount still available to purchase future merchandise, the computerized report, Figure 37, controls the merchandising facts planned and identifies deviation between the planned goals and the actual reports so that necessary corrective measures can be taken. Generally, it is prepared on a weekly basis.

Explanation of Open-to-Buy Report (Figure 37)

Figure 37 illustrates the information that is contained in a typical OTB report (e.g., sales, stocks, markdowns, outstanding orders, and open-to-receive). The report format and frequency of issuance can vary with organizational size and needs. This particular report shown gives the reviewer the opportunity to analyze the department's performance by individual store or on a combined all-store basis. The annotated information on Figure 37 is numbered (1) to (9), and the following information corresponds to those numbers:

(1) Date: Published date of the report, example: 10/10/99.

(2) WEEK 01 OF 04: Week of the month being viewed.

(3) DEPT 736 BRIDGE SUITS: Department number and name.

(4) Branch store listing: Listing of all the stores by location, example: NY (left-hand column). At the bottom of the sheet is the total (T) section, which designates the total for all stores.

(5) SALES: Net sales, by store, and the % change, which indicates the variance of CURRENT sales figures from PL and LY's actual. This category is divided into the following sections:

(a) CURRENT WK: Sales in $ and % by store, for the current week, example:

For store NY, CURRENT WEEK:

	$	%
TY	$18.6	
PL	$14.4	29%
LY	$22.2	−16%

These figures show that for the current week, store NY had net sales of $18.6, which was 29% ahead of PL, but 16% behind LY.

(b) LAST WEEK: Sales in $ and % by store, for the prior weeks, example:

For Store NY, LAST WEEK:

	$	%
TY	$ 9.7	
PL	$14.2	−32%
LY	$24.2	−60%

Figure 37. Open-to-Buy Report

(1) 10/10/99 (2) WEEK 01 OF 04 FALL 2000 OPEN TO BUY (3) DEPT 736 BRIDGE SUITS

1	(4)	(5) SALES (d) PRIOR 4 WKS		(c) 2 WKS AGO		(b) LAST WEEK		(a) CURRENT WEEK		(e) MTD		(f) STD		OCT $	(g) NOV $	DEC $	ENDING JULY $	ENDING AUG $	(6) STOCKS (a) LAST WK	(b) CURENT WK	OCT $	(c) NOV $	DEC $	(d) WKS OF STOCK (i) ON PL	(ii) ON TRD	
TY	+ – +	24.2		23.3		9.7		18.6		18.6		126.7							141.5	126.7				11	8	TY
PL	NY	28.5	–15	14.2	64	14.2	–32	14.4	29	14.4	29	110.5	15	57.8	43.1	49.9			177.3	166.4	166.4	142.1	99.3			PL
LY		26.5	-9	17.0	37	24.2	–60	22.2	–16	22.2	–16	135.2	–6	70.2	70.2	73.3			272.0	289.7	270.4	283.9	305.3	24		LY
TY	+ – –	1.8		2.2		1.7		1.1		1.1		13.1							23.4	21.0				10	6	TY
PL	BR	1.1	67	.6	263	.6	188	1.3	–17	1.3	–17	5.4	145	5.4	8.4	14.2			22.2	26.2	26.2	38.1	40.6			PL
LY		1.0	84	2.4	–9	3.5	–50	2.7	–60	2.7	–60	15.8	–17	10.7	10.7	6.0			40.1	40.1	26.3	18.9	39.3	33		LY
TY	– – +	6.5		3.6		2.1		4.4		4.4		22.4							45.9	42.5				37	12	TY
PL	BC	3.2	102	1.6	124	1.6	29	1.5	193	1.5	193	12.4	80	6.0	6.6	8.0			37.1	41.7	41.7	33.7	24.6			PL
LY		1.7	283	1.5	138	1.7	22	–1.0	–552	–1.0	–552	8.1	177	1.8	1.8	3.3			20.0	20.9	16.9	6.7	17.8	44		LY
TY	+ + –	7.2		3.6		4.0		3.8		3.8		26.1							32.7	37.4				19	8	TY
PL	SH	3.5	106	1.8	100	1.8	120	1.9	102	1.9	102	15.9	64	7.3	9.5	11.1			38.8	34.2	34.2	34.2	22.0			PL
LY		5.3	37	4.6	–23	5.2	–24	3.3	16	3.3	16	25.8	1	8.9	8.9	8.2			52.3	45.9	50.0	38.7	52.2	21		LY
TY	+ – –	5.3		4.9		4.0		3.8		3.8		33.9							109.8	111.4				58	58	TY
PL	NM	8.3	–36	4.2	17	4.2	–4	4.3	–11	4.3	–11	32.2	5	17.4	14.7	15.8			71.3	58.9	58.9	60.4	44.3			PL
LY		8.2	–35	4.4	13	7.0	–43	8.5	–55	8.5	–55	31.5	8	17.8	17.8	10.3			55.9	50.2	45.2	62.4	59.7	21		LY
TY	– – –	2.9		1.6		1.6		–.3		–3		10.6			20.3	22.0					23	38				TY
PL	GC	2.7	7	1.3	25	1.3	24	1.6	–116	1.6	–116	10.7	–1	6.1	4.3	5.8			23.4	19.3	19.3	17.8	17.8			PL
LY		2.0	46	1.5	7	2.4	–32	3.2	–108	3.2	–108	11.3	–7	6.5	6.5	5.2			31.4	33.5	20.5	19.1	23.7	42		LY
TY	+ + –			.9		1.4		.1		.1		3.0							12.0	11.9				23	6	TY
PL	PG	.2	–90	.1	844	.1	256	.2	–56	.2	–56	1.3	141	1.0	1.5	2.5			2.9	6.4	6.4	9.4	12.5			PL
LY		1.1	–98	.3	216	.3	329	.2	–63	.2	–63	2.4	28	.8	.8	1.9			17.1	18.6	15.1	6.0	7.8	99		LY
TY	+ + –	2.7		1.1		1.7		.2		.2		8.6							18.2	21.0				38	54	TY
PL	CH	2.4	12	1.2	–4	1.2	38	1.2	–87	1.2	–87	9.1	–6	5.1	4.3	4.8			21.1	17.7	17.7	16.8	13.6			PL
LY		3.0	–9	.5	115	3.2	–49	2.0	–92	2.0	–92	11.1	–23	4.3	4.3	3.5			22.5	17.1	16.5	7.6	20.4	99		LY
TY	+ – –	2.6		2.3		1.5		.7		.7		10.0							15.0	16.0				74	13	TY
PL	WP	1.2	118	.6	280	.6	153	.7	1	.7	1	5.0	100	2.8	1.8	2.7			13.1	10.7	10.7	9.9	7.2			PL
LY		2.2	20	.5	318	2.8	–46	.9	–22	.9	–22	8.0	25	1.1	1.1	.6			15.3	16.2	16.2	8.5	103	41		LY
TY	+ – –	5.4		4.7		3.3		.9		.9		19.4							31.2	30.5				34	15	TY
PL	WF	3.5	54	1.8	161	1.8	81	1.8	–49	1.8	–49	14.1	38	7.2	5.3	5.8			29.1	27.3	27.3	22.3	15.2			PL
LY		2.5	118	4.1	16	4.5	–27	3.1	–70	3.1	–70	20.5	–5	8.9	8.9	7.9			28.2	27.1	24.9	28.9	41.8	19		LY
TY	+ – +	2.8		1.9	42	.8		2.5		2.5		13.2							16.3	16.8				16	10	TY
PL	TC	2.6	9	1.3	–41	1.3	–39	1.2	109	1.2	109	10.3	28	5.1	1.3	5.8			26.7	23.0	23.0	19.3	13.3			PL
LY		.8	269	3.2		.5	63	1.6	57	1.6	57	11.2	18	5.7	5.7	5.8			31.9	31.6	25.1	15.7	26.0	58		LY
TY	+ – +	2.7		6.1		2.3		2.9		2.9		22.0							29.6	26.6				15	8	TY
PL	KP	5.0	–46	2.5	146	2.5	–9	2.3	25	2.3	25	18.3	20	9.2	7.9	9.2			37.1	36.3	35.3	28.7	19.7			PL
LY		2.9	–6	5.3	17	5.3	–57	4.5	–36	4.5	–36	25.7	–14	13.0	13.0	7.7			68.5	68.4	60.1	28.7	52.1	43		LY
TY	+ – –	.8		1.9		1.7		1.1		1.1		10.2							32.2	27.1				63	36	TY
PL	WG	2.2	–65	1.1	74	1.1	53	1.1	–3	1.1	–3	8.6	19	4.4	3.8	4.5			21.7	16.1	16.1	13.4	7.6			PL
LY		3.9	–80	.7	183	1.9	–10	1.2	–8	1.2	–8	8.5	20	2.4	2.4	3.6			12.2	12.58	12.3	11.3	12.7	22		LY
TY												1.2														TY
PL	FA	1.3	–100	.7	–100	.7	–100	1.1	–100	1.1	–100	6.1	–80	4.1	4.3	6.9			11.4	18.2	18.2	22.3	22.7			PL
LY		1.4	–100	1.7	–100	3.1	–100	1.3	–100	1.3	–100	11.2	–89	3.4	3.4	4.5			24.9	25.6	23.6	10.3	23.0	30		LY
TY	+ – +	6.0		2.4		.9		1.7		1.7		21.9							43.1	43.4				47	63	TY
PL	MI	4.4	35	2.2	11	2.2	–3	1.8	–3	1.8	–3	17.2	27	7.2	6.3	9.2			38.2	33.7	33.7	26.7	18.6			PL
LY																										LY
TY																										TY
PL	RTV																		7.6				99	99		PL
LY																										
TY																										
PL																										
LY																										
TY																										
PL																										
LY																										
TY																										
PL																										
LY																										
TY																										
PL																										
LY																										
TY																										
PL																										
LY																										
TY																										
PL																										
LY																										
TY	+ – –	40.7		34.9		25.9		21.2		21.2		192.5							386.5	384.2				27	16	TY
PL	EB	35.9	13	18.1	93	18.1	43	19.1	11	19.1	11	143.2	34	77.0	72.4	90.2			343.5	816.8	316.8	304.0	238.4			PL
LY		34.3	19	29.0	21	38.3	–32	30.3	–30	30.3	–30	179.9	7	81.9	81.9	64.1			395.3	382.4	329.1	252.6	363.8	30		LY
TY	+ – +	65.0		58.2		35.6		39.8		39.8		319.2							528.0	511.0				22	13	TY
PL	ES	64.4	1	32.3	80	32.3	10	33.5	19	33.5	19	253.6	26	134.8	115.5	140.1			520.8	483.2	483.2	446.1	337.7			PL
LY		60.9	7	46.0	27	62.5	–43	52.5	–24	52.5	–24	315.1	1	152.1	152.1	137.4			667.3	672.0	599.5	536.5	669.1	27		LY
TY	+ – +	70.9	1	60.6		36.5		41.6		41.6		342.3							571.1	562.0				22	14	TY
PL	T	70.1	14	35.2	72	35.2	4	36.4	14	36.4	14	276.9	24	146.1	126.1	156.2			570.4	535.1	535.1	495.1	379.0			PL
LY		62.3		47.7	27	65.6	–44	53.7	–23	53.7	–23	326.3	2	155.5	155.5	141.9			692.2	897.6	623.1	546.7	692.0	27		LY

2		(7) ORDERS (a) PRIOR MOS. PAST DUE	OCT $	(b) NOV $	DEC $	(c) FUTURE $	(d) TOTAL $	(e) S & O	(8) MARKDOWNS (a) CUR-RENT WEEK	(b) MTD	(c) STD	(d) STD % SLS	(9) OPEN TO REC OCT $	NOV $	DEC $	
TY	NY	37.0	76.9	27.0			103.9	230.7	8.0	8.0	27.7	21.9	–23.7	13.4	28.3	OTR
LY		17.2	117.2				117.2	406.9	.3	.3	43.3	32.0	65.1	40.4	28.3	PL REC
TY	BR	16.3	28.4	10.9			39.3	60.3	1.3	1.3	6.2	47.3	–16.6	14.2	23.6	OTR
LY		1.2	6.2				6.2	46.3	.2	.2	2.7	17.1	11.8	25.1	23.6	PL REC
TY	BC	6.6	6.6				6.6	49.1	2.4	2.4	8.1	36.1	4.2	2.2	3.4	OTR
LY								20.9	1.8	1.8	5.9	73.4	14.1	2.2	3.4	PL REC
TY	SH	16.5	22.7				22.7	60.1	1.4	1.4	4.8	18.4	–26.2	14.3	3.7	OTR
LY		.4	17.1				17.1	62.9			6.6	25.7	6.4	14.3	3.7	PL REC
TY	NM	9.7	10.2	8.5			18.7	130.1	–.1	–.1	7.2	21.3	–4.3	15.9	7.7	OTR
LY			8.0				8.0	58.2	.8	.8	5.7	18.0	11.3	24.4	7.7	PL REC
TY	GC	4.8	9.4				9.4	31.4	1.9	1.9	7.0	65.8	–8.3	6.2	9.3	OTR
LY								33.5	.2	.2	2.3	20.6	4.5	6.2	9.3	PL REC
TY	PG	4.9	7.2	8.2			15.3	27.3			.5	17.5	–2.1	-2.8	6.9	OTR
LY								18.6			.5	19.1	5.1	5.4	6.9	PL REC
TY	CH	11.6	12.1				12.1	33.1	.6	.6	3.1	36.4	–11.5	5.8	5.0	OTR
LY								17.1	.3	.3	4.8	42.7	4.1	5.8	5.0	PL REC
TY	WP	2.4	2.4				2.4	18.4	1.3	1.3	2.7	27.0	–3.7	2.1	1.3	OTR
LY								16.2			1.7	21.2	1.7	2.1	1.3	PL REC
TY	WF	4.8	9.4				9.4	39.9	3.3	3.3	4.9	25.4	–5.0	3.7	2.2	OTR
LY		2.3	6.6				6.6	33.7	–.2	–.2	7.0	34.4	7.9	3.7	2.2	PL REC
TY	TC	6.6	11.3				11.3	28.1	.4	.4	4.4	33.5	–9.9	3.5	3.3	OTR
LY			2.2				2.2	33.8	.1	.1	2.3	20.1	4.8	3.5	3.3	PL REC
TY	KP	9.5	15.0				15.0	41.6	2.3	2.3	11.1	50.6	–5.4	6.4	5.0	OTR
LY		7.6	12.9				12.9	81.3			11.0	42.9	11.7	6.4	5.0	PL REC
TY	WG	2.4	2.9				2.9	30.0	2.5	2.5	6.6	64.6	–.4	3.8	1.1	OTR
LY								12.8			.7	8.6	1.0	3.8	1.1	PL REC
TY	FA			3.0			3.0	3.0			.8	70.2	12.3	7.8	10.8	OTR
LY		1.7	4.5				4.6	30.2	.2	.2	3.2	28.5	12.3	10.8	10.8	PL REC
TY	MI	7.7	13.5				13.5	56.9	3.0	3.0	5.4	24.9	–12.8	4.9	5.8	OTR
LY													6.3	4.9	5.8	PL REC
TY	RTV							7.6	–10.0	–10.0	–10.0		2.4			OTR
LY																PL REC
TY																OTR
LY																PL REC
TY																OTR
LY																PL REC
TY																OTR
LY																PL REC
TY																OTR
LY																PL REC
TY																OTR
LY																PL REC
TY																OTR
LY																PL REC
TY																OTR
LY																PL REC
TY																OTR
LY																PL REC
TY	EB	96.1	137.5	27.5			165.0	549.3	17.3	17.3	66.7	34.7	–89.4	75.4	72.5	
LT		11.5	52.9				52.9	435.3	3.3	3.3	51.2	28.5	84.4	102.9	72.5	
TY	ES	133.1	214.5	54.5			268.9	779.9	25.4	25.4	94.4	29.6	–113.	88.8	100.8	
LY		28.7	170.2				170.2	842.2	3.6	3.6	94.5	30.0	149.5	143.3	100.8	
TY	T	140.8	228.0	57.5			285.5	847.5	18.9	18.9	90.7	26.5	–111.	101.5	117.4	
LY		30.3	174.8				174.8	872.4	3.8	3.8	97.7	29.9	168.1	159.0	117.4	
TY	LST	152.2	347.6				347.6	918.7	.6							
LY	WK	32.4	205.4				205.4	897.6	9.1							
TY	2WK	26.4	154.6	202.9			357.5	979.9	1.5							
LY	AGO	4.6	168.8	139.9			308.8	975.7	18.2							
TY	3WK	32.6	218.2	206.8			425.0	1.051	1.7							
LY	AGO	11.4	261.0	115.4			376.5	1.023	6.7							
TY	EOM	7.298	51.16	28.82			79.96	79.98								
LY	AUG	96.1	456.2	111.6			567.8	567.8								
TY	EOM	24	321.5	347.2			816.3	816.3								
LY	JUL	267.8	535.4	247.3			869.1	869.1								
TY	IMP															
LY	MEM	3														

These figures show that for LAST WEEK, store NY had net sales of $9.7, which was 32% under PL, and 60% behind LY.

(c) 2 WKS. AGO: Sales in $ and % by store, for 2 weeks prior, example:

For store NY, 2 WKS. AGO:

	$	%
TY	$23.3	
PL	$14.2	64%
LY	$17.0	37%

These figures show that for 2 WKS. AGO, store NY had net sales of $23.3, which was 64% ahead of PL, and 37% over LY.

(d) PRIOR 4 WKS: Total sales in $ and % by store, for 4 weeks prior, example:

For store NY, PRIOR 4 WKS.:

	$	%
TY	$24.2	
PL	$28.5	−15%
LY	$26.5	− 9%

These figures show that for PRIOR 4 WKS., store NY had net sales of $24.2, which was 15% under PL, and 9% behind LY.

(e) MTD (Month to date): Total sales in $ and % by store, for fiscal month, example:

For store NM, MTD:

	$	%
TY	$ 3.8	
PL	$ 4.3	−11%
LY	$ 8.5	−55%

These figures show that for MTD, Store NM had net sales of $3.8, which was 11% under PL, and 55% behind LY.

(f) STD (Season to date): Total net sales in $ and % by store, from beginning of seasons to the current date, example:

For store BR, STD:

	$	%
TY	$13.1	
PL	$ 5.4	145%
LY	$15.8	− 17%

These figures show that for MTD, store BR had net sales of $13.1, which was 145% ahead of PL, but 17% behind LY.

(g) OCT $, NOV $, DEC $: Planned sales in dollars for the present month and the next two months, compared to the same months LY, example:

For store BC:

OCT	NOV	DEC
$6.0 PL	$6.6 PL	$8.0 PL
$1.8 LY	$1.8 LY	$3.3 LY

(6) STOCK: Retail dollar value of stock currently received, which is planned by the month. This category is divided into the following sections:

(a) LAST WK: Dollar value of stock LAST WK, compared to PL and LY amounts for the same week, example:

For store NY LAST WK:

TY	$141.5
PL	$177.3
LY	$272.0

(b) CURRENT WK: Current week's dollar value of stock compared to PL and LY amounts for the same week, example:

For store NY CURRENT WK:

TY	$126.7
PL	$166.4
LY	$289.7

(c) OCT $, NOV $, DEC $: Comparison of the PL EOM with LY's stock dollars for the current month, and the next two months, example:

For store NY:

OCT	NOV	DEC
$166.4 PL	$142.1 PL	$ 99.3 PL
$270.4 LY	$283.9 LY	$305.3 LY

(d) WKS. OF STOCK: This subcategory is divided into two sections:

(i) WKS. OF STOCK ON PL: Number of weeks merchandise should last based on planned sales. They indicate how many future weeks of planned sales will be covered by the current week's stock, example:

For store NY: 11 (weeks)

(ii) WKS. OF STOCK ON TRD: Weeks of stock adjusted for actual vs. planned sales performance, example:

For store NY: 8 (weeks)

(7) ORDERS: Commitments by retail value of merchandise ordered. This category is divided into the following sections:

(a) PRIOR MOS. PAST DUE: Alerts the buyer to past due orders, TY vs. LY, example:

For store NY:

TY	$37.0
LY	$17.2

(b) OCT $, NOV $, DEC $: Orders due for the current month, and the next two months, example:

For store NY:

OCT	NOV	DEC
$ 76.9 TY	$27.0 TY	
$117.2 LY		

(c) FUTURE: Figures for orders that would be due in future months, subsequent to the current month, and the next two months. Blank spaces indicate no future commitments.

(d) TOTAL: Figures that are the total of orders due for the present month, and next two months, example:

For store NY:

TY	$103.9
LY	$117.2

(e) STOCK AND ORDERS: Figures, which are a combination of the stock with the total orders, used to compare TY figures with LY figures, example:

For store NY:

TY	$230.7
LY	$406.9

(8) MARKDOWNS: Dollar reductions taken. This category is divided into the following sections:

(a) CURRENT WEEK: Markdowns for the current week, comparing TY with LY, example:

For store NY:

TY	$8.0
LY	$0.3

(b) MTD $: Total dollar reductions taken month-to-date, comparing TY with LY, example:

For store NY:

TY	$8.0
LY	$0.3

(c) STD $: Total dollar reductions taken season-to-date, comparing TY with LY, example:

For store NY:

TY	$27.7
LY	$43.3

(d) STD % SLS: Total reductions expressed as percentages of sales, comparing TY with LY, example:

For store NY:

TY	21.9%
LY	32.0%

(9) OPEN TO REC.: Comparison of the planned and actual receipts at a given point in time during the month. It lists by month the retail dollar amount of merchandise open to be bought and received and is calculated by subtracting the month's orders from the month's planned receipts (i.e., planned purchases) figure. The positive numbers indicate money still available while the negative numbers show an overextended or overbought condition. This overbought condition occurs when the month's orders placed exceed that month's planned receipts, example:

For store NY:

OCT	NOV	DEC
−$23.7 TY	$13.4 TY	$28.3 TY
$65.1 LY	$40.4 LY	$28.3 LY

A. Calculating Retail Open-to-Buy at the Beginning of a Month

CONCEPT:

OTB: – Planned purchases for the month minus outstanding orders to be delivered that month

PROBLEM:

A buyer has planned January sales of $60,000, with an opening January stock planned at $50,000, a closing stock of $30,000, and markdowns planned at $500. If the orders that have already been placed for January delivery amount to $10,000 at retail, what is the buyer's January open-to-buy?

SOLUTION:

January EOM stock	$30,000
+ January sales	+60,000
+ January markdowns	+ 500
Total merchandise requirements =	$90,500
– January BOM stock	–50,000
January planned purchases =	$40,500
– January on order	–10,000
January OTB at retail =	$30,500

When the retail open-to-buy for any period is established, it can be converted to a cost open-to-buy figure. For example, $30,500 retail open-to-buy is converted to a cost figure by multiplying the retail open-to-buy by 100% (minus the planned markup percentage).

B. Calculating Retail Open-to-Buy During the Month

If the buyer wishes to calculate the OTB figure at a certain time during the period, the calculations may be based either on the predetermined planned purchases or the open-to-buy figure may be determined for the balance of the period using the planned closing stock figure. The problems that follow illustrate these calculations.

OTB for Balance of Month Based on Predetermined Planned Purchases

CONCEPT:

OTB for balance of month =

Planned purchases for month
– Merchandise received to day
– On order

= Open-to-buy

PROBLEM:

The merchandise plan shows that the planned purchases for September amounts to $17,000. The store's records indicate that from September 1 to September 15 the department received $8,300 worth of new goods and there is an order of $700 for September delivery. What is the open-to-buy for the balance of the month?

SOLUTION:

September planned purchases	$17,000
− Merchandise received	− 8,300
− On order	− 700
September OTB balance	$ 8,000

OTB for Balance of Month Based on Planned Closing Stock

CONCEPT:

OTB for balance of month =

	Planned EOM stock
+	Planned sales for balance of month
+	Planned markdowns for balance of month
=	Total merchandise requirements
−	Actual stock-on-hand
−	On order
=	OTB for balance of the month

PROBLEM:

On September 15, an infants' department has a stock of $26,000 and merchandise on order amounting to $700. The planned sales for the balance of September are $8,000, with planned markdowns for the balance of the month at $500. The stock planned for September 30 is $31,800. What is the OTB for the balance of the month?

SOLUTION:

	Planned sales for balance of month		$ 8,000
+	Planned markdowns for balance of month		+ 500
+	Planned EOM stock		+31,800
	Total merchandise requirements	=	40,300
−	Actual stock-on-hand		−26,000
−	On order		− 700
	September OTB balance		$13,600

For assignments for the previous section, see practice problems 43–47.

PRACTICE PROBLEMS

Calculating Retail Open-to-Buy

43. What is the open-to-buy for a department that has planned purchases of $71,500 and outstanding orders of $74,000?

44. The actual stock on April 1 is $116,000 with "on order" in April amounting to $18,000. Sales are planned at $75,000, with markdowns estimated to be 3.5%, and the stock on April 30 planned at $112,000. What is the OTB for this month?

45. On March 13, stock-on-hand is $16,300, with planned sales for the balance of the month at $9,000. Merchandise on order comes to $3,000 and the planned April 1 stock is $10,000. Find the balance of the OTB for March.

46. The May portion of a six-month plan for a shop is as follows:

Planned May sales	$37,500
Planned May markdowns	10%
Planned May BOM stock	66,000
Planned June BOM stock	59,000
Planned markup	49%

(a) What are the planned May purchases at retail?

(b) On May 1, the buyer is notified that $8,000 worth of goods (retail value) is on order. What is the open-to-buy at cost for May?

47. Find the OTB balance for December when on December 10 the stock-on-hand is $265,000 and the planned sales for the balance of the month are $171,000. Markdowns are planned at $11,000, planned inventory for December 31 is $150,000, with outstanding orders totaling $71,500.

Notes

48. A major West Coast retail store has a housewares department that operates on a planned stock turn figure of 4.0 for the six-month period August 1 to February 1. Find the number of weeks supply.

49. The annual turnover figure for a plus-size apparel department is projected at 5.0. Express the stated relationship in terms of weeks supply.

50. Average weekly sales in an automotive supply department of a major national chain is stated at $3,400,000. Turnover in this classification of merchandise is 4.0 annually. Using the weeks supply method, calculate the appropriate stock figure.

51. Turnover is planned at 2.5 for the six-month period starting February 1 through July 31. Average weekly sales for that period are $75,000. What average stock should be carried in this situation?

52. After careful analysis of economic projections from the U.S. Department of Commerce, a major department store chain set a figure of 7.5% as a realistic increase for this year's business volume over last. The previous year, the corporate volume was $3,700,000,000. What figure is projected for this year?

53. A Dallas-based specialty chain had sales of $196,000,000 last year. It plans $216,000,000 for the coming year. What percentage increase is being projected?

54. March figures for a shoe department are:

Planned sales	$510,000
Planned markdowns	6,000
Planned March 1 stock	906,000
Planned April 1 stock	630,000
Outstanding March orders	126,000
Planned markup	52%

Calculate:

(a) The planned March purchases at retail.

(b) The March open-to-buy at cost.

55. A junior sportswear buyer was shown the following data:

Planned sales	$22,000
BOM stock June	44,000
BOM stock July	40,000
Planned June markdown	1,000

Find:

(a) The OTB at retail, if "on order" for June delivery is $16,000 at retail.

(b) The OTB at cost, if the planned markup is 56%.

56. Note the following figures:

Planned sales	$ 85,000
Planned markdowns	1,000
Planned BOM stock	151,000
Planned EOM stock	105,000
Merchandise on order	21,000
Planned markup	51%

Determine:

    (a) The original planned purchases at cost.

    (b) The OTB at retail.

57. What is the OTB for a coat department with planned purchases of $56,000 and an "on order" of $19,000?

58. The stock-sales ratio in the men's shirt department has been set at 3.4 for June. Sales are planned at $34,500. What is the BOM stock for June?

59. Determine the BOM stock-sales ratio when the planned sales for April are $56,000 and the retail value of stock-on-hand for April 1 is $84,000.

60. The shoe department planned the following figures for October:

Planned sales	$46,000
Planned markdowns	6,500
Planned September EOM stock	68,000
Planned October EOM stock	54,000
Planned markup	48%

(a) Find the planned purchases for October at retail and at cost.

(b) On October 1, the buyer calculates that $16,000 worth of merchandise at retail is on order. What is the OTB at cost for October?

61. A boutique had net sales of $760,000 for a six-month period ending July 31. The monthly retail inventories were:

Dates	Stock-on-hand
Feb. 1	$ 78,000
March 1	130,000
April 1	217,600
May 1	306,600
June 1	197,840
July 1	132,880
July 31	118,700
	$1,181,620

(a) Find the turnover for the six-month period.

(b) Calculate the stock-sales ratio for May, if sales for the month were $146,000.

62. An infants' wear buyer takes a physical inventory of stock every three months. Last year, the stock counts showed the following inventory valuations:

Dates	Stock-on-hand
January 3	$16,390
April 2	18,412
July 1	14,473
October 2	19,670
December 31	15,880
	$84,825

What was the department's average stock for last year?

63. In a junior dress department, planned sales for the six-month period February through July were $250,000. The monthly inventories at retail for this period were:

Dates	Stock-on-hand
February 1	$90,000
March 1	87,000
April 1	92,000
May 1	90,000
June 1	84,000
July 1	79,000
July 31	62,000
	$584,000

(a) What is the planned average stock for the period?

(b) What is the planned annual turnover based on the performance of this six-month period?

(c) If planned sales in April were $23,000, what is the stock-sales ratio for April?

64. For the Fall season, a boutique with a 3.0 turnover has planned the following sales:

August	$100,700	November	$116,900
September	113,500	December	118,200
October	150,000	January	100,000

Using the basic stock method, find the BOM stock figures for each month.

65. Consider the following figures:

	BOM stocks	Net sales
January	$ 50,000	$ 15,000
February	46,000	18,000
March	46,000	20,000
April	46,000	14,000
May	40,000	12,000
June	40,000	16,000
July	45,000	14,000
August	45,000	14,000
September	50,000	18,000
October	60,000	18,000
November	80,000	38,000
December	44,000	16,000
January (following year)	46,000	
	$638,000	$213,000

Find:

(a) The yearly average stock figure.
(b) The turnover for the year.
(c) The turnover for September.
(d) The stock-sales ratio for June.

66. The statistical division provides an accessories buyer with the following computerized information:

Planned sales for balance of month	$162,000
Planned markdowns for balance of month	4,000
Planned EOM stock	200,000
Merchandise on order this month	64,000
Stock figure this date	214,000

Determine the balance-of-the-month OTB.

67. Research and Discussion: Describe how a buyer may use turnover and stock-sales ratio figures in planning a future departmental operation.

68. Research and Discussion: Are turnover and stock-sales ratio related? Explain.

69. Research and Discussion: Does an increased turnover rate always mean that the department is functioning more effectively and profitably? Explain.

70. When the buyer for the junior dress department started to develop the merchandise plan for the Spring season, the following data was received. It represents the department's performance of last year. Preparing to plan the goals of the department for this year, the buyer refers to the factors of the plan located on the six-month merchandising plan in Figure 38.

(a) What judgmental decision must be made first? Why?

(b) What figures can be calculated from the incomplete information in the plan to either improve or repeat last year's results?

71. Under the present conditions, the buyer plans a 7% sales increase because it is realistic. On the basis of this planned sales increase, project, for the forthcoming Spring season only, the monthly sales, stocks, markdowns, and retail purchases on the six-month merchandising plan provided on Figure 38. Attach a separate sheet showing all calculations.

(a) Justify why a particular month was changed in the monthly sales distribution.

(b) State the method of stock planning used in calculating the BOM stocks. The ending stock is $300,000, which is the same as last year.

(c) Justify a change, if any, in monthly planned dollar markdowns and/or seasonal total percentage.

(d) Calculate the monthly planned retail purchases.

Figure 38. Six-Month Merchandising Plan

			PLAN (This Year)	ACTUAL (Last Year)
Department Name _____		Department No. _____		

<table>
<tr><td rowspan="7">SIX-MONTH
MERCHANDISING
PLAN</td><td></td><td>PLAN
(This Year)</td><td>ACTUAL
(Last Year)</td></tr>
<tr><td>Workroom cost</td><td></td><td></td></tr>
<tr><td>Cash discount %</td><td></td><td></td></tr>
<tr><td>Season stock turnover</td><td></td><td></td></tr>
<tr><td>Shortage %</td><td></td><td></td></tr>
<tr><td>Average Stock</td><td></td><td></td></tr>
<tr><td>Markdown %</td><td></td><td></td></tr>
</table>

SPRING 1996		FEB.	MAR.	APR.	MAY	JUNE	JULY	SEASON TOTAL
SALES $	Last Year	140,000	160,000	200,000	175,000	165,000	160,000	$1,000,000
	Plan							
	Percent of Increase							
	Revised							
	Actual							
RETAIL STOCK (BOM) $	Last Year	325,000	475,000	550,000	500,000	375,000	275,000	
	Plan							
	Revised							
	Actual							
MARKDOWNS $	Last Year	20,000	20,000	30,000	35,000	45,000	50,000	200,000
	Plan (dollars)							
	Plan (percent)							
	Revised							
	Actual							
RETAIL PURCHASES	Last Year	310,000	255,000	180,000	85,000	110,000	235,000	
	Plan							
	Revised							
	Actual							
PERCENT OF INITIAL MARKON	Last Year	50.4	49.8	50.8	51.3	48.0	50.8	
	Plan							
	Revised							
	Actual							
ENDING STOCK JULY 31	Last Year	300,000						
	Plan							
	Revised							
	Actual							

Comments

Merchandise Manager _____   Buyer _____

Controller _____

Figure 39. Six-Month Merchandising Plan

SIX-MONTH MERCHANDISING PLAN	Department Name _____			Department No. _____			
					PLAN (This Year)	**ACTUAL (Last Year)**	
	Workroom cost						
	Cash discount %						
	Season stock turnover				2.0		
	Shortage %						
	Average Stock				$530,000		
	Markdown %				5.0%		

SPRING 1996		**FEB.**	**MAR.**	**APR.**	**MAY**	**JUNE**	**JULY**	**SEASON TOTAL**
SALES $	Last Year							
	Plan	80,000	120,000	145,000	300,000	315,000	100,000	$1,060,000
	Percent of Increase							
	Revised							
	Actual	78,194	119,873					
RETAIL STOCK (BOM) $	Last Year							
	Plan	350,000	550,000	650,000	700,000	650,000	450,000	
	Revised							
	Actual	325,312	552,100	651,325				
MARKDOWNS $	Last Year							
	Plan (dollars)	3,000	5,000	5,000	8,000	16,000	16,000	53,000
	Plan (percent)							
	Revised							
	Actual	3,000	5,000					
RETAIL PURCHASES	Last Year							
	Plan							
	Revised							
	Actual							
	Outstanding Orders				$160,000	50,000		
ENDING STOCK JULY 31	Last Year							
	Plan	360,000						
	Revised							
	Actual							

Comments

Merchandise Manager _____   Buyer _____
Controller _____

Open-to-Buy

It is the beginning of the third week in April. Mr. Johnston, the handbag buyer for a women's specialty store in California, studies the position of this department as he approaches the second quarter of the Spring season.

Before Mr. Johnston analyzes the actual results of the season-to-date performances, he examines the classification reports for the department to ascertain if the composition of his stock is in balance with the sales records. He finds that the leather handbag category—in which the price lines are highest—has fewer unit sales, which result in a high dollar inventory. The "fashion" fabrication of the season—sisal and straw, combined with new styling—has caused an out-of-proportion increase in the unit sales of this group when compared to the sales of previous years. This trend has surpassed even Mr. Johnston's originally high expectations of this fashion. Additionally, the weather, which has turned unusually warm for this time of year, has been a catalyst to this vigorous selling in the Spring-Summer look. On the six-month merchandise plan, the season-to-date figures for the department are shown in Figure 39.

As Mr. Johnston examines these figures, he considers the following facts:

■ The February and March sales are almost on target for the plan, but the post-Easter sales sagged. (Mr. Johnston estimates that there will be a 10% decrease in sales from the plan during the first quarter because the sales before Easter were slightly off and have been decreasing since that time.) A 5% increase is required over planned sales for the second quarter to achieve, if not surpass, the total seasonal planning goals in relation to sales, markdowns, and turnover.

■ Unless immediate action is taken, the lowered actual sales, to date, will result in a higher than planned May 1 inventory figure.

■ Both the dollar amount in the inventory and the outstanding orders in the straw category are entirely too low to generate possible sales increases because the demand for this merchandise has exploded. (This requires instant correction.)

■ The sales at the beginning of the third week for the month are $60,000, and the inventory figure is $795,000.

To accomplish the second quarter objectives (i.e., to attain the originally planned figures regarding sales, markdowns, and turnover), what actions must Mr. Johnston take? What are the alternatives, if any? What adjustments do you recommend? Justify your suggestions mathematically.

PLANNING FOR EFFECTIVE BUYING

You were recently promoted to the position of buyer for the Hosiery Department in a large specialty store. Your market is about to open, and in anticipation of this, you must be prepared with certain dollar goals for the coming season.

It is the policy of your store that the buyer be responsible for the formulation of the departmental dollar six-month plan. You know that if this plan is to be of value, the figures established must be ones that you can actually achieve. You also know that despite your inexperience you will have to be prepared to explain and justify the plans and strategies you will use as guidelines when merchandising for the period under consideration.

Where shall you begin? You know a sound basis for future planning is to analyze the past results of your "new" department. So before you develop your plan for Fall, you decide to review the figures below, which show the performance achieved by the Hosiery Department for Fall of last year.

Month	BOM Stock	Sales	Markdowns
August	$455,500	$ 75,000	$ 2,000
September	850,000	205,000	2,000
October	550,000	135,000	7,500
November	600,500	135,000	7,500
December	850,000	230,000	8,300
January	440,000	120,000	24,000
February	454,000		
	Total	$900,000	$51,300

Turnover for Period	1.5
Markdown %	5.7

Your Divisional Merchandise Manager (DMM) informed you that though the sales increases for the Fall season of last year had been greater than planned, there were other areas in the overall operation that needed improvement.

You are aware of the following facts: the nation-wide economy is moving briskly; top management has planned on an overall store-wide sales increase of 7%; legwear has had a strong surge of sales for the first six-month period (sales were planned with a 15% increase but actually were ahead 23% over the year before); fashion influences of long, leggy looks with slits in dresses and skirts continue as important apparel looks; the rising trend for legwear in the Spring season, after 4 dismal years, also saw the revival of body suits which has stabilized to a fair contribution of total sales. The textured hosiery introduced in the spring retailing at 20% higher retail prices is expected to create an explosion. . . .

Your DMM requested a meeting with you to discuss your projected goals for the six months before they are finalized. You feel the following issues will be addressed:

- How should the L.Y. figures to be used by you in preparation for your plan for the Fall season of this year?
- It would seem as if the sales trend in your department lends itself to a further increase of sales. Why must you estimate as accurately as possible (neither too high nor too low) the amount of sales you can generate during this season?
- As the buyer, what 3 strategies can you plan in order to achieve the sales gain you propose?
- Having set your projected sales figures, you now want to adjust your stocks to the proper size in order to achieve the planned monthly sales figures. Your DMM gave you August 1 stock figures of $460,000 and February 1 stock figures of $450,000. He told you to work out the BOM stock figures for each of the other months in your six-month plan. There are three approaches to planning the amount of stock necessary for projected sales figures. Which will you choose? Why?
- After you have determined all BOM stock figures for the entire period, what measurement will tell you how well you balanced your stock and sales for the entire period?
- In addition to planning sales and stocks, the markdown amounts are to be included. The typical markdown percentage in the industry for the hosiery department is 8%. The amount taken by your predecessor was 5.7. In planning the amount of reductions for the entire period, how will you plan the markdowns on your current plan? In dollars? In percentages? Higher? Lower?
- Because your predecessor only achieved a turnover of 1.5, and the typical turnover in the industry for your department is 3.7, you realize that this was one of the "areas that needs improvement." How can you show an increased T.O. on the *dollar plan* you are going to submit at present?

It is September 15. Below are the figures of your 6-month plan. Should you make any revisions in your plan in light of the fact that your department for August had a 10% decrease in planned sales? If so, why and what revision(s) would you make? If not, why not?

	Aug	Sept	Oct	Nov	Dec	Jan	Seasonal total
Sales	$100.00	$235.00	$165.00	$165.00	$265.00	$150.00	$1,080.00
L.Y.	75.00	205.00	135.00	135.00	130.00	120.00	900.00
Plan	100.00	235.00	165.00	165.00	265.00	150.00	1,080.00
Actual	90.00						
Revised							
BOM stock	$460.00	$840.00	$525.00	$655.00	$860.00	$410.00	
L.Y.	455.50	850.00	550.00	600.50	850.00	440.00	
Plan	460.00	840.00	525.00	655.00	860.00	410.00	
Actual							
Revised							

Outstanding Orders

			Oct	Nov	Dec		
			200.00	250.00	450.00		

From this information, calculate the OTB figure for the month of November.

What could cause the OTB figure for September to change after it is once established?

Can you convert an overbought condition to an OTB position? If so, how? If not, why?

During the course of the six-month period, as you review your actual sales performance, should the actual results be compared to last year's sales or the planned sales figures, or both, in order to have a meaningful comparison. Which? Why?

The sales performance of the Luggage Department in a Sporting Goods Store last Fall was:

August $80,000, September $90,000, October $100,000, November $140,000, December $160,000, and January $120,000 = $690,000 Total Seasonal Sales.

As the six-month merchandising plan for this department was being formulated for this fall season, the following decisions were made:

1. An 8% sales increase could be attained this year due to the introduction and addition of a new classification of carry-on travel luggage that is well priced and of exceptional value.
2. The planned BOM stock-to-sales ratio for each month this year would be the same as last year, i.e. August 3.3, September 3.1, October 2.9, November 2.5, December 2.2, January 2.6 with an ending retail inventory for the period of $288,000.
3. The planned total reductions for last year were 11.6% and were distributed with 7% for August, 9% in September, 18% in October, 12% in November, 26% in December and 28% in January.

Compute:

1. The planned monthly retail receipts (purchases) for each month.
2. The planned average stock and the planned stock turnover.

Notes

UNIT VI

INVOICE MATHEMATICS: TERMS OF SALE

Objectives

- Identification and recognition of the different types of discounts, including:
  Trade discounts.
  Quantity discounts.
  Cash discounts.
- Calculation of net cost.
- Identification and understanding of the different types of dating terms, including:
  COD.
  Regular (Ordinary).
  Extra.
  EOM.
  ROG.
  Advance (Postdating).
- Calculation of discount dates and net payments dates.
- Knowledge and understanding of anticipation.
- Identification and recognition of the different types of shipping terms.

Key Terms

advanced dating	list price
anticipation	loading
cash discount	net cost
COD dating	net payment date
dating	net terms
discount period	postdating
discount date	prepaid
EOM dating	quantity discount
extra dating	regular or ordinary dating
FOB city or port of destination	ROG dating
FOB factory	terms of sale
FOB retailer	trade discount

hen retail buyers select merchandise, they not only agree on the cost price, they also negotiate other factors that influence final cost. These conditions of the sale that are agreed on when the merchandise is purchased are called **terms of sale.** These terms deal with discounts granted, dating for payments, transportation arrangements, and shipping charges. When the discounts granted are deducted from the billed cost, **net cost** remitted to the vendor is the resultant figure. When shipping charges are to be paid by the retailers, they are added to the net cost that is due the vendor, and the final or total amount to be sent the vendor is determined. Lack of familiarity with terms of sale is a serious handicap because one of the best ways to improve profits is to lower the cost of goods, assuming other factors remain constant. Consequently, any factor that will increase the ever-significant gross margin figure is essential.

I. Terms of Sale

In this chapter, the various types of discounts, dating, and shipping terms involved in buying goods by the retailer will be examined because much of the secondary negotiation between vendors and retail buyers revolves around these three factors.

A. Different Types of Discounts

A discount is a deduction (expressed as a percentage) off the quoted or billed cost of the merchandise. Discounts are granted by a vendor to a purchaser for various negotiated terms. While discount practices and schedules vary from one industry to another, and from firm to firm, and even within merchandise classifications, there are three basic types of discounts. Generally, these discounts are taken in the following order: (1) trade discounts; (2) quantity discounts; and (3) cash discounts. These three types of discounts are examined in the following sections.

Trade Discount

Trade discount is a percentage or a series of percentages deducted from the **list price** (i.e., the theoretical retail price recommended by the manufacturer). The price that a buyer pays for merchandise is determined by deducting a percentage (called a trade discount) from the list price. It is a means of establishing the cost price of the goods. The number and/or amount of trade discounts varies according to the classification of the purchasers (i.e., retail stores, jobbers, other middlemen, or industrial buyers) and the amount of marketing services performed by that group. For example, a flashlight manufacturer quotes trade discounts to general retailers at 35%, department stores at 40%, chain stores at 45%, and wholesalers at 50%.

Trade discounts are deducted regardless of when the invoice is paid. In merchandise lines that customarily offer trade discounts, the list price minus the trade discount(s) is a way of quoting the cost. In some cases, this type of discount is quoted as a single percentage (e.g., $100 list price, less 45%), or is offered as a series of discounts (e.g., $100 list price, less 30%, less 10%, less 5%). Generally, the clothing industries do not use the trade discount approach to determine the cost of an item; usually cost prices are quoted directly (e.g., style #332 costs $18.75 each or scarves cost $120/dozen). Trade discounts deducted from an established list price provide a vendor with a mechanism for changing cost easily. For example, when a supplier shows and describes merchandise through a catalog, the price change is done expeditiously by printing new price lists with a change in the discount. It is a device whereby the various middlemen in the channels of distribution can get larger and/or more discounts than retailers either because of the functional services they provide for the manufacturer or because of the larger quantities that they purchase. On the same item, a wholesaler might receive discounts of 40% and 10%, while the retailer may receive a discount of 40% only.

CONCEPT:

Billed cost = List price − Trade discount(s)

PROBLEM:

Trade discounts on a lawnmower that "lists" as $200 are 25%, 10%, 5%. Find the billed cost on an item quoted at $200 list, less 25%, 10%, and 5%.

SOLUTION:

List price   = $200

Less 25% $200.00 List Price
                 − 50.00 ($200 × 25%) = 1st discount
                 _____
                  $150.00 (resultant figure)

Less 10% $150.00
                 − 15.00 ($150 × 10%) = 2nd discount
                 _____
                  $135.00 (resultant figure)

Less 5% $135.00
                 − 6.75 ($135 × 5%) = 3rd discount
                 _____
                  $128.25 (resultant figure)

Billed cost = $128.25

Or use your calculator, press

$200 − 25% − 10% − 5% = $128.25 Billed Cost

Note that even though the list price is $200, the retailer does not necessarily offer the consumer the manufacturer's suggested list price. It is common practice for the buyer to use the billed cost and the appropriate markup percentage to calculate the retail price desired.

Quantity Discount

Quantity discount (QD) is a percentage off the billed cost given by a vendor when a stipulated quantity is purchased and is deductible regardless of when invoices are paid. Usually the purchase of a large amount of goods is involved. Although quantity discounts are not customary practice in the fashion industries, they are common in home furnishings and hard goods lines. Depending on custom and practice within individual industries, this kind of discount is offered either when the stipulated quantity is purchased, or it is given for accumulated purchases over a specified period of time. The amount of discount is based on a sliding scale (i.e., the larger the purchase, the greater the percentage of quantity discount). A quantity discount is offered as an incentive for buyers to commit to purchase large amounts of goods. This is a legal practice under specific provisions of the Robinson-Patman Act of 1936.[1] Additionally, it is the buyer's responsibility to judge the merits of savings through this quantity discount against the risks of tying up more than the normal planned amounts of open-to-buy money.

CONCEPT:

$ Quantity discount = $ Billed cost × Quantity discount %
$ Net billed cost = $ Billed cost − Quantity discount

PROBLEM:

A cookware manufacturer's established price schedule is:

- A minimum initial order of $500 receives a 1% QD.
- An initial order of $1,250 receives 1.5%.
- An initial order of $2,500 receives 2%, and so on.

On an order of assorted cookware amounting to $2,000, use this discount schedule to determine:

(a) The quantity discount.
(b) The net cost of this order.

---

[1]Federal legislation regulating wholesale pricing practices.

SOLUTION:

(a)   Quantity discount   = $2,000 Billed cost × 1.5% Quantity discount

$$\$2,000 \times 1.5\%$$

Quantity discount = $30

(b)   Billed cost   = $2,000
    − Quantity discount   −   30

Net cost   = $1,970

Cash Discount

Cash discount, the most common kind of discount, is a stated percentage of the billed cost allowed by a vendor if payment of the invoice amount is made within a stipulated time. The full utilization of cash discounts is another approach to decreasing the total cost of merchandise that results in an increased profit potential. Although any invoice or bill must be paid within some specified time, the intent of the cash discount is to offer the purchaser an incentive to make early payment. The vendor sacrifices a fraction of the cost that is due to receive payment more rapidly. Cost prices that are subject to quantity and/or trade discounts may also be subject to cash discounts. Eligibility for a cash discount is contingent on the time element only. The cash discount percentage is not only written on the purchase order, but also on the vendor's invoice (e.g., 8/10 terms refers to an 8% discount if the invoice is paid within 10 days).

Calculating Net Cost When Billed Cost and Cash Discount Are Known

CONCEPT:

Net cost = Billed cost − Cash discount

PROBLEM:

The cost of a microwave oven is $60. The cash discount earned is 6%. What is the net cost paid to the manufacturer?

SOLUTION:

Cash discount   = $60.00 Billed cost × 6% Cash discount

$$\begin{array}{r} \$60.00 \\ \times\ \ 6\% \end{array}$$

Cash discount = $ 3.60

Billed cost   = $60.00
− Cash discount   − 3.60

Net cost   = $56.40 (Amount to be remitted)

Calculating Net Cost When List Price Is Quoted and Cash Discount Is Given

When the cost of goods is stated by quoting a list price with a series of trade discounts, and the buyer is also eligible for a cash discount, the amount to be paid is determined by calculating the billed cost first, and then deducting the cash discount.

CONCEPT:

Net cost = List price − Trade discount(s) − Cash discount

PROBLEM:

The list price of a lawnmower is $200 less 25%, less 10%, less 5%. There is a 2% cash discount offered for payment within ten days. What is the amount to be remitted if the cash discount is earned?

SOLUTION:

List price	$200.00	$200.00	List price
Less 25%	× 25%	− 50.00	1st dollar discount
	$ 50.00	$150.00	
Less 10%	$150.00	$150.00	Intermediate price
	× 10%	− 15.00	2nd dollar discount
	$ 15.00	$135.00	
Less 5%	$135.00	$135.00	2nd intermediate price
	× 5%	− 6.75	3rd dollar discount
	$ 6.75	$128.25	
Billed cost =		$128.25	Billed cost
		× 2%	Cash discount
		$ 2.57	Cash discount
		$128.25	Billed cost
		− 2.57	Cash discount
Net cost		$125.68	Amount remitted

To use your calculator, press $200 − 25% − 10% − 5% − 2% = $125.68 Net cost.

Calculating Net Cost When Quantity and Cash Discounts Must Be Considered

When the purchase is large enough to become eligible for a quantity discount, and a cash discount is offered, the amount to be paid is calculated by first deducting the amount of the quantity discount and then deducting the cash discount.

CONCEPT:

Net cost = Billed cost − Quantity discount − Cash discount

PROBLEM:

A cookware manufacturer has established price schedules of:

- A minimum initial order of $500 receives 1% QD.
- An initial order of $1,250 receives 1.5%
- An initial order of $2,500 receives 2%, etc.

In addition, there is a 3% cash discount offered for payment within ten days. Based on this discount schedule, what is the net cost for a $2,000 order of assorted cookware if it is paid within 7 days?

SOLUTION:

Quantity discount = $2,000.00 Billed cost × 1.5% QD

$$
\begin{array}{r}
= \$2,000.00 \\
\times \quad 1.5\% \\
\hline
\end{array}
$$

Quantity discount = $ 30.00

$$
\begin{array}{r}
\text{Cost} \qquad = \$2,000.00 \quad \text{Billed cost} \\
-\quad 30.00 \quad \text{QD} \\
\hline
\end{array}
$$

Cost   = $1,970.00

$$
\begin{array}{r}
\text{Cash discount} = \$1,970.00 \\
\times \qquad 3\% \quad \text{Cash discount} \\
\hline
\end{array}
$$

Cash discount   = $ 59.10

$$
\begin{array}{r}
\text{Net cost} \qquad = \$1,970.00 \\
-\quad 59.10 \quad \text{Cash discount} \\
\hline
\end{array}
$$

Net cost   = $1,910.90

To use your calculator, press $2,000 − 1.5% − 3% = $1910.90 Net cost.

Calculating Net Cost When a List Price Is Quoted and Quantity Discounts and Cash Discounts Are Allowed

When the cost of goods for some types of merchandise is stated by quoting a list price with a series of discounts and the buyer is granted a quantity discount and is also eligible for a cash discount, the amount to be remitted to the vendor is calculated by:

- First, deducting the series of trade discounts to find the billed cost.
- Second, determining the eligibility for the quantity discounts offered and deducting the percentage of dollar amount from the calculated billed cost.
- Third, subtracting the cash discount from this amount.

The reason for this order is that when merchandise is quoted with trade discounts, the cost price of the goods must be established first. Only then can the buyer determine if the amount purchased satisfies the quantity specified for the quantity discount, regardless of when the invoice is paid. After this cost price is calculated, then the cash discount subtracted—but only if payment is made within the stipulated time. Savings realized by these discounts alone have an impact on the department's profit margin and should be thoroughly understood for what they are and how they are calculated to determine the remitted cost price.

CONCEPT:

Net cost = List price − Trade discount(s) − Quantity discount − Cash discounts

PROBLEM:

A silverware buyer purchases 75 pairs of sterling salt and pepper shakers directly from a manufacturer who quotes the list price of this item for $125 less 25%, 10%, and 5%. The vendor's price schedule is as follows:

■ A minimum order of $4,000 receives a 3% quantity discount.
■ An initial order of $4,500 receives a 4% quantity discount.
■ An initial order of $5,000 receives a 7% quantity discount.

In addition, there is a 2% cash discount offered for payment made within 10 days. What is the net cost of this order if it is paid in eight days?

SOLUTION:

List price: $125 × 75 pairs	=	$9,375.00
− First trade discount 25%	×	25%
	=	$2,343.75
Total list price	=	$9,375.00
− First $ discount		−2,343.75
First intermediate price	=	$7,031.25
		$7,031.25
− Second trade discount 10%	×	10%
	=	$703.125
First intermediate price	=	$7,031.25
− Second $ discount		− 703.13
Second intermediate price	=	$6,328.12

		$6,328.12
− Third trade discount 5%	×	5%
	=	$316.406
Second intermediate price	=	$6,328.12
− Third $ discount	−	316.41
Billed cost	=	$6,011.71
		$6,011.71
− Quantity discount 7%	×	7%
	=	$ 420.82
Billed cost	=	$6,011.71
− Quantity discount	−	420.82
	=	$5,590.89
		$5,590.89
− Cash discount 2%	×	2%
Cash discount	=	$111.82
Billed cost	=	$5,590.89
− Cash discount	−	111.82
Amount remitted	=	$5,479.07

To use your calculator, press $125.00 × 75 pairs − 25% − 10% − 5% − 7% − 2% = $5479.07 Net cost remitted.

B. Net Terms

Net terms is the expression used to refer to a condition of sale if a cash discount is neither offered nor permitted. When an item is sold under these conditions, it is expressed as a "net" arrangement.

PROBLEM:

A buyer purchases an item costing $500 with net terms. The invoice is dated October 5 and the bill is paid within 30 days. What is the amount of the bill that was paid?

SOLUTION:

$500 billed cost with "net terms" means no cash discount is allowed, so $500 is paid.

For assignments for the previous section, see practice problems 1–13.

Notes

Practice Problems

Discounts

1. The Robner Electronic Company lists a top-of-the-line answering machine for $175. The trade discount offered is 30%. What is the billing price?

2. A guitar manufacturer sells electric guitars at $450 less 30% and 10%. What is the net cost to the buyer?

3. Dealer A sells stereo sets for $975 with a 30% trade discount. Competitor B offers a similar model at $760 with a 15% discount. Which is the better buy? By how much?

4. The quantity discount schedule of a china importer is 0.5% discount on orders for $1,000, 1% discount on orders for $1,5000, 1.5% discount on orders for $2,500, and a 2% discount on orders for $3,000. A retailer's order of bone china luncheon sets amounted to $2,800. No other discounts were allowed on this particular group. How much should the retailer pay the importer?

5. As an incentive, a supplier of motor bikes offers an additional 10% quantity discount on orders of more than 5 bikes. The normal trade discount offered by the supplier is 40%, 10% on the suggested list price of $250 each. How much would a retailer remit if 8 bikes are purchased?

6. What is the net cost on an $850 order if the cash discount earned is 4%?

7. Calculate the net cost on an order for 6 dozen boys' swim trunks at $84/dozen. The cash discount earned is 3%.

8. If a buyer purchases 120 coats at $52 each and earns an 8% cash discount, what amount must be paid to the manufacturer?

9. A gift store received an invoice in the amount of $8,200, which represents the manufacturer's suggested retail price. The invoice also shows that a trade discount of 45% is allowed, as well as a 2% cash discount. Determine the amount of payment to the vendor.

10. A sporting goods buyer purchased 50 individual golf clubs of one style that cost $35 each. When the merchandise was received, the invoice indicated that an additional 5% quantity discount was allowed when more than 36 clubs of any one style were purchased. Additionally, a 3% cash discount was allowed when payment was made within 10 days. What amount should have been remitted to the manufacturer if payment was made in 7 days?

11. The housewares department placed an order for two dozen food processors that have a list price of $300 each, with trade discounts of 30%, 10%, and 5%. The supplier's price schedule is:

- A minimum order of $3,000: 1%.
- An initial order of $4,000: 1.5%.
- An initial order of $5,000: 2%.
- Payments within 10 days: 2% cash discount.

If this invoice was paid in nine days, what amount should have been remitted to the seller?

12. A retailer has in stock a microcomputer that lists for $1,950. Trade discounts of 35% and 10% were quoted.

    (a) What is the billed cost?

    (b) At what price would the microcomputer sell if the retailer decided to apply a 48% markup?

13. If you were a buyer with an invoice that came to a list price of $100, which set of series trade discounts would you favor?

    (a) 25%, 20%, and 15%

or

    (b) 50% and 10%

Explain your choice.

II. DATING

Dating is an agreement between the supplier and retailer whereby a specified time period for payment of an invoice is arranged. Dating arrangements vary within any particular industry and from one industry to another. Dating usually implies a cash discount and is expressed as a single term of sale (e.g., 2/10). This means that the buyer will deduct a 2% cash discount from the billed cost if the payment is remitted to the manufacturer on or before the stipulated 10-day period.

For example:

Industry	Common dating practice
Ready-to-wear	8/10 EOM
Jewelry	2/10, net 30
Home furnishings	2/10, net 30

In the home furnishings example, 2/10, net 30 means that a 2% discount off the billed cost is permitted if the invoice is paid within 10 days following the date of invoice. The payment of the net amount (i.e., total amount of billed cost) is required between the 11th and the 30th day following the date of the invoice.

PROBLEM:

An invoice, dated March 1, for 10 folding chairs at a cost of $24 each, carries terms of 2/10, net 30. If the bill is paid on any day from March 1 to March 11, 2% may be deducted. How much should be paid if the invoice is paid on March 8?

SOLUTION:

Each chair	$ 24.00	
× Quantity	× 10	
Total cost	= $240.00	
	$240.00	Billed cost
	× 2%	Cash discount
Cash discount	= $ 4.80	
	$240.00	Billed cost
	− 4.80	Cash discount
Net cost	= $235.20	

However, if the bill is paid on or after March 12, the full amount of $240 is due, as listed in the payment schedule following:

Cash Discount Period		Net Period		Penalty Period
Date of invoice	Last Date for cash discount	First date for net payment	Last date for net payment	Penalty period starts
March 1	March 11	March 12	March 31	April 1

In dating that allows a 10-day **discount period,** the last day for the net payment can be determined by adding another 20 days to the last discount day (i.e., date). For example:

Starting with a March	1	Invoice date
+	10	Discount days
March 11		**Last discount date**
+	20	Net payment days
March 31		**Last net payment date** (TRADITIONAL CALENDAR)

or

Last Net Payment Date = March 1 invoice date + 30 days = March 31

A. Different Types of Dating

There are many different types of dating used in all industries. As stated before, variations can even occur within a particular industry. Generally, the nature of the goods influences the prevalent dating practices. For example, some segments of the apparel industry offer a relatively high cash discount (e.g., 8%) to induce purchasers to take advantage of the savings inherent for early or prompt payment. This is vital in an industry composed of many small businesses that are frequently undercapitalized. From the standpoint of the purchaser (i.e., retailer) who invokes the cash discount privileges, the cost of the merchandise is considerably reduced, which has potential implications for increased profits. In the determination of when to pay an invoice, the buyer must be able to distinguish between the discount date and the net payment date. The **discount date** is the date by which the invoice may be paid to take advantage of the discount granted, and the **net payment date** is the date by which the invoice must be paid to acquire a favorable credit rating and avoid possible late penalties.

The previous explanations and problems used in the material pertaining to the time period of payment reflect the customary, accepted U.S. practices that are associated with the various types of invoice payment dating. However, in buyer vs. seller markets and in certain other economic conditions (e.g., a recession) the adherence to these rules can and frequently does change. For example, when economic conditions are not favorable, a retailer may be prone to disregard or possibly extend the traditional negotiated time period. Under these conditions, the vendor usually makes exceptions and concentrates on invoice payment rather than the strict observance of datings. Nonetheless, the most important negotiation is to set a specific date for payment of an invoice, and then be able to calculate the exact payment date. Even though there are different numbers of days for each month throughout the year, to simplify the payment calculations, many businesses will base their calculations on a 30-day month. Many businesses who want to take advantage of all possible days in the payment period prefer using the traditional calendar. Since individual arrangements can vary, for the purpose of identification and the application of the various types of dating, the problems and illustrations used in this text calculate the discount and net payment dates on a 30-day month.

COD Dating

COD dating (cash-on-delivery) is a type of dating that means payment must be made "on the spot" as delivery takes place. Generally, COD dating is applicable to purchasers with poor or unproven credit ratings.

PROBLEM:

Goods valued at $500 cost are purchased by a retail store under COD dating terms. What amount must be remitted? When?

SOLUTION:

Invoice amount = $500; Amount remitted = $500
When = As delivery takes place

Regular (or Ordinary) Dating

Regular or **ordinary dating** is one of the most common kinds of dating. The discount period is calculated from the date of the invoice, which is usually the same date that the merchandise is shipped.

PROBLEM:

What payment should be made on an invoice for $500 dated November 16, carrying terms of 4/10, net 30?

SOLUTION:

If paid on or before November 26 (November is 16 + 10 days)

Billed cost	$500.00
− Cash discount ($500 × 4%)	− 20.00
Remitted	= $480.00

If paid between November 27 and December 17 (i.e., 20-day net payment period), no discount is permitted, and the full $500 is remitted. The vendor reserves the right to charge carrying fees after the expiration of the net payment period. The exercising or bypassing of this option depends on individual cases (e.g., credit history, the relationship of the vendor to the retailer, etc.).

Extra Dating

Extra dating (written as an X) is calculated from the date of the invoice, with a specified number of extra days granted, during which the discount may be taken. Consequently, 2/10–60X means that the bill is payable in 10 days plus 60 extra days (i.e., a total of 70 days) from the date of the invoice to earn the 2% discount. The full amount is due after the expiration of the 70 days and the customary, though often unstated, 20-day additional net payment period follows.

PROBLEM:

An invoice dated March 16 has a billed cost of $1,800 and terms of 3/10–60X. Determine:

(a) Final date for taking cash discount.
(b) Cash discount earned if bill is paid June 14.
(c) Amount due if paid in full on April 17.
(d) Last date for net payment.

SOLUTION:

(a) Final date for cash discount:
    March 16 through 30 = 14 days
    April (entire month) = 30 days
    May 1 through 26   = 26 days

    End of cash discount period = May 26 = 70 days
    Cash discount allowable through May 26 only.

(b) **None**

(c) Eligible for cash discount:
    $1,800 Billed cost
    –   54 ($1,800 × 3% Cash discount)
    ───────
    $1,746 Amount due

    $1,746 **Amount due if paid in full on April 17.**

(d) Last date for net payment:
    20 days after May 26 = June 16

    Last date for net payment: June 16.

EOM Dating

EOM dating (end of month) means the cash discount period is computed from the end of the month in which the invoice is dated rather than from the date of the invoice itself. Thus, 8/10 EOM (invoice dated April 1) means that the time for payment is calculated from the end of April, Additionally, an 8% cash discount may be taken if the bill is paid by May 10, that is, ten days after the end of April. Again a twenty-day net period occurs from May 11 through May 31 (implied), during which the retailer may pay the bill in full.

(Note: Traditionally, under EOM dating only, invoices dated on or after the 25th of any month are considered to be part of the next month's transactions.[2] For example, a bill with 8/10 EOM dated on August 26, is considered a September 1 bill and the discount period extends to October 10. Of course, arrangements of this kind vary.)

PROBLEM:

An invoice for $1,000 dated March 17 has terms of 8/10 EOM.

(a) What is the last date for deducting 8% cash discount?
(b) What amount will be due if the bill is paid on that date?

SOLUTION:

(a) Discount date = April 10 (ten days after end of March)

April 10 is the last date for 8% discount.

(b) $1,000 Billed cost

−   80 ($1,000 × 8% Cash discount)

$ 920 Amount due

$920 due if paid by April 10.

If this invoice was dated March 26 through to March 31 (using the traditional calendar), the discount date of payment would be May 10.

ROG Dating

ROG dating (receipt of goods) is when the discount period is calculated from the date the goods are delivered to the retailer's premises, rather than from the date of the invoice. This type of dating is often requested by buyers located at a considerable distance from the market (or shipping point). These retailers typically receive bills a few days after shipment, but may not get delivery of the merchandise itself for a considerably longer time. Therefore, 5/10 ROG, for example, means that the bill must be paid within 10 days after receipt of goods to earn the cash discount.

---

[2]Presently, it is common to apply this concept for invoices dated after the 25th of a month to other types of dating as well.

PROBLEM:

An invoice for $100 is dated April 4 and carries terms of 5/10 ROG. The goods arrive in the store on May 7.

(a) What is the last date that the discount may be deducted?

(b) How much should be remitted if payment is made on that date?

SOLUTION:

(a) Date Goods Were Received + 10 days

May 7 + 10 days   = May 17

Last day for discount = May 17

(b) $100 Billed cost − $5 ($100 × 5% Cash discount) = $95

$95 amount due on or before May 17.

Advanced or Postdating

Advanced or **postdating** (seasonal discount) is the type of dating that indicates the invoice date is advanced so that additional time is allowed for payment to be made and, ultimately, for the cash discount to be deducted. The discount period is then calculated from this advanced date agreed upon by the buyer and the seller. Generally, this type of dating is used by manufacturers to persuade buyers to buy and/or receive goods earlier than they would normally. Also, it is requested by purchasers who are momentarily short of cash. Consequently, if a shipment was made on February 10 and the invoice date was May 1, terms of 2/10 would mean that payment was due on or before May 11 to qualify for a 2% cash discount. (Please note that on invoices with advance or postdating, the payment of the invoice, at net, is delayed until the last day of the month in which the cash discount is earned, after which it is considered overdue.)

PROBLEM:

An invoice for merchandise shipped on August 18 is postdated October 1 and carries terms of 3/10, net 30. When does the discount period expire?

SOLUTION:

3% may be deducted if payment is made on or before October 11. The full amount is due at the end of the customary net period on October 31, using the traditional calendar.

B. Net Payment Dates

Net payment dates refer to that date by which an invoice must be paid. This date is expressed as n/30. It is considered overdue—and may be subject to an interest charge—if paid after the net payment period. Of course, there are variations for determining the final net payment date of an invoice (see Figure 40). The net payment date is determined by the type of cash discount dating that has been agreed upon. The commonly used practices are:

- Regular dating: the full amount of the invoice is due exactly 30 days from the date of invoice.
- EOM, ROG, and extra dating: the net payment date of the invoice is determined by adding 20 days from the expiration of the cash discount period.
- Advanced or postdating: the payment of the net invoice is delayed until the last day of the month in which the cash discount is earned.

Figure 40. Summary of Discount Dates[3]

Type of Dating	Invoice date	Last date eligible for discount	Net amt. paid between dates below	Bill past due if paid on or later than
1. Regular (2/10 or net 30)	11/16	11/26	11/27 through 12/17	12/18
2. Extra Dating (X) (3/10–90X)	6/7	9/17	9/17 through 10/7	10/8
3. End of Month (EOM) (8/10 EOM)	3/17	4/10	4/11 through 4/30	5/1
4. Receipt of Goods (ROG) (5/10 ROG; Rec'd 4/16)	4/4	4/26	4/27 through 5/16	5/17
5. Advanced or Post Dating (3/10 net 30 as of 10/1)	8/18	10/11	10/12 through 10/31	11/1

For assignments for the previous section, see practice problems 14–23.

---

[3]Deadline dates used in this chart are based on a 30-day month.

Notes

Practice Problems[4]

Dating

14. Determine the final dates on which a cash discount may be taken for different terms on invoices dated May 15. Assume that the merchandise is received in the stores on June 2. The different terms are:

    (a) 8/10, net 30.
    (b) 2/10 EOM.
    (c) 2/10–60X.
    (d) Net 30.
    (e) 3/10 ROG.

15. An electronics retailer buys several color TV sets that list for $725 each and is billed with trade discounts of 20% and 10%. Terms are net. What is the actual net cost price of each TV?

---

[4]All dating problems are based on the 30-day month method. When solving practice problems, unless advised otherwise, the calculations for Unit VI in Selected Answers are based on the 30-day month method.

16. Your department receives an invoice dated October 10 in the amount of $6,750. How much must be paid on November 10 if terms are:

(a) 10/10, net 30.

(b) 10/10 EOM.

(c) Net.

17. Merchandise that amounts to $650 at cost is shipped and invoiced on August 14. Terms are 4/10 EOM. Payment is made on August 26. How much should be remitted?

18. A buyer purchased 75 ginger jar lamps at a list price of $40 each. The trade discounts were 30%, 20%, and 5% with terms of 2/10, net 30. The lamps were shipped and billed on October 18 and were received October 22. The bill was paid on October 31. What amount was paid?

19. An invoice dated March 2 carries terms of 3/10–60X. When does the discount period expire? Explain.

20. Goods are invoiced and shipped on July 1 and received on July 15. Terms are 5/10 EOM and the invoice is for $5,600. Payment is made on August 10. How much should be remitted?

21. An invoice for $3,290, dated April 26th, covering merchandise received May 19th, carries terms of 8/10 EOM, ROG. It is paid on June 10.

    (a) How much should have been remitted?

    (b) What would have been remitted had ROG not been included? Why?

22. Goods that are invoiced on July 26 are received on August 10. Indicate the final discount date for net payment and the final date for net payment if terms are:

	Final discount date	Net payment date
(a) 3/10 EOM	_____	_____
(b) 2/10, net 30	_____	_____
(c) 1/20–30x	_____	_____
(d) 8/10 EOM as of Sept. 1	_____	_____
(e) 8/10 EOM, ROG	_____	_____

23. On June 24, a buyer received a purchase that amounted to a total list price of $16,000. This merchandise had a trade discount of 37.5%. The buyer wanted to negotiate with the supplier the last date possible to take a cash discount. The invoice on this purchase was dated June 22. Determine the various cash payment dates for the buyer under the following purchase terms:

(a) 2/10, n/30.
(b) 2/10, n/30 ROG.
(c) 2/10, n/30 EOM.
(d) 2/10–60X, anticipation allowed.

III. ANTICIPATION

Anticipation is an extra discount, which is usually calculated at the prevailing prime rate of business interest and is subject to change based on economic conditions. This extra discount is often permitted by vendors when an invoice is paid prior to the end of the cash discount period and, again, is subject to change based on economic conditions. For the purpose of illustration only, this text will use a 6% annual rate, which equates to 0.5% per month, or a decimal equivalent of .005 per month.

The number of days of anticipation is based upon the number of days remaining between the actual date of payment of an invoice and the last date on which the cash discount could be taken. While some vendors do not permit an anticipation discount, alert retailers deduct it, unless a notation on the invoice expressly forbids it. Many retailers, when sending in a confirmed order, specify "anticipation allowed." Anticipation is taken by retailers because, in effect, the vendor has the use of the retailer's money ahead of the date arranged by the terms of the sale, and because of this the retailer is charging the vendor "interest" for its use. An anticipation deduction is taken in addition to any other discounts that may apply, and the deduction percentage customarily is combined with the regular cash discount percentage.

Currently, however, some retailers are anticipating invoices based on the number of days from the date of payment to the end of the net period. When using this policy, a bill that is paid after the cash discount period has ended can still be anticipated for the balance of the net period.

(Note: In the practice problems illustrating anticipation that follow this section, only the more traditional cash discount period method should be used. The following example, however, shows the calculations used for both the cash discount period method and the net payment period method.)

PROBLEM:

An invoice for $100 is dated December 4 and carries terms of 2/10–30X. Anticipation is permitted. If the bill is paid on December 14:

(a) Calculate the number of days that were anticipated and the remittance due using the cash discount period method.

(b) Determine the number of days that were anticipated and the remittance due using the net payment period method.

SOLUTION:
(a) Using the traditional cash discount period method.

The cash discount period is 40 days.
Because the bill is paid in 10 days the anticipation period is 30 days.

Total $ amount of goods	= $100
Anticipation	= .5% for 30 days
Cash discount	= 2%
Cash discount + anticipation	= 2% + .5% = 2.5%
Total discount	= $100 × 2.5% = 2.50
Net cost	= $100 − $2.50 = $97.50
Amount remitted	= $97.50

(b) Using the net payment period method or an alternate approach to anticipation.

The cash discount period is 40 days and the net payment period is 60 days. Because the bill is paid in 10 days, the anticipation period is 50 days.

(Note: Using the net payment period method, if this invoice was paid after 40 days, that is, after the cash discount period had elapsed, the buyer would still be allowed an anticipation discount for the 20 days remaining in the net payment period.)

Total $ amount of goods	= $100
Anticipation	= .82% for 50 days
Cash discount	= 2%
Cash discount + anticipation	= 2% + .82% + 2.82%
Total discount	= $100 × 2.82% = $2.82
Net cost	= $100 − $2.82 = $97.18
Amount remitted	= $97.18

IV. LOADING

Loading is the practice of intentionally increasing the amount of the invoice to a price that would allow a theoretically greater cost discount, but results in paying the net amount that the vendor quotes. The standardized cash discount percentage arbitrarily set by top management does not reflect the true cash discount allowed by the vendor. When loading is practiced, the retailer may request the vendor to bill a "loaded" cost that is then adjusted by the required cash discount percentage to achieve the true net cost. In other cases, the store will make the adjustment statistically when the invoices are processed.

PROBLEM:

A manufacturer quotes the cost of an item at $30 with terms of 3/10, n/30. The buyer desired an 8% cash discount. What is the "loaded" cost?

SOLUTION:

Net cost of invoice = $30 Billed cost − 3% Cash discount

$\qquad\qquad\qquad\quad$ = $30 − .90 (3% × $30)

Net cost $\qquad\qquad\quad$ = $29.10

Loaded cost $\qquad\quad$ = $29.10 Net cost

$\qquad\qquad\qquad\quad$ = $29.10 Net cost

Loaded cost $\qquad\quad$ = 92% (100% − 8% loaded discount)

$\qquad\qquad\qquad\quad$ = $31.63

V. Shipping Terms

As with dating, shipping charges vary in different industries and in different situations. They are expressed as free-on-board (FOB) at a designated location. The place that is designated defines the point to which the vendor pays transportation charges and assumes risk of loss or damage and the legal title to the merchandise being shipped to a purchaser. Because the factors that determine the total cost of goods include inward freight charges, it is important that the retailer negotiate advantageous shipping terms as a means of reducing the total cost of goods. The buyer should apply ethical but firm pressure on merchandise resources for appropriate and favorable terms of sale and discounts. The most common arrangements are:

- **FOB retailer.** Vendor pays transportation charges to the retailer's store or warehouse and, unless otherwise agreed upon, bears the risk of loss until goods are received by the retailer.
- **FOB factory.** Purchaser pays transportation charges from factory to purchaser's premises and, unless otherwise agreed, bears the risk of loss from the time the goods leave the factory.
- **FOB city or port of destination.** Vendor pays the transportation charges to a specified location in the city of destination and then the purchaser pays delivery charges from that point to the purchaser's premises. Unless otherwise agreed upon, the risk of loss passes from seller to buyer when goods arrive at the specified location in the city of destination.
- **Prepaid.** Vendor pays transportation (freight) charges to the retailer's store or warehouse when the merchandise is shipped from vendor's premises. The FOB agreement, made at the time of sale, determines whether the vendor or purchaser pays the freight charges.

For assignments for the previous section, see practice problems 24–33.

Practice Problems[5]

Anticipation, Loading, and Shipping Terms

24. On June 10, the buyer for the Charm Stores placed an order for 24 dozen turtleneck tops costing $81 per dozen with AOK Inc. The vendor offered the terms of 8/10 EOM, ROG, anticipation allowed, FOB Store.

    (a) Complete the accompanying purchase order indicating a delivery date of November 10, complete.

    (b) What amount should be remitted if the shipment was received October 26 and paid on November 10?

Figure 41. Purchase Order for Charm Stores

CHARM STORES

3025 PALM CANYON DRIVE

PALM SPRINGS, CA. 92264

INVOICE INSTRUCTIONS

ORIGINAL INVOICE MUST ACCOMPANY THE MERCHANDISE FOR ALL SHIPMENTS.

FOR LOCAL SHIPMENTS DELIVERED TO OUR PLATFORMS:
- Driver present invoice with merchandise.

FOR { LOCAL SHIPMENTS DELIVERED TO U.S. PACKING AND SHIPPING CO.
ALL PARCEL POST AND RAILWAY EXPRESS SHIPMENTS
ALL OTHER OUT-OF-TOWN SHIPMENTS

- Enclose invoice in an envelope glued to outside of the "lead" carton.

For Out-of-Town where the above instructions cannot be followed, Mail Original Invoice to:

And also Enclose PACKING SLIP in an envelope glued to outside of "lead" carton.

FIRM AOK Inc.

STREET 1300 Broadway

CITY New York, New York 1000

ORDER NUMBER

Serial	Store	Dept.
2 4 6	8	2 4

Order Number, Weight and Pkg. No. MUST be shown on all packages and inv ject to refusal.

SHIP VIA: ❑ TRUCK ❑ FRT. ❑ P.P. ❑ R.E.A

oices or shipment is sub-

DATE WRITTEN	TO BE SHIPPED FROM	DELIVERY DUE	F.O.B.	Charges on Shipments bought F.O.B. XXXX XXXXX our premises must be prepaid.		FREIGHT ALLOWED		TERMS Dating is From Date of Receipt of Goods

CLASS.	HOUSE & STYLE OR LOT NO.	DESCRIPTION	S	M	L	XL			QUAN.	DOZEN COST	TOTAL COST
CT	5107	LS. Cotton Turtleneck							24 doz.	81 00	
		Camel	12	24	24	12					
		Navy	12	24	24	12					
		Wine	12	12	12	12					
		Black	12	24	36	24					

[5] In the practice problems illustrating anticipation, only the cash discount period method should be used. For the purpose of illustration, use a 6% annual rate.

25. Merchandise amounting to $6,800 was shipped on March 23 and was received the same day. Terms were 7/10 EOM and anticipation was permitted. The bill was paid on April 10. How much should have been remitted?

26. The following goods, shipped on June 7 and received on July 2, are:

- 50 occasional tables at $75 list price.
- 200 folding chairs at $20 list price.

Trade discounts are 40% and 5%, with terms of 5/10 ROG, and anticipation is permitted. What amount must be remitted if the bill is paid on July 12?

27. An invoice for $4,500 is dated and received on March 15, along with the merchandise it covers. Terms are 1/10 EOM, ROG, anticipation permitted. If the bill is paid on March 25, how much should be remitted?

28. An invoice is dated and received on April 6, which carries terms of 2/10, net 30. Anticipation is permitted. It is paid on April 16. What is the discount taken?

29. An invoice dated August 28 carrying terms of 4/10–90X is paid on October 8. Anticipation is permitted. If the billed amount is $875, what should be the remittance?

30. An invoice for $1,800 dated August 10 is paid on August 20. Terms are 5/10, net 30. Anticipation is not permitted. What is the "loaded" cost when the buyer requested an 8% cash discount?

31. An invoice was received by Grandma's Closet in the amount of $2,100 with terms of 2/10–30X, n/90. If the invoice is dated April 20, what payment would be made on April 30? If the buyer desired a 6% cash discount, what is the "loaded" cost?

32. Calculate the payment that should be made on August 26 by Tom's Swift Shop for merchandise amounting to $5,600. The invoice is dated August 16 and terms are 8/10–60X, anticipation allowed.

33. Marie's Book Shop received an invoice dated March 26 for books amounting to $2,500, with terms of 2/10 EOM, anticipation permitted. Indicate the amount to be remitted if payment is made on April 10.

Notes

34. An invoice for a shipment of luggage is dated September 27 and is paid on October 25. The trade discount is 45% and 5%, with terms of 2/10 EOM, anticipation permitted, FOB retailer's warehouse. There is a quantity discount of 1% on initial orders of $6,000 or more. What amount should be remitted to the vendor if the bill was for:

Quantity	Luggage item	List price
50	2 Suiter	$45
120	Overnighter	25
70	Dress Bag	30
90	Vacationer	60

35. A bill for $6,000 is dated November 8 for merchandise that is to arrive on November 25. What is the last date for taking the discount if terms are 7/10 ROG?

36. An invoice for $2,300 has terms of 2/10–30X, net 60, FOB factory, anticipation permitted. The vendor prepaid the shipping charges of $34. The invoice was dated August 29 and was paid on September 24. How much should the vendor have received?

37. The infants' and nursery department receives an invoice for merchandise with a list price value of $10,750. It is dated January 28 and is paid on February 25. Terms are 2/10 EOM, FOB store, with trade discounts of 40% and 10%. Anticipation is not forbidden. The manufacturer prepaid the freight of $125.

(a) What is the last date on which a discount may be taken?
(b) What is the last date for payment without penalty?
(c) What amount should be remitted under the conditions given in this problem?

38. An athleticwear buyer receives a shipment of 30 dozen pairs of 50/50 sweatpants costing $9 each. The invoice is dated April 26 and terms are 6/10 EOM, FOB factory. Anticipation is not permitted. Shipping charges of $92 are prepaid by the vendor.

(a) What is the last possible date that a discount may be taken?
(b) If the bill was paid on May 11, how much was remitted to the vendor?

39. What amount must be remitted on an invoice for $3,200 that is dated April 26 and paid on May 10? Terms are 8/10 EOM, anticipation permitted.

40. Research and Discussion: If you were a small, independent dress manufacturer in a very competitive market, what terms of sale would you offer to your customers? Explain your reasoning.

41. Research and Discussion: Your department receives a bill dated July 16, which is paid July 26. Which set of terms (5/10–30X or 7/10, net 30, anticipation permitted for both) would you choose as the most advantageous to your department? Explain your choice with supporting calculations.

42. Research and Discussion: If you were an owner/buyer for a medium-sized specialty shop, would you always take advantage of the anticipation option when offered? Why or why not? Explain your answer.

43. For the Fall season, a gift boutique received an invoice dated April 23. In negotiating terms of purchase with the resource, a series discount of 35%, 25%, and terms of 2/10, n/30 ROG were agreed upon. The retail value of the merchandise received in the store on April 28 was $1,800. How much should have been remitted to the resource if the bill was paid on May 6?

44. Jean's Fashion placed an order for 12 dozen silk scarves that cost $120 per dozen with freight charges of $18. The terms negotiated on this purchase were 2/10–30X, n/60 EOM, FOB store, anticipation permitted. If the invoice is dated June 10, determine the payment to be made to the manufacturer on July 10.

45. On June 10, the junior sportswear buyer for a large department store placed an order with a resource who offered terms of 8/10, n/30 EOM, FOB warehouse, freight prepaid. Determine the required payment if the date of the invoice was August 10, the amount of the invoice was $8,700, and the bill was paid August 18.

TERMS OF SALE

Mr. Williams, the silverware buyer for a specialty store located in San Francisco, decides to review his vendor analysis report before making his forthcoming season's purchases. The report shows that among the top six resources, there are three relatively strong and three relatively weak suppliers in relation to the gross margin each generated. Mr. Williams realizes that some important aspects of his job as buyer are negotiating trade discounts, quantity discounts, cash discounts, and dating, as well as transportation charges. Because any and/or all of these factors can increase the essential gross margin figure, he examines copies of past orders to determine the terms of sale on previous purchases. He discovers that some suppliers granted all his requests pertaining to discount and dating elements, certain vendors negotiated these factors only after an initial order was placed, and a considerable number allowed only the absolute minimum discount that prevailed in the market.

Because business conditions have been less than favorable, Mr. Williams feels that the success of the next season depends not only on his ability to select the most desirable items from his key resources, but also to negotiate with those vendors who offer the most advantageous terms of sale, to help maintain or improve the gross margin performance.

The first classification he shops in the market is sterling flatware. He had and continues to have strong sales in one well-advertised national brand that is distributed and can be bought directly from the manufacturer or from a jobber (i.e., middleperson). Customarily, Mr. Williams places his order for these goods with the manufacturer because he is able to view the complete line of patterns and buy any quantity he needs. Additionally, he has developed rapport with one of the salespeople who served him. This salesperson would rush special orders, would call Mr. Williams about special promotions, etc. Consequently, during market week, Mr. Williams visits the manufacturer's showroom, shops the entire line, gets delivery dates, and inquires about the current terms of sale, which are:

- Trade discounts from list price: 40%, less 25%.
- Quantity discounts offered: none.
- Cash discount: 2/10, n/30.
- FOB: Factory/shipping charges are running 0.5%.

When Mr. Williams returns to the store, he studies his open-to-buy for this category and decides to purchase:

- 15 sets of Pattern A: List price $175 for each 5-piece place setting, 40-piece service.
- 10 sets of Pattern B: List price $200 for each 5-piece place setting, 40-piece service.
- 8 sets of Pattern C: List price $225 for each 5-piece place setting, 40-piece service.

He is interrupted in his calculations by his assistant who informs him that the salesperson of an out-of-town jobber would like to speak with him. This particular supplier has tried for several reasons to get the store as an account. In the past, Mr. Williams had used local jobbers, often for immediate shipment of various items when his stock would become "low" on fast-moving items, but he had not done business before with this particular firm. Mr. Williams invites the salesperson into his office and during their conversation, Mr. Williams senses the salesperson's eagerness to open an account with him now. He deduces this because of all the concessions the salesperson is willing to offer the store. Because this jobber carries the same brand of silverware Mr. Williams has just seen at the manufacturer's showroom, he asks the prices, terms, etc. They are:

- Trade discount from list price: 40%, less 20%, less 5%.
- Quantity discount: an additional 1% for orders over $10,000; 1.5% for orders over $15,000; and 2% for orders over $20,000.
- Cash discount: 2/10–60X, anticipation allowed.
- FOB store.

With which resource should Mr. Williams place his order—the manufacturer, the jobber, or both? Justify your choice mathematically.

RESOURCES INFLUENCED BY TERMS OF SALE

Mr. Green is the owner of a three-store shoe chain called TRED-RITE. The merchandise featured in these stores, which are located in small strip malls, could be described as fashion forward at moderate to high prices. The strength of his operation is the services offered the customers combined with merchandise that has a unique twist.

Mr. Green has developed over the 15 years of the store's existence an extensive mailing list. During the year, periodically, he has sent out a direct mail brochure which has successfully produced plus business because of the items featured.

In April, as he covers the market for the Fall season, he is on the lookout for THE promotional item to be selected and promoted in this year's Christmas mailing piece.

He finally decides on a very trendy, attractive slipper that can be worn outdoors. It is a lamb-lined scuff with a leather suede upper, made in China. The slipper has a 1/2" platform with a hard sole, available in this season's four most desirable fashion colors. It would be priced at $45 and represents exceptional value. This item is being offered by X-Cel Co., an importer, from whom Mr. Green has bought consistently because this resource has had superior sales performance. Their deliveries and terms have been exactly as negotiated, and their offerings are synonymous with good value. The X-Cel Co. has quoted on this particular item a landed cost of $20 per pair, requiring a minimum order of 3,000 pair with terms of n/30, FOB store. The date of mailing this brochure is set for Oct. 15, and X-Cel has agreed on an Oct. 1, complete, delivery date. Mr. Green is confident about the item, but he questions the stores' capacity to meet the demand of this quantity in a relatively short selling period.

Mr. Green saw in the market a similar, though not identical, branded slipper manufactured by a medium-sized local factory, that is quoted with a cost of $21.25. This resource does not require a minimum quantity, yet guarantees shipment of sufficient quantities as needed (by the response to the brochure), with prompt delivery throughout the holiday season and the life of the "mailer." The terms for this resource are 5/10 EOM, anticipated allowed, FOB store. He will write the order with a delivery date of September 26 and should Mr. Green write the order for 3,000 pairs, he will ship half September 26 and then the balance by November 1.

With which resource should Mr. Green negotiate? Would the terms offered by each vendor affect the profitability of this purchase? How? Explain mathematically.

Additional markup   Adjustment that raises the price on merchandise already in stock.

Advanced dating (seasonal discount)   The invoice date is advanced so that additional time is allowed for payment and the deduction of the cash discount.

Allowance to customer   A partial refund or credit compensates for a merchandising deficiency, such as missing buttons, dry cleaning, and so on.

Alteration and workroom costs   A charge to selling department when it is necessary to put merchandise in condition for sale (i.e., assembling, polishing, making cuffs).

Anticipation   A discount earned by retailers, under certain conditions, for the payment of invoices prior to expiration of cash discount period.

Average cost   The proportioning of different cost amounts that can carry retail prices that achieve the desired markup percentage.

Average retail   Price that will achieve desired markup percentage.

Average retail stock   Sum of retail inventories at the beginning of each year, season, month, or week.

Average stock   The total of BOM dollar inventory figures divided by the number of stocks considered.

Averaging markups   The adjustment of the proportions of goods purchased at different markups. A composite of the relationship between all cost and retail for a department or grouping of goods during a specified time.

Averaging retails   The proportioning of different retail prices on purchases that may have two or more costs to achieve a desired markup percentage.

Basis stock method   Stock size using a constant basic stock figure with a turnover rate.

Billed cost   The manufacturer's price for goods offered to a retailer.

BOM stock   The beginning of the month stock figure in dollars.

Book inventory (perpetual or running book inventory)   Statistical records that show the value, at retail, of goods on hand at a given time.

Cash discount   A percentage deducted from the cost of goods for conformance to prearranged terms of payment of an invoice between the vendor and retailer.

Charge-back   Form on which the amounts of merchandise returned to resources by retailer for credit or refund is recorded.

Closeout   A grouping of goods, usually composed of a broken assortment, offered by a resource to a retailer at a reduced price.

Closing inventory   The value of merchandise in stock at the end of an accounting period. It can be expressed in cost or retail.

Closing physical stock   The retail value of aggregate retail prices of a stock determined by a physical count at the end of a designated time period.

COD dating   A form of dating in which payment must be made "on the spot" as delivery occurs.

Complement   The difference between 100 and any number less than 100. E.g., the complement of 60 is 40.

Contribution or controllable margin   The technique that evaluates the buyer's performance based on those expenses that are direct, controllable, or a combination of direct and controllable expenses. It is the amount a department contributes to indirect expenses and profit.

Controllable expenses   Many, but not all direct expenses are controllable. See *Direct Expenses*.

Cost   The amount a retailer pays a resource for purchases.

Cost of goods sold   The cost of merchandise that has been sold during a given period.

Cumulative markup   The markup percentage achieved on all goods available for sale from the beginning of a given period. It is the markup in dollars or percentages obtained on the accumulated inventory at the beginning of the given period, plus the markup of all the new purchases received season-to-date.

Customer allowances   After a sale has been made, the amount of reduction in price the customer has been given.

Customer returns   Dollar amount value returned to retailer by customer for credit or refund.

Dating   An agreement specifying time period for payment of an invoice.

Department   A grouping of related merchandise for which common records are kept.

Direct expenses   Expenses that exist only with a given department and cease if that department is discontinued (i.e., department advertising).

Discount date   The date by which an invoice must be paid to take advantage of the discount granted.

Dollar merchandise plan   A "roadmap" indicating projected sales, stocks, markdowns and purchases as well as the desired markups . . . usually it is prepared biannually in advance of the selling season.

Employee discounts   A percentage deducted from a regular retail price as a courtesy to employees of a retail organiza-

tion. Ranges from 10 to 30%. It is a "retail reduction."

EDP (electronic data processing)   The planned conversion of facts (as by the computer) into storable form to achieve a desired result.

EOM   End of month. Usually designates dollar value of stock at the end of a month.

EOM dating   The cash discount period is computed from the end of the month in which the invoice is dated rather than from the date of the invoice itself.

Expenses   The overhead of doing business, e.g., salaries, rent, advertising, delivery, utilities.

Extra dating   A specific number of days granted during which a discount may be taken.

Final profit and loss statement   The basic profit factors (i.e., sales, cost of goods and expenses) are developed in detail so that every transaction is clearly seen.

Final selling price   Price received when an item is sold.

Flash report   Daily report indicating sales amount.

FOB (Free-on-board)   The way of expressing who is responsible for payment of transportation and the point at which title is transferred.

FOB city or port of destination   Vendor pays transportation charges to a specific city or destination.

FOB factory   The retailer pays transportation.

FOB retailer   The resource pays transportation.

GMROI (gross margin return on investment)   The relationship between the average inventory at cost and gross margin. Gross margin divided by average inventory at cost.

Gross margin   The remainder after subtracting total cost of goods sold from the total retail amount of sales. Also called gross profit. The difference between net sales and the cost of goods sold.

Gross markdown   Original price reduction.

Gross sales   Retail value of total initial sales prior to deduction of dollar amount returned by customers.

Indirect expenses   Expenses that consist of some store expenses which are prorated to all selling departments on the basis of sales volume.

Initial markup   The difference between the cost of goods and the original retail price. The first price placed on merchandise for resale. Planned markups specified on orders for merchandise; a projected markup goal.

Inventory (n.)   Synonymous with the term "stock."

Inventory (v.)   To actively count and record quantities of merchandise.

Invoice   A bill presented by a vendor to a retailer for goods purchased.

Inward freight   The amount charged for transporting merchandise to designated premises, e.g., trucking, freight, postage, and so on. Charges are paid by either vendor or retailer according to an agreement between them at the time of purchase.

Journal or purchase record   Consolidated listing of purchases by invoice amounts, transportation charges, discounts, vendors, and so on.

List price   A theoretical retail price set by manufacturers.

Loading   Intentionally increasing the amount of the invoice to a price which would allow a theoretically greater cash discount, but results in paying the net amount that the vendor quotes.

Maintained markup   The difference between the cost of goods and the actual selling price of the merchandise sold.

Markdown   A reduction in retail price. The lowering or reducing of the original or previous retail price on one item or group of items. The difference between the original or present retail price and the new retail price. Taken in dollars and can be expressed as a percentage.

Markdown cancellation   The restoration of a markdown price to the former retail.

Markdown percentage   Markdown expressed as a percentage of net sales.

Markup   The difference between cost and retail price, expressed either in dollars or percentage.

Markup cancellation   A downward price adjustment that offsets an original inflated markup.

Merchandise loans   Goods given temporarily to another department or division for purposes other than resale, such as display.

Merchandise plan   A combination of a dollar merchandise plan and an assortment plan.

Merchandise transfers   Goods "bought or sold" internally, from one department to another for purposes of resale to the ultimate consumer.

Net   What remains when nothing more is to be taken away.

Net cost   No additional discounts are earned on merchandise purchased.

Net loss   When the operating expenses are greater than the gross margin.

Net markdown   Difference between gross markdown and markdown cancellation.

Net payment date   The date by which an invoice must be paid to acquire a favorable credit rating and avoid late penalties.

Net period Span of time between expiration of eligibility for cash discount and start of the penalty period.

Net profit The difference between gross margin and operating expenses.

Net sales The sales total after customer returns and allowances have been deducted from gross sales.

Net terms A condition of sale in which a cash discount is neither offered nor permitted.

On order Unfilled orders, also known as open orders.

Open-to-buy (OTB) The amount of unspent money available for purchasing merchandise.

Opening book inventory The value of merchandise in stock at the beginning of an accounting period. It can be expressed at retail or cost.

Opening inventory The retail value of merchandise in stock.

Operating expenses Disbursals incurred in running an organization. There are two types, direct and indirect.

Operating income In retailing, this is the net sales.

Ordinary dating See *Regular Dating*.

Overage Dollar difference between book stock figure and physical count when the latter is the larger of the two.

Perpetual inventory See *Book Inventory*.

Physical inventory The retail dollar value of all goods physically present in a periodic stock count.

Planned purchases Known as planned receipts, the dollar amount of merchandise that can be brought into a stock during a given period.

Planned receipts See *Planned Purchases*.

POS Point-of-sale.

Point of sale markdown Recording of the markdown as the reduced offering when an item is being sold.

Prepaid Payment of transportation charges by vendor when merchandise is shipped.

Price change form Form on which markdowns, markdown cancellation, additional markup and markup cancellation or any price change made is recorded.

Price line A predetermined retail figure or a specific price point which is aimed at a specific customer market segment.

Price lining The predetermination of retail prices at which an assortment of merchandise will be carried.

Price range Spread from highest to lowest price lines.

Price zone Series of price lines likely to appeal to one group of a store's customers. These can be referred to as volume, promotional or prestige price zones.

Profit The dollar amount remaining after costs and expenses are paid.

Profit and loss statement Statement prepared periodically by either department, store or organization that summarizes the basic merchandising factors that affect profit results.

Quantity discount A percentage deduction from billed cost allowable when the dollar or unit amount on an order for goods (or a cumulative figure for a period of time) falls within certain predesignated limits.

Regular dating Discount date calculated from date of invoice. See *Ordinary Dating*.

Remit or remittance Payment.

Retail Price at which stores offer merchandise for sale.

Retail merchandising The science of offering goods to the ultimate consumer at the right price, the right form, at the right location, and at an appropriate time.

Retail method of inventory An accounting system used in retail stores that values merchandising at current retail prices that can then be converted to cost value by markup formula.

Retail price The price at which goods are sold to the ultimate consumer.

Retail reductions Markdown plus stock shortages and employee discounts.

Return to vendor See *Charge-Back*.

ROG dating Receipt of goods used in dating terms to denote the beginning of a discount period.

Running inventory See *Book Inventory*.

Sales volume Indicates in dollars how much merchandise has been sold.

Season letter A code letter indicating date of item's entry into stock.

Shortage Dollar difference between book stock figure and physical count figures, when the former is the larger of the two.

Shrinkage Lessening of retail value of stock on hand, generally due to theft or breakage. See *Shortage*.

Skeletal profit and loss statement A quick method to determine at any given time profit or loss.

Stock Goods on hand at a given time expressed as a dollar amount.

Stock-sales ratio The proportion between the BOM stock figure and the dollar amount of sales for the same month.

Terms of sale Arrangement between merchandise source or vendor and retailer relative to time period of invoice, cost of merchandise, shipping charges and transportation arrangements.

Total cost of goods Combines the cost of merchandise purchased and inward transportation charges.

Total cost of goods sold Results from subtracting cash discounts and adding alteration and workroom costs to the gross cost of merchandise sold (total merchandise handled less the cost of the closing inventory).

Total merchandise handled Opening inventory, at cost, plus new purchases at cost plus inward freight or the sum of the opening inventory plus the total cost of the purchases that is all merchandise available for sale.

Trade discount A percentage or series of percentages deducted from a list price, thereby determining cost price.

Transfers Change of ownership of merchandise between departments or stores.

Turnover The number of times at which the average retail stock has been sold and replaced.

Vendor A merchandise resource such as a manufacturer, importer, jobber, distributor, etc.

Vendor analysis An investigation of the profitability of each vendor's products sold by a retailer.

Volume The retail value of sales for a given period, usually expressed annually. See *Sales Volume*.

Weeks supply method The method of planning stock size on a weekly basis.

Workroom charges A charge to a selling department when it is necessary to put merchandise in condition for sale, i.e., assembling, polishing, putting on cuffs, etc. See *Alteration and Workroom Charges*.

Selected Answers

UNIT I

1. 5%

3. $49,122.00

5. $40,000.00

7. 1.5% (Junior Dept.); 4.5% (Misses Dept.)

11. $2,917.40

13. $59,045.00

15. (a.) $1,374.00; (b.) $1,420.26

19. $8,100.00; 2.9%

21. $225,500.00; 46%

23. $2,500.00

25. (a.) $9,000.00; (b.) 41.25% or 41.3%

27. $38,400.00; 48.0%

33. 51%

35. (a.) $261,000.00; (b.) $139,000.00

37. $608,000.00

41. (a.) $236,160.00; (b.) $238,040.00; (c.) $15,800.00; 3.2%

43. $5,620.00

45. $9,561.93

47. $350,000.00

49. 50.4%

51. $50,000.00

53. $25,000.00

55. 50.19% or 50.2%

UNIT II

2. $29.95

4. $93.00

6. 45%

8. (a.) $88.54; (b.) $90.00; (c.) 46.5%

12. $75.43; 50%

16. $22.00

18. 48.77%

20. $41.67

22. $23.07

24. (a.) $25.00; (b.) $10.83

31. $1,225.00

37. $669.75

39. (a.) $1,330.00; (b.) 15.3%

45. $20.57

47. $8.57

49. 47.95% or 48%

51. (a.) 47%; (b.) 2.98% or 3%

52. 54.4%

54. $4,240.00

56. $67.90

58. (a.) $117,000.00; .5% More

UNIT III

1. 51.4%

3. 49.15% or 49.2%

5. 53%

7. 53.8%

9. 48.3%

11. 53.7%

13. (a.) 55.3%; (b.) 54.9%

15. 50.1%

17. 37.3%

21. 13.4%

23. (a.) $8,704.00; (b.) $108.80 per dozen

25. $1,774.50

27. $27.41

28. $25.51

29. $26.00

31. 53.7%

33. 49.6%

35. 47.2%

37. 47.6%

38. 13%

40. (a.) 41.6%; (b.) 47.6%

42. 53.6%

45. $21.68

46. 61.5%

47. $5.83

48. $47.14

50. $60.41

53. 49.5%

55. 49.57% or 49.6%

58. (a.) $130,000.00; (b.) $139,200.00

UNIT IV

1. $62,875.00

3. $95,000.00

5. (a.) $23,000.00; (b.) $11,730.00

7. (a.) $1,311,000.00; (b.) $672,543.00

9. $162,382.00

10. (a.) $937,000.00; (b.) $475,996.00

13. .41%

15. 1.5%

17. 2.07% or 2.1%

19. $70,000.00

21. (a.) .1% Higher; (b.) $2,000.00 More

26. (a.) $284,100.00; (b.) $282,550.80

UNIT V

1. 10%

3. August–$900,000.00

September–$840,000.00

October–$960,000.00

November–$1,080,000.00

December–$1,500,000.00

January–$720,000.00

5. 20%

8. $80,000.00

10. $300,000.00

12. 3.88 or 3.9

15. 2.5

16. (a.) $40,000.00; (b.) 4.95 or 5

18. 3.2

20. 1.10

22. 3.0

24. $312,000.00

26. 4.245 or 4.3

28. $117,000.00

30. $126,150.00

31. $275,000.00

33. $60,000.00

35. $80,000.00

37. (a.) $20,000.00; (b.) $9,700.00; (c.) .36 or .4

39. (a.) $28,000.00; (b.) $33,000.00

41. $61,800.00

43. None

45. None

47. None

49. 10.4

51. $780,000.00

53. 10.2%

55. (a.) $3,000.00; (b.) $1,320.00

57. $37,000.00

59. 1.5

61. (a.) 4.5; (b.) 2.1

63. (a.) 583,428.57; (b.) 6; (c.) 4

64. August–$217,250.00 BOM

September–$230,050.00 BOM

October–$266,550.00 BOM

November–$233,450.00 BOM

December–$234,750.00 BOM

January–$216,550.00 BOM

66. $88,000.00

UNIT VI

1. $122.50

5. $972.00

7. $488.88

9. $4,419.80

11. $4,159.67

13. B.

15. $522.00

17. $624.00

19. May 12

20. $5,320.00

27. $4,443.75

29. $831.25

33. $2,437.50

34. $6,446.86

35. December 5

37. (a.) March 10; (b.) March 30; (c.) $5,674.39

39. $2,928.00

44. $1,404.00

Reference Readings

Berman, Barry, and Joel R. Evans, *Retail Management,* Englewood Cliffs, NJ: Prentice Hall, 1995.

Diamond, J., and G. Pintel, *Retail Buying, 5th edition,* Englewood Cliffs, NJ: Prentice Hall, 1997.

Donellan, J., *Merchandise Buying and Management,* New York: Fairchild Publications, 1996.

Dunne, Patrick and Robert F. Lusch, *Retailing, 3rd edition,* Orlando, FL: Dryden Press, Harcourt Brace College Publishers, 1999.

Eskew, Robert and Daniel Jensen, *Financial Accounting,* New York: McGraw-Hill, 1992.

Horngren, Charles and Gary Sundem, *Introduction to Management Accounting,* Englewood Cliffs, NJ: Prentice Hall, 1990.

Levy, Michael and Barton Weitz, *Retailing Management,* Chicago, IL: Irwin, 1995.

Risch, E., *Retail Merchandising,* New York: Macmillan, 1991.

Index